WOMEN, MILITARISM, AND WAR

New Feminist Perspectives Series

General Editor: Rosemarie Tong, Davidson College

WOMEN, MILITARISM, AND WAR

*Essays in History,
Politics, and Social Theory*

edited by
JEAN BETHKE ELSHTAIN
AND
SHEILA TOBIAS

ROWMAN & LITTLEFIELD
Publishers, Inc.

ROWMAN & LITTLEFIELD PUBLISHERS, INC.

Published in the United States of America
by Rowman & Littlefield Publishers, Inc.
8705 Bollman Place, Savage, Maryland 20763

Library of Congress Cataloging-in-Publication Data

Women, militarism, and war: essays in history,
politics, and social theory.
Bibliography: p.
Includes index.
1. Women and the military.   2. Women and war.
3. Women and peace.   I. Elshtain, Jean Bethke,
1941–   . II. Tobias, Sheila.   III. Title.
U21.75.W67   1988   355'.0088042   88–26409

ISBN 0–8476–7469–X
ISBN 0–8476–7470–3 (pbk.)

Printed in the United States of America

to
Errol L. Elshtain
and Carl T. Tomizuka,
our partners

Contents

Preface

This book represents a cluster of vital political and historical concerns that are matters of deep theoretical and moral complexity. When we think of war, we inescapably immerse ourselves in the horror and allure of collective violence, a violence from which women have been officially separated, at least in the era of modern nation-states, but to which they are, and have been, essential. Women may not be history's prototypical citizen-soldiers, but they are the homefront helpmeets for whom men fly to arms; they are the "Spartan Mothers" whose civic identity is bound up with the warrioring of sons.

Although women have long been identified with antiwar and antimilitarist efforts—so much so that an ironic result of such activities is to shore up the canard that women are more pacific by nature than men—they *appear* to have had little overall effect on the political culture of war/peace. This leads to yet another irony, that peace has been forged in opposition to war. These ironies have required and mirrored one another. To talk of war is to call forth its opposite. Antiwar activists have long been vexed with their lack of success in garnering and sustaining popular energy for their cause, the sort of energy wars—or good, popular wars—historically incite and channel. "Peace" does not appear in the title of this book, but, without the hope for peace variously understood, few of the contributors to this volume would be thinking about war and militarism and where women and men have fit and might fit with reference to the complex and contested human possibilities that peace symbolizes.

War/peace—twin apocalyptic fears and dreams of a more, if not perfect, peaceable kingdom. The subject of war is elusive, and becomes more so as one takes it up theoretically and critically. "Just War" thinkers have long suggested that we must not think simply in terms of war *versus* peace. A number of contemporary feminists urge us in this direction as well and point us to the existence of a "false peace" or unjust order. That is, they insist that "peace," as an absence of overt collective violence, may prevail, but the social order may nonetheless harbor, even institutionalize, many forms of violence against the dignity of human beings. Recall St. Augustine's blistering commentary on that peace that was the *Pax Romana:* "Peace and war had a competition in cruelty, and Peace won the prize." An unjust peace can be as devastating, he argued, as outright violence. There are many forms of brutality, exploitation, and devastation, and not all of them come at the point of the sword.

For these reasons, this book includes the word "militarism" in its title in order to reflect the concern of the editors and contributors with a deep and wide infrastructure that sustains a war-like peace, that revolves not only around preparation for collective conflict but also around a war-like politics. We are not in search of what Jane Addams called a "goody-goody" peace. Rather, we believe it is important to show the many ways that war permeates the body politic and works itself into the interstices of the social fabric to shape our dominant imagery and metaphors. We offer no tidy, stipulative definition of militarism, nor do any of our essayists. Rather, we alert the reader to the possibility that "war" versus "peace" cannot capture the daunting complexities of contemporary political and social life.

Having touched upon the grand, contested words in our title—women, militarism, and war—it might be helpful for us to explain, briefly, how we came to this editorial collaboration and what we hope this book will do. Sheila Tobias has long been concerned with several war-related issues. First, she is interested in the ways in which technical information, especially that having to do with modern weaponry and defense strategies, seem to intimidate and are used to intimidate, women. While on tour to talk about her book on "math anxiety" in 1979, the same period when the SALT II treaty had bogged down in the Senate, Tobias found that very few of the people she talked to knew what the "S" in SALT stood for. Despite wide media coverage on the topic, they failed to appreciate that the SALT II agreement had to do only with nuclear weapons of intercontinental range. Second, Tobias began puzzling over the connection between feminism and peace. Some feminists assimilated the two; others, including then-president of the National Organization for

Women, Eleanor Smeal, articulated the belief that "Peace is not a feminist issue."

As the texts in this volume make abundantly clear, peace has long been a *women's* issue—women as mothers, women as victims, women as preservers of the nation's—now the world's—good health. From these perspectives, many women historically found their way to peace as a moral and political priority. Indeed, it was part of the overoptimistic promise of nineteenth-century women's suffrage efforts that, once in power, women would see to it that politics was sanitized and wars were forbidden. So, where do women's peace politics—in the many bewildering varieties currently on display—fit, or not fit, with feminist politics? What are the current feminist approaches to militarism, to relations between liberal capitalist and state socialist systems, between developed and developing nations in our nuclear era? Just as these political questions began to be posed with growing insistency, the enterprise of women's studies expanded to include peace and conflict-resolution courses.

About the time Tobias was directing her efforts toward combatting the widespread ignorance of the vocabulary and syntax of debates on national security, efforts that culminated in an introductory primer called *What Kinds of Guns Are They Buying for Your Butter?*,[1] Jean Bethke Elshtain was completing her book, *Public Man, Private Woman,*[2] that exposed and criticized the many ways public and private spheres had been conceptualized in the tradition of Western political thought and among contemporary feminists. Although it was not then her major concern, Elshtain was struck by the close ties between citizenship and soldiering and the ways in which women's historic identities, as those who do not make war but mourn and support the men who do, had located them symbolically and politically as lesser civic beings. It was then that President Jimmy Carter's call for draft registration for men and women canalized Elshtain's energy and scholarship toward matters of men and women, war and peace. The result was *Women and War,*[3] and the beginning of our collaboration, a collaboration of mutual interest marked by debates over our different approaches to this subject. What we share is a strong conviction that a transformed polity might find it within itself to break the deadlock between war/peace; warriors/victims.

This book is organized into four parts, each devoted to a particular theme that overlaps with what precedes and what follows. We offer no comprehensive history of peace politics. Nor will the reader find a systematic model or blueprint of what is to be done. Rather, we provide, through the scholarship of our contributors, a sampler of ideas and narratives, critiques and exhortations that we have woven together with commentaries. We hope this way of structuring our effort promotes a dialogue among our contributors as well as among them and our readers.

As in all lively collections, there is diversity in perspective and voice. We hope that the essays will help you read more closely and think more analytically, with moral passion and concern, about subjects that tend to generate confusion and even despair. We see the book as a contribution to women's studies, international relations, history, philosophy, ethics. But we also hope it captures a moment in the ongoing debate about women, militarism, and war.

Jean Bethke Elshtain and Sheila Tobias

Notes

1. The full title is *What Kinds of Guns Are They Buying for Your Butter: A Beginner's Guide to Defense, Weaponry and Military Spending* (New York: Wm. Morrow, 1982); retitled for the paperback edition as *The People's Guide to National Defense* (New York: Wm. Morrow, 1984).

2. Princeton University Press, 1981.

3. Basic Books, 1987.

Part I

Mothers, Feminists, and the Politics of Peace in the Nuclear Age

Comments

We begin with this piece by Amy Swerdlow because it provides a moving story of women succeeding in peace politics in the nuclear era. What we see through Swerdlow's recapturing of an important moment in the history of the Women Strike for Peace is a form of politics that does not mimic dominant male forms—forms that exist not only among militarists but among a male-dominated politics of peace. Even when called before the House Un-American Activities Committee, these 1960s women for peace did not succumb to the temptation to ferret out nonconformists or to protect themselves by engaging in their own kind of politics of repression. Long before the second feminist wave embraced a nonhierarchical ideal, the Women Strike for Peace showed its power.

Women of the Women Strike for Peace made the most of a particular historic construction of women as mothers, demonstrating the latent political power of that role, just as the Mothers of the Plaza de Mayo in Argentina have done in more recent years. Those "Mothers of the Disappeared" wore scarves during their demonstrations, simulated diapers embroidered with the names of their tortured and "disappeared" children. These and other historic episodes show how the strengths of mothers can and have been forged and maternal identities politicized to oppose state power.

As Swerdlow tells the story, a great strength of the Women Strike for Peace was its inclusivity. Although not all women involved were mothers, all women were welcome to participate in a nonsectarian movement. Since the early 1960s, feminism has both built on and questioned this

3

kind of political action. At its worst, feminist politics sometimes exhibits the sectarianism that has long undermined the left in American politics. Those espousing the model of androgyny, which was powerful in articulating a new feminist program in the 1970s, are made uneasy by images of the power and authority of mother. One result of this ambivalence is that the story of women's peace politics has gone underreported.

One can understand a feminist's unease: the symbols of milk and baby-carriages coupled with the self-proclaimed amateurism of the strategy and tactics all fly in the face of the androgynous ideal—narrowly construed—as does the rejection of a politics of "expertise." Feminists can point to the reactionary mobilization of "motherhood" (especially in the fascist models) as evidence of the dangers of proceeding in this direction. However, nazism enforced a mobilization of mothers; here mothers mobilized themselves under a politics they *defined* in opposition to a regime or state of affairs.[1]

Swerdlow reminds us of its power and its efficacy, for the Women Strike for Peace *did* succeed in its goal: in 1963, the United States and the Soviet Union signed a limited test ban treaty prohibiting testing of nuclear weapons in the atmosphere—a treaty that has never been broken. In signing the document, President John F. Kennedy acknowledged the contribution of the Women Strike.[2]

Given a more expansive view of citizenship—a theme that will reverberate throughout this volume—the women participating in the Women Strike for Peace were not just mobilizing as mothers. They were entering the public sphere as citizens, legitimating a civic voice most often excluded from considerations of national security and foreign policy. Indeed, Swerdlow insists on conceptualizing motherhood as a social and communal and not just a private activity.

In addition to the points she makes about motherhood and citizenship, Swerdlow shows the grand deconstructive power of a politics of humor, irony, evasion, and ridicule. The Women Strike for Peace didn't proclaim that the Emperor had no clothes; rather, it put him in a position where, to his own astonishment, he found he had disrobed himself with his own tactics and strategies. Too often our politics becomes solemn and brittle— just like that of those we are opposing. Swerdlow recaptures images that exhibit the compelling force of a form of political theatre, more akin to classic comedies of reversal (Aristophanes' *The Congresswomen*) than to tragedies riddled with plots, violence, and victories bought at a terrible cost in human lives.

4

Note

1. See Leila J. Rupp, *Mobilizing Women for War* (Princeton, N.J.: Princeton University Press, 1978); also Claudia Koontz, *Mothers in the Fatherland: Women, the Family and Nazi Politics* (New York: St. Martin's Press, 1987).

2. We do not suggest of course that the women's efforts alone led to the test ban treaty.

1

Motherhood and the Subversion of the Military State: Women Strike for Peace Confronts the House Committee on Un-American Activities

Amy Swerdlow

This essay situates itself within the current theoretical and historical debates among feminist scholars and activists regarding the relationship of gender difference to gender equality. One of the most pressing political questions for feminists today is whether separatist women's peace groups advance or undermine the social and political changes they espouse. There are those, like Simone de Beauvoir, who charge that those women's movements that stress female identification with nurturance and moral guardianship project an essentialist view of women that not only rein-

This is a revised version of "Ladies' Day at the Capitol: Women Strike for Peace Confronts HUAC," which appeared in *Feminist Studies* 8 (Fall 1982): 493–520.

forces our secondary status but also lays the basis for all other forms of social oppression, including militarism. On the other hand, a number of historians of women point out that since the nineteenth-century women's organizations have used the ideology of domesticity to undermine it, and that this dialectic has been an essential component of all the important women's political movements in the United States, from moral reform and temperance to abolition and peace.[1]

This essay seeks to reconstruct a confrontation between Women Strike for Peace (WSP), a newly-formed separatist women's peace movement, and the House Un-American Activities Committee (HUAC), which took place twenty-five years ago. By analyzing the ideology, consciousness, political style, and public demeanor of the WSP women as they defended their rights as mothers "to influence the course of government," we can learn a great deal about the strengths and weaknesses of women's movements for social change that build on traditional sex role ideology and on female culture.

HUAC's intention in issuing subpoenas in 1962 to thirteen female peace activists was, in its own words, "to determine the extent of Communist Party infiltration into the peace movement, in a manner and to a degree affecting the national security."[2] The women of WSP interpreted the summons as an attempt to "intimidate women who might become active." "This we can't allow," WSP declared, "because . . . more and more it's obvious that it has to be *the women* who speak for mankind."[3]

The tactics and rhetoric WSP employed to meet the fearsome challenge from HUAC were cool, feminine, nonideological, and pragmatic—far different from those of earlier radical groups called before the committee. The WSP strategy was to stress the rights of ordinary mothers to protect children from nuclear death over the rights of governments to kill them. In their organizational response to the HUAC summons and in their testimony at the hearings, the women of WSP were so effective and witty in evoking traditional assumptions regarding a woman's role that they succeeded in holding the committee up to public ridicule, and damaging its image and reputation with the press, the public, and Congress. In fact, Eric Bentley, in a history of the committee, which he called *Thirty Years of Treason*, gives WSP the credit for striking the crucial blow in "the fall of HUAC's Bastille." Other historians have concurred.[4] The battle of the sexes between WSP and HUAC demonstrates that reliance on female culture can give women the freedom, creativity, and courage that rigid ideological male-led groups often lack. It also reveals that women's movements are not static in that women who invoke traditional culture to

8

justify their struggle against patriarchal institutions can find themselves in direct contradiction to the sex role ideology they formerly espoused.

WSP burst upon the American political scene on November 1, 1961, when an estimated fifty thousand women in over sixty cities in the United States walked out of their kitchens and off their jobs in a one-day women's peace strike. As a radioactive cloud from a Russian nuclear test hung over the American landscape and the United States was threatening to hold its own series of atmospheric tests, these women staged the largest female peace action of the twentieth century.[5] After a decade marked by Cold War consensus and the feminine mystique, the women strikers seemed to be coming from nowhere. They were, in fact, responding to a call from a handful of Washington, D.C., women who had become alarmed by the acceleration of Cold War confrontations between the United States and the USSR, which they feared could turn into a push-button nuclear holocaust. They were so disheartened by the passivity of traditional peace groups in the face of what they perceived to be a world crisis that they contacted women friends all over the country, urging them to suspend their regular routine of home, family, and jobs in a dramatic one-day strike "To End the Arms Race—Not the Human Race."[6]

The call to strike, which was composed in Washington, spread rapidly from coast to coast through typical female networks: telephone and Christmas card lists, contacts in PTAs, the League of Women Voters, church and temple groups, and flyers left in doctors' offices and supermarkets. Established peace organizations such as the Women's International League for Peace and Freedom (WILPF) and the Committee for a Sane Nuclear Policy (SANE) also spread the word. The nature of the strike in each community depended entirely on what the local women were willing and able to do. Some marched while others visited local officials. A few groups took ads in local newspapers, and thousands sent telegrams to the White House and to the Soviet Embassy, calling upon the first ladies of the two nuclear superpowers, Jacqueline Kennedy and Nina Khrushchev, to urge their husbands to "stop all nuclear tests—east and west." Impressed by the numbers and the composition of the turnout, *Newsweek*[7] commented:

> They were perfectly ordinary looking women, with their share of good looks; they looked like the women you would see driving ranch wagons, or shopping at the village market, or attending PTA meetings. It was these women by the thousands, who staged demonstrations in a score of cities across the nation . . . protesting atomic testing. A "strike for peace" they

9

called it and—carrying placards, many wheeling baby buggies or strollers— they marched on city halls and Federal buildings to show their concern about nuclear fallout.

The women's peace strike, however, did not end on the first day of November. By the end of 1962, the participants had transformed a one-day action into a national movement with local groups in sixty communities and offices in ten cities. With no paid staff and no designated leaders, thousands of women in different parts of the country, most of them previously unknown to each other, managed to establish a loosely structured communications network capable of swift and effective direct action on a national and international scale. From its inception, WSP was a participatory movement of women consciously opposed to rigid hierarchical organizational structures. They called their much debated format "our un-organization," but they showed little understanding of its significance for feminist process.[8] Eleanor Garst, one of the Washington founders, explained the attractions of the WSP un-organization this way:

> No one must wait for orders from headquarters—there aren't any headquarters. No one's idea must wait for clearance through the national board. No one waits for the president or the director to tell her what to do—there is no president or director. Any woman who has an idea can propose it through an informal memo system; if enough women think it's good, it's done. Those who don't like a particular action don't have to drop out of the movement; they just sit out that action and wait for one they like. Sound "crazy"?—it is, but it also brings forth and utilizes the creativity of thousands of women who could never be heard from through ordinary channels.[9]

From its first day, WSP tapped a vast reservoir of moral outrage, energy, organizational talent, and sisterhood—female capacities that had been submerged and silenced for more than a decade by McCarthyism and the national celebration of female domesticity. The women used standard pressure group tactics, such as lobbying and petitioning, coupled with direct action and face-to-face meetings with women across national and ideological boundaries, executed with imagination and "feminine flair." The WSPers' talent for creating human interest stories succeeded in placing women's political demands on the front pages of the nation's newspapers, from which they had all but disappeared since the days of the suffrage campaign. WSP also managed to influence public officials and public policy. At a time when peace marchers were ignored or condemned as "commies" or "kooks," President John F. Kennedy gave public recognition to the women strikers. Commenting on a WSP march at the White House on January 15, 1962, the President told the nation in his regularly scheduled news conference that he thought the WSP women were "extremely earnest."

> I saw the ladies myself. I recognized why they were here. There were a great number of them, it was in the rain. I understand what they were attempting to say, therefore, I consider their message received.[10]

In 1970, *Science* reported that Jerome Wiesner, President Kennedy's Science Advisor, "gave the major credit" for moving President Kennedy toward the Limited Test Ban Treaty of 1963 not to arms controllers inside the government but to the Women Strike for Peace and to SANE and Linus Pauling."[11]

Although WSP, in its first year, was well received by liberal politicians and journalists, the surveillance establishment and the right-wing press were wary of what a researcher for the Rand Corporation saw as the WSP potential "to impact on military policies."[12] Jack Lotto, a Hearst columnist, charged that although the women described themselves as a "group of unsophisticated housewives and mothers who are loosely organized in a spontaneous movement for peace, there is nothing spontaneous about the way the pro-Reds have moved in on our mothers and are using them for their own purposes."[13] *The San Francisco Examiner* claimed to have proof that "scores of well-intentioned, dedicated women . . . were being made dupes of by known Communists . . . operating openly in the much publicized Women Strike for Peace demonstrations."[14] The fact is that WSP was under FBI surveillance from its first planning meetings for the November strike. FBI records on WSP, which have been made available under the provisions of the Freedom of Information Act, show that FBI offices in major cities, North, East, South, and West—and even in such places as Mobile, Phoenix, and San Antonio, not noted particularly for WSP activities—were sending and receiving reports on the WSP women, often prepared in cooperation with local "red squads."[15]

Having just lived through the Cuban missile crisis, WSPers celebrated their first anniversary with a deep sense of urgency and pride in their new movement. As the women were making plans to increase their numbers and expand their activities, they were stopped in their tracks by subpoenas to thirteen women in the New York metropolitan area, as well as to Dagmar Wilson of Washington, D.C., the movement's founder and national spokesperson.[16]

It is difficult today to comprehend the emotions and fears such a summons could evoke, as HUAC was known for destroying the lives, careers, and reputations of those it labeled un-American. Lillian Hellman's *Scoundrel Time* gives a picture of the tension, isolation, and near hysteria she felt as she prepared her defense against the committee in 1953.[17] By 1962, cold war hysteria had abated somewhat, as the United States and the USSR were engaged in test-ban negotiations. But HUAC represented those forces in American politics that opposed such negotiations and, as a committee of Congress, still possessed the power to command headlines and cast suspicion. By labeling organizations as subversive it could eliminate them from political contention.

As the key women of WSP were attempting to cope with the shock of the HUAC summons, they discovered that three of those subpoenaed were not even involved in WSP. They were members of the Conference of Greater New York Peace Groups, an organization founded by New Yorkers who had either been expelled or who had willingly withdrawn from SANE because of its internal red hunts. Of these three women, two had already been named as communists in previous HUAC hearings, and one, Elizabeth Moos, had achieved considerable notoriety when she was identified by accused Russian spy William Remington as his mother-in-law and a card-carrying communist. Given these circumstances, it was clear that the WSP women across the country had some important decisions to make about how they would conduct their defense against HUAC. As WSP had no official membership list, the first question was: Should the movement embrace any subpoenaed woman working for peace even if she was not directly involved in WSP activities? The second question was: Should WSP disavow women within the movement who had past or present communist affiliations. The question of Communist affiliation raised fears, for if WSP did not disavow them, the movement questioned whether it would lose its political credibility.

The key to WSP unity in the face of the "communist issue," which had divided and disrupted peace, labor, and civil liberties organizations in the past, was a sense of sisterhood that transcended ideological differences. WSP had, even before the HUAC summons, decided to reject political screening of its members, deeming it a manifestation of outdated Cold War thinking. This decision, the women claimed, was based not on fear or expediency but on principle. The issue of accepting communists in the movement had been brought to the floor of the first national conference by the Los Angeles coordinating council. A statement by the Los Angeles group declared: "Unlike SANE and Turn Toward Peace, WSP must not make the error of initiating its own purges." Treating the issue of communist membership as a question of personal conscience, the Los Angeles group asked, "If there are communists or former communists working in WSP, what difference does that make? We do not question one another about our religious beliefs or other matters of personal conscience. How can we justify political interrogation?" The Los Angeles statement continued: "If fear, mistrust and hatred are ever to be lessened, it will be by courageous individuals who do not hate and fear and can get together to work out tolerable compromises."[18] The argument that "this is a role women would be particularly equipped to play" won over the conference and resulted in a section of the official national policy statement that declared that WSP included "women of all races, creeds and political persuasions who are dedicated to the achievement of general and complete disarmament under effective international control."[19]

The first decision made by WSP after the HUAC summons was that it would live up to its inclusionary policy, and that it would embrace and support all the women summoned before HUAC, regardless of their past or present affiliations, as long as they opposed both Russian and American nuclear policies. This meant that WSP would support the three women from the Greater New York Peace Council along with its own activists from New York. All would be given access to the same lawyers and would not be isolated or attacked either for their affiliations or for the way they chose to conduct themselves at the hearing. This decision contrasted sharply with the action taken by SANE in 1960 when it expelled a leading member of its New York chapter after he invoked the Fifth Amendment at a Senate Internal Security Subcommittee hearing and refused to tell Norman Cousins, a cochairman of SANE, whether or not he had ever been a communist.[20]

The decision made by the New York and Washington key women not "to cower" before the committee, to conduct no internal purges, to acknowledge each woman's right to act according to the dictates of her conscience, was bold for its day. The women themselves arrived at this position without consultation with the male leaders of more traditionally organized peace and civil liberties groups, many of whom disagreed with the WSP policy.[21] The policy was based not only on the decision to resist the demonology of the Cold War but also on empathy for the women who had been singled out for attack. Working together at a feverish pace, night and day for three weeks, writing, phoning, speaking at rallies, the key women of WSP, including all those subpoenaed, acted like a family under attack for which all personal resources and energies had to be

13

marshalled. But the family, this time, was the WSP movement, and it was the sisters, not the fathers, who were in charge.

An anti-HUAC statement was composed, which spoke so well to the concerns and the consciousness of the WSPers that it succeeded in unifying a movement in confusion and shock. The anti-HUAC statement declared:

> Differences of politics, economics or social belief disappear, when we recognize man's common peril. . . . We do not ask an oath of loyalty to any set of beliefs. Instead we ask loyalty to the race of man [sic]. The time is long past when a small group of censors can silence the voice of peace.[22]

These words would be the WSP *leitmotif* in the HUAC hearings. The women were saying once again, as they had throughout their first year, that the Cold War and the arms race were obsolete concepts in the nuclear age.

WSP took the offensive against the committee, publicizing the subpoenas even before HUAC did. The memorandum proposed that "the usual response of protest and public statements is too traditional and ineffectual. . . . Let's Turn the Tables! Let's meet the HUAC challenge in the Good New WSP way!" The "new way," suggested simultaneously by different women from different parts of the country, was to insist on the right of any WSP woman to testify at the hearings, rather than to refuse to talk as many principled radicals and civil libertarians had done in the 1940s and 1950s. Over one hundred WSPers volunteered to "tell all" about their movement. Carol Urner of Portland, Oregon, spoke for those who volunteered. She made it clear that she wanted to talk about the WSP program because she was proud of it, but she vowed not to be a "friendly witness." "I could not, of course, divulge the names of others in the movement," she wrote to Representative Francis Walter, Chairman of HUAC.

> I suppose such a refusal could lead one to "contempt" and prison and things like that . . . and no mother can accept lightly even the remote possibility of separation from the family which needs her. But mankind need us too.[23]

The WSP offers to testify were refused by HUAC, but the publicity around the committee's refusal cheered and heartened the women, as it pointed up the fact that HUAC was less interested in gathering information than in exposing and smearing dissenters. Some WSP groups objected to the volunteer testimony strategy on the grounds that there was a contradiction between denying the right of the committee to exist and offering to cooperate with it. But these groups were in the minority.

Only three weeks time elapsed between the arrival of the subpoenas from HUAC and the date scheduled for the hearings. In that short period, the WSPers managed to develop a legal defense, collect the funds to support the subpoenaed women, and launch a national campaign against the hearings and the committee. But the most important factor in WSP's triumph over HUAC was the fact that WSP's performance at the hearings was so original, so winning, and so unexpectedly "feminine" that it succeeded in captivating the media. For once a HUAC investigation strengthened the group under attack and weakened the committee.

The hearings opened on December 11, 1962, at 10:00 A.M. in the caucus room of the Old House Office Building of the United States Congress. Fear turned to exhilaration as each WSPer in the audience became aware that almost every seat in the room was occupied by sisters who had come from eleven states, some from as far as California. All the women rose as one when the committee called its first witness, Blanche Posner, a retired schoolteacher who was the volunteer office manager of the New York WSP. The decision to rise with the first witness, to stand *with* her, was spontaneous. It was proposed only a few minutes before Posner was called, as a note from an unknown source was circulated around the room. Posner refused to answer any questions about the structure or the individual women involved in WSP. She resorted to the Fifth Amendment forty-four times, which the press pointed out in dozens of news stories. The media also reported the way in which Posner took matters into her own hands, lecturing the committee members as though they were backward boys at DeWitt Clinton High School in the Bronx where she had taught in her youth. Talking right through the interruptions and objections raised by the committee chairman, Clyde Doyle, and by counsel, Alfred Nittle, Posner declared:

> I don't know, sir, why I am here, but I do know why you are here, . . . because you don't quite understand the nature of this movement. This movement was inspired and motivated by mothers' love for children. . . . When they were putting their breakfast on the table, they saw not only the Wheaties and milk, but they also saw strontium 90 and iodine 131. . . . They feared for the health and life of their children. . . . If you gentlemen have children or grandchildren you should be grateful to the Women Strike for Peace.[24]

15

Each time Posner resorted to the Fifth Amendment, she did it with a condescending and witty quip directed at the committee. This endeared her to the women in the hearing room who needed to keep up their spirits in the face of charges that Posner had been identified by an FBI informer as a member of the Communist party while she was working as a New York City schoolteacher. One exchange between Nittle and Posner led to particularly enthusiastic applause and laughter from the WSPers. Nittle asked, "Did you wear a colored paper daisy to identify yourself as a member of the Women Strike for Peace?" Posner answered, "It sounds like such a far cry from communism it is impossible not to be amused. I still invoke the Fifth Amendment."[25]

Most of the women subpoenaed were chosen because the committee apparently believed it had evidence to link them with the Communist party through identification by FBI informers or because they had signed Communist party nominating petitions. This strategy backfired with Ruth Meyers of Roslyn, Long Island. She stepped forward, according to a report in the *Washington* (D.C.) *Evening Star*, "swathed in red and brown jersey, topped by a steeple crowned red velvet hat," and "was just as much of a headache to the committee as Posner had been."[26] There was much sparring between Meyers and the committee about the nature and structure of WSP. "Are you presently a member of a group known as Women Strike for Peace?" Nittle asked. "No, sir," Meyers replied, "Women Strike for Peace has no membership."[27] When asked by Nittle if the New York group had been responsible for the idea of sending a delegation of women to a Geneva disarmament conference, which Nittle characterized as the "most spectacular accomplishment of WSP," Meyers replied:

> The conception of the program gets so lost when hundreds of women are thinking about it. Sometimes we find that we are coming to the same idea at the same time, and no one looks for credit. We just look for activity.[28]

Nittle then asked Meyers the crucial question. "Mrs. Meyers," he intoned, "it appears from the public records that a Ruth Meyers, residing at 1751 East 10th Street, Brooklyn, New York, on July 27, 1948, signed a Communist Party nominating petition. . . . Are you the Ruth Meyers who executed that petition?" Meyers shot back, "No, sir." She examined the petition carefully, and announced, "I never lived in Brooklyn, and this is not my signature."[29] Although the official transcript does not contain the following statement, many, including the author, remember that Meyers added, "My husband could never get me to move there." This domestic remark brought an explosion of laughter and applause. Meyers also invoked the Fifth Amendment. As she left the witness stand she received a one-minute ovation for humor, grace, and mistaken identity. In front of TV cameras outside the hearing room, Meyers told reporters that she had never been a communist. "But I'll never acknowledge the committee's right to ask me that question."

Another witness, Lyla Hoffman, chose to reveal her own past communist affiliation, asserting that she had left the party. However, she would not cooperate in naming names or in citing the cause of her resignation. In a statement to WSP written after the hearings, Hoffman explained: "I felt that it was high time to say, 'What difference does it make what anyone did, or believed, many years ago? That's not the problem facing humanity today.' But I had to say this in legal terms." This she could not do because the committee was interested only in whether she was a genuine anticommunist or a secret fellow-traveler.[30] Hoffman invoked the First Amendment, which could have sent her to jail.

The witnesses who followed Posner, Meyers, and Hoffman, each in her own style, invoked whatever rhetorical or legal strategy her conscience, her talents, and her particular situation dictated. The women lectured the committee eloquently and courageously on the danger of nuclear holocaust and on women's responsibility and right to work for human survival in the nuclear age. In attempting to explain WSP's loose structure, several witnesses suggested laughingly that the movement was too fluid, too democratic, and too chaotic for the male members of HUAC to comprehend.

In their most optimistic projections, the WSP women could not have predicted the overwhelmingly favorable press and public response they would receive, and the support and growth for the movement that resulted from the HUAC investigation. The WSP leadership had understood that HUAC needed the press to make its tactics of intimidation and punishment work. So, WSP played for the press—as it had done from its founding—and won! The Washington and New York leadership knew that it had two stories, and both were developed to the hilt. The first was motherhood under attack and the second was the age-old battle of the sexes. The contest between the sexes, according to the WSP version, involved female common sense, openness, connectedness, humor, and hope versus male solemnity, rigidity, abstraction, and suspicion. The WSPers, in their pointedly feminine style, turned the hearings into an episode of the familiar and funny "I Love Lucy," which was far different from the tragic and scary inquisitions of Alger Hiss and the Hollywood Ten. For the first time, HUAC was belittled with humor, and treated successfully to a dose of its own moral superiority.

At the end of the first day of the hearings, headlines critical of the committee and supportive of WSP were featured on the front pages of prominent newspapers from coast to coast. The Chicago *Daily News* declared: "It's Ladies' Day at the Capitol: Hoots, Howls—and Charm; Congressmen Meet Match." Russell Baker's column was headed "Peace March Gals Make Red Hunters Look Silly," and a *Detroit Free Press* story carried the title, "Headhunters Decapitated." A cartoon by Herblock in *The Washington Post* showed three aging and baffled HUAC members seated at their hearing table. One turns to another and whispers, "I Came in Late, Which Was It That Was Un-American—Women or Peace?"[31] A story in the *Vancouver* (B.C.) *Sun* of December 14 was typical of many other reports:

> The dreaded House Un-American Activities Committee met its Waterloo this week. It tangled with 500 irate women. They laughed at it. Kleig lights glared, television cameras whirred, and 50 reporters scribbled notes while babies cried and cooed during the fantastic inquisition.

The question most often asked about the WSP response to HUAC is: "Were the WSPers cleverly manipulating female culture for political advantage, or had they internalized the anti-feminist consciousness of the 1950s so thoroughly that they didn't even suspect that they were relying on sex role stereotypes? After studying the rhetoric and tactics of WSP and its internal documents, interviewing a dozen of the most influential leaders, and looking back to my own memories as a key woman in WSP, I can offer no clear-cut answer to this question. The WSPers, it seems to me, were using the gender consciousness of the 1950s at the same time as they were stressing its contradictions. An examination of the backgrounds of the WSP activists reveals that the WSPers based themselves on both their gender and their political consciousness, which were tempered by the constraints engendered by the political repression and the antifeminism of the previous decade. The key women of WSP were, for the most part, in their thirties and forties at the inception of the movement. Most of them reached adulthood in the late 1930s and early to mid-1940s. They had been students or workers in the years of political ferment preceding World War II, and had married just before, during, or right after the war. The majority of the women had contributed to the postwar baby boom, and they had participated in the domesticity, the privatism, and the consumerism of the previous decade. The WSPers seem to have enjoyed the benefits of middle-class economic mobility to the point of losing their class consciousness. The issue of class was never discussed in the early years of WSP, whereas racial injustice was constantly referred to. Eleanor Garst, one of WSP's image makers, proclaimed the women's pride in their middle-class status and their preference for acceptable politics.

> The women [WSPers] continue to attract recruits until the movement now numbers hundreds of thousands. . . . Furthermore, . . . they are no oddball types, but pillars of the community long courted by civic organizations. Others—perhaps the most numerous—are apolitical housewives who have never before lifted a finger to work for peace or any other social concern.[32]

Despite the fact WSP proclaimed itself a network of political neophytes, the movement was actually initiated by five women who were already active members of SANE in Washington, D.C. They had gravitated toward each other because of their mutual distaste for SANE's internal red hunts and their frustration with the organization's concentration on lobbying instead of direct action. The women were most disenchanted, however, with the fact that the male leadership of SANE did not give top priority to such "mother's" issues as contamination of milk by radioactive fallout from atmospheric atomic testing.

Dagmar Wilson was forty-five years old and unaccustomed to political leadership when she called a few friends to her home in the late summer of 1961 to discuss what they could do in response to the escalating nuclear arms race and the Berlin wall crisis, which she feared would turn into a push-button nuclear war. At this meeting WSP was born. Wilson was, at the time, a successful children's book illustrator, the mother of three daughters, and the wife of Christopher Wilson, a commercial attaché at the British Embassy. She had been born in the United States but had spent most of her early years in England. Her father, Cesar Searchinger, was a broadcast reporter for CBS and later for NBC. Wilson returned to the United States prior to World War II, held a variety of professional jobs as an artist and teacher, and eventually became a free-lance illustrator. Following the advice of Dr. Spock and other child development specialists, Wilson worked from a studio at home in order to be available to her children and to insure a smooth-running household. Despite the fact that Wilson was so successful an illustrator that one of her books had

19

become a best-seller, she identified herself to the press and public as a housewife. During an interview in 1976 she explained:

> My idea in emphasizing the housewife rather than the professional was that I thought the housewife was a downgraded person, and that we, as housewives had as much right to an opinion, and that we deserved as much consideration as anyone else. I wanted to emphasize . . . this was an important role and it was time we were heard.[33]

A gifted artist, an intelligent person of grace and charm, Wilson possessed the charisma of those who represent the feelings and perceptions of their constituency but excell them in passion and the capacity for creative expression. Having been a "nonjoiner" most of her life, and having spent her student days in England, Wilson had not been involved in radical U.S. politics of the 1940s. Consequently, she was free of the self-consciousness and timidity that plagued many WSPers who had been involved in leftist organizations and who still feared either exposure or persecution. Wilson claims she "never bought the Cold War." She recalled that "the State Department line . . . was being repeated without challenge or question by press, and by government officials, and accepted by intelligent, educated, intellectual, liberal Americans. . . . Was everyone brain-washed but me?" she wondered. She told an audience of WSPers in 1979 that:

> I was not only disturbed by our policies but angered by the gutlessness of the professional men who were a part of the social circle to which my husband and I belonged.[34]

Among the women who came to Dagmar Wilson's house to discuss what they could do to end the nuclear crisis was Eleanor Garst, whose direct, friendly, political prose played a powerful role in energizing and unifying WSP in its first year. Garst, who came from a conservative Baptist background, recalls that everything in her upbringing told her that the only thing a woman should do was to marry, have babies, care for her husband and babies, and "never mind your own needs." Despite this, Garst was the only one of the inner circle of Washington organizers who was a completely self-supporting professional woman, living on her own. The mother of two grown children, Garst worked as a community organizer for the Adams Morgan Demonstration Project, sponsored by American University to maintain integrated neighborhoods in Washington. Garst recalled that she had become a pacifist at the age of ten, after reading about war in poems and novels. Her husband, a merchant seaman, refused to be drafted for World War II, a decision he and Eleanor made together without consulting any pacifists because they had never met any. They spent their honeymoon composing an eighty-page brief against peacetime conscription and waiting for him to be arrested.

After the war, Garst became a professional political worker, writer, and peace activist. She was a founder of Los Angeles SANE before coming to Washington and an editor of its newsletter. Garst had been published in the *Saturday Evening Post, Reporter, Ladies Home Journal,* and other national publications when she was asked to draft the letter that initiated the successful November 1 strike.

Folly Fodor, who was also one of the WSP founders, had come to Washington in 1960 to follow her husband's job in the U.S. Labor Department. She joined SANE on her arrival and was elected to its local board. Thirty-seven years old at the time of the founding of WSP, Fodor was the mother of two and an old hand at political activism. She was the daughter of parents who had been involved in liberal-to-communist causes and had, herself, been a leader in radical organizations since her youth. As an undergraduate at Antioch College, Fodor was active in the Young People's Socialist League, eventually becoming "head of it," as she put it. In retrospect she believed that she had spent too much time fighting communists on campus, and "never did a goddamn thing."[35] Fodor had also been chairperson of the Young Democrats of California, yet she had secretly supported Henry Wallace in 1948. During the mid-1950s after the birth of her second child, Fodor organized an unaffiliated mothers group against nuclear testing. By 1961 Fodor was ready, willing, and able to become a key woman in a separatist women's peace group.

Two other women who helped to found WSP, Jeanne Bagby and Margaret Russell, were also active in the peace cause in 1961. Bagby, a former beatnik and committed pacifist, was a contributor to *Liberation,* the radical-pacifist journal. Russell was active in civil rights and peace organizations and was working with Garst as a community organizer. All the founders of WSP were politically conscious and interested in issues that went beyond the kitchen and the nursery. None were feminists, but they shared a conviction that the men in the peace movement and the government had failed them and that women had to insist on their share of political decision-making to save the planet. Together the founders and organizers of WSP possessed research, writing, organizing, speaking, and

21

public relations talents not unusual for women active in their communities in the 1950s.

But what of the thousands of other women who participated in the WSP movement in its first year? What were their social and political backgrounds and their motivations for taking to the streets in peace protest? Elise Boulding, a sociologist and long-time peace activist, who for the first six months after the strike edited the *Women's Peace Movement Bulletin*, an information exchange for WSP groups, kept wondering whether the majority of the WSPers were really political newcomers or "old pros" with a well-defined idea of some kind of world social order? She decided to find out. Using the resources of the Institute for Conflict Resolution in Ann Arbor and with the help of WSPers in the Ann Arbor chapter, she composed a questionnaire. It was sent to every eighth name on the mailing lists of 45 local groups. By the fall of 1962, shortly before the HUAC subpoenas, 279 questionnaires had been returned from 37 localities in 22 states. According to Boulding, the respondents represented a cross section of the movement—not only leaders.

Boulding found that the overwhelming majority of the WSP women were well-educated mothers, and that 61 percent were not employed outside the home. She concluded that the women who went out on strike in November 1961 and stayed on in the movement in the following months were a more complex and sophisticated group than the "buggy-pushing housewife" image the movement conveyed. Boulding characterized the WSPers as "largely intellectual and civic-minded people, most of the middle class"—very much like the Washington founders.[36]

In the 1940s, most of the women strikers were liberals, radicals, communists, socialists, Quakers or non-religious pacifists. Although few had been political leaders, they shared the 1940s belief that society could be reformed in the interest of peace and social justice through the direct efforts of ordinary people of good will like themselves. Dorothy Dinnerstein has described the psychological process of depoliticization and privatization that pushed them out of politics in the 1950s. According to Dinnerstein, people like the WSPers had spent the decade of the 1950s in moral shock caused both by McCarthyism and Stalinism. They lost their optimism and their capacity for social connectedness. "In this condition, Dinnerstein suggests, they withdrew from history.[37] What the WSPers withdrew into, with society's blessing, was the manageable sphere of children, home, husbands, and local community. When their children no longer required full-time care, many of the WSPers were propelled by earlier social, political, and humanitarian concerns into the

PTA, the League of Women Voters, the Democratic party, church, or temple. Some were returning to school and to work, but few of those who considered themselves key women in WSP were employed full-time outside the home.

It took the escalation of the nuclear arms race and the civil rights sit-ins to give the WSPers the sense of urgency and possibility. When the WSPers took to the streets, they were a disorganized band of middle-class housewives pleading for the children in the domestic terms they had been taught since childhood. But once in the political arena, the WSPers found that they were as intelligent, capable, articulate, and courageous as the men in government and in the peace movement to whom they had previously deferred. They realized that they could learn as much about radioactive isotopes as members of the Atomic Energy Commission, and that they already knew as much about the history of disarmament as members of the Arms Control and Disarmament Agency and more about the dangers of atomic holocaust than most of the men in Congress. Their commitment to the societal role prescribed for them, their disillusionment with the obsolete thinking of male leaders, and their determination not to be pushed back into the kitchen, made the WSPers unafraid of a mere congressional committee before which others had quaked.[38] In their confrontation with HUAC, the women of WSP stressed their role as mothers because it was that role that was being threatened both by the government's atomic policies and by HUAC. According to HUAC, it was communism that subverted the family, and they wanted to point out that, on the contrary, it was nuclear war that was the greatest threat to the family. For that reason, they wanted to use motherhood to subvert anticommunism. Another factor that made motherhood the focal point of the WSP testimony was the fact that carrying out their societal role was the WSPers' best claim to consideration.

In their concern for the fate of their children, the WSPers were no different from millions of other American women. However, they did differ in their broader perception of motherhood as a social and communal function, rather than as a purely private role. In addition, the WSPers were women ideologically and politically opposed to militarism and in favor of détente with the Soviet Union. In this regard they were closer to male pacifists and radicals than to women like Phyllis Schlafly, who testified against the ratification of the test ban treaty on the grounds that she, too, wanted to save her five children—not from fallout, but from communism.[39] When the WSPers acted on what they called their "rights and responsibilities to influence the course of government," they, like

23

Phyllis Schlafly, were acting not only on their maternal thought but also on their political assumptions as well.

Did the WSP campaign for the test ban treaty of 1963, including its rhetorical victory over HUAC, reinforce sex role stereotypes and thus weaken women politically? I believe the answer is no. The women of WSP had neither the historical memory of the pacifist feminist movement of the World War I era nor the analytical tools to make a connection between women's secondary status in the family and their political powerlessness in government, or between domestic violence and state violence. Lacking this understanding, WSP was never able to offer a feminist critique of war. But WSP did propel women into the political arena during a period of political and gender repression. The WSP movement made public speakers, political strategists, pamphlet writers and local, national, and international leaders out of formerly unknown housewives and mothers. In speaking, writing, talking, and walking for peace, in standing up to HUAC, and in traveling to Geneva to demand progress at the seventeen-nation disarmament conference, WSP demonstrated that women could be militant political thinkers and actors while still referring to themselves only as mothers and housewives. The Birmingham [England] Feminist History Group has suggested that the feminism of the 1950s seemed to be more concerned with integrating and foregrounding femininity than in transforming it in a fundamental way.[40] The tactics WSP used in its confrontation with HUAC follows this pattern. The WSP women were not concerned with transforming sex role ideology but rather with using it to enhance women's political power. But in so doing, they were transforming that ideology and foreshadowing the feminism that emerged later in the decade.

WSP also helped to change the image of the good mother from meek to militant, from private to public. In proclaiming that the men in power could no longer be counted on for protection, WSP challenged one of the most important myths regarding the male/female sex role contract: that wars are waged by men to protect women and children.

By stressing global issues and international cooperation among women rather than private family issues, WSP challenged the key element of the feminine mystique: the domestication and privatization of the middle-class white woman. By making recognized contributions to the achievement of an atmospheric test ban, WSP also raised women's sense of political efficacy and self-esteem. The struggle of WSPers against the bomb illustrated, despite the fact that women did not have the vocabulary to make that point themselves, that the familial and the personal are political, and that the private and public sphere are one.

Notes

1. Alice Schwartzer, "Simone de Beauvoir Talks About Sartre," *MS.*, August 1983, pp. 87–90; see Ellen DuBois *et al.*, *Feminist Studies* 6 (Spring 1980), pp. 26–64; Temma Kaplan, "Female Consciousness and Collective Action: The Case of Barcelona, 1910–1918," *Signs* 7 (Spring 1982), pp. 54–66; Micaela Di Leonardo, "Morals, Mothers, and Militarism: Antimilitarism and Feminist Theory," *Feminist Studies* 11 (Fall 1985), pp. 599–617.

2. United States Congress, House Committee on Un-American Activities, *Communist Activities in the Peace Movement (Women Strike for Peace and Certain Other Groups), Hearings Before the Committee on Un-American Activities on H. R. 9944*, 87th Cong., 2nd sess., 1962, p. 2057.

3. Letter from Women Strike for Peace, Washington, D.C. to "Dear WISPs," 16 December 1962, mimeo. WSP Document Collection. The WSP documents used in this essay were in the custody of the author until 1987. They are now in the Swarthmore College Peace Collection, which has a substantial collection of WSP documents.

4. Eric Bentley, *Thirty Years of Treason* (New York: Viking Press, 1971), p. 95; Charles de Benedetti, in *The Peace Reform in American History* (Bloomington, Ind.: Indiana University Press, 1980), pp. 167–78, states: "WSP activists challenged for the first time the House Un-American Activities Committee's practice of identifying citizen peace seeking with Communist subversion. . . . The open disdain of the WSP for HUAC did not end the Congress's preference for treating private peace actions as subversive. But it did help break the petrified anti-Communism of Cold War American politics and gave heart to those reformers who conceived peace as more than military preparedness."

5. The figure of fifty thousand claimed by the Washington founders after November 1 was accepted in most press accounts and became part of the WSP legend. It was based on reports from women in sixty cities and from newspapers across the country. Often the women's reports and those of the newspapers differed, but even using the highest figures available, I can substantiate only a count of approximately twelve thousand women who joined the strike. Nevertheless, this was still the largest women's peace demonstration to date in the twentieth century.

6. "Help Wanted," 25 October 1961, Washington, D.C., mimeo, WSP Document Collection. The prospect of human extinction through nuclear holocaust was also invoked by other peace activists during the early 1960s. The Port Huron statement, adopted at the founding convention of Students for A Democratic

Society (SDS) in 1962, stated: "Our work is guided by the sense that we may be the last generation in the experiment with living."

7. *Newsweek*, 13 November 1961, p. 21.

8. It is interesting to note that the young men of SDS, who were more aware of their place in the radical political tradition, more cognizant of the power of naming and of foreshadowing, called their loose structure "participatory democracy." WSP perceived its dedication to "un-organization" as a reaction to hierarchy in the state and in the peace movement, but the women did not understand the significance of their innovations for feminist process. See Swerdlow, "Politics of Motherhood," pp. 511–14. Jeanne Bagby, one of the founders of WSP, still referred to the WSP organizational methods as "naive" despite the fact that she recognized that "other organizations invariably suffered from the hierarchical, formalist impediments we so briskly ignored" (*Liberation*, December 1966, p. 33).

9. Eleanor Garst, "Women: Middle-Class Masses," *Fellowship* 28 (1 November 1962), pp. 10–12.

10. "Transcript of the President's News Conference on World and Domestic Affairs," *The New York Times*, 16 January 1962, p. 18.

11. *Science* 167 (13 March 1970), p. 1476.

12. A. E. Wessel, *The American Peace Movement: A Study of Its Themes and Political Potential* (Santa Monica: The Rand Corporation, 1962), p. 3.

13. *New York Journal American*, 4 April 1962.

14. *San Francisco Examiner*, 21 May 1962.

15. Copies of the FBI files on WSP are located in the offices of the Washington, D.C., law firm, *Gaffney, Anspach, Shember, Klimasi, and Marx*. As early as 23 October 1961, one week before the strike, the Cleveland office of the FBI had already identified one of the WSP planning groups as communist-infiltrated (FBI Document 100-39566-8). When WSP sent a delegation to lobby the Geneva Disarmament Conference in April 1962, the FBI enlisted the Swiss federal police and covert Central Intelligence Agency agents in the American embassy to spy on the women ("Legat Bern to Director," 4 April 1962, FBI Document 100-39566-222).

16. Those subpoenaed were, in order of appearance, Blanche Posner, Ruth Meyers, Lyla Hoffman, Elsie Neidenberg, Sylvia Contente, Rose Clinton, Iris Freed, Anna MacKenzie, Elizabeth Moos, Ceil Gross, Jean Brancato, Miriam Chesman, and Dagmar Wilson. Norma Spector was also supboenaed but never testified due to illness (*Hearings before Committee on Un-American Activities*, p. 111).

17. Lillian Hellman, *Scoundrel Time* (Boston: Little, Brown & Co., 1976), p. 99.

18. Los Angeles WISP, Statement I, Ann Arbor Conference, June 9–10, 1962 (WSP Document Collection).

19. "WSP National Policy Statement," *Women Strike for Peace Newsletter, New York, New Jersey, Connecticut,* Summer 1962, pp. 1–2.

20. Milton Steven Katz, "Peace Politics and Protest: SANE and the American Peace Movement, 1957–1972" (Ph.D. dissertation, St. Louis University, 1973), pp. 122–26.

21. Homer A. Jack, "The Will of the WSP Versus the Humiliation of HUAC," transcript of talk on Radio Station WBAI, New York, 28 December 1962, WSP Document Collection (mimeo).

22. Women Strike for Peace, letter to "Dear WISPs," "Statements on HUAC Subpoena," 6 December 1962, WSP Document Collection (mimeo).

23. From Carol Urner to Representative Francis Walter reprinted in *The Women's Peace Movement Bulletin* 1 (20 December 1962), p. 5.

24. *Hearings Before the Committee on Un-American Activities,* pp. 2074–75.

25. *Ibid.,* p. 2085.

26. Mary McGrory, "Prober Finds Peacemakers More Than a Match," *Washington,* (D.C.) *Evening Star,* 12 December 1962, p. A–1.

27. *Hearings Before the Committee on Un-American Activities,* p. 2095.

28. *Ibid.,* p. 2098.

29. *Ibid.,* p. 2101.

30. Lyla Hoffman, typewritten statement, n.d. (WSP Document Collection).

31. Thirty-seven favorable news stories, columns, and editorials were reprinted in a WSP pamphlet published two weeks after the hearings, among them pieces in *The Detroit Free Press, The Chicago Daily News, The Washington Post.*

32. Eleanor Garst, "Women: Middle-Class Masses," *Fellowship* 28 (1 November 1962), pp. 10–11.

33. Interview with Dagmar Wilson, Leesburg, Va., September 1977.

34. Speech by Dagmar Wilson, Hotel Roosevelt, N.Y., November 1979.

35. Interview with Folly Fodor, Washington, D.C., 6 November 1976.

36. Sixty-five percent of the women had either a B.A. or a higher degree in the early 1960s when only 6 percent of the female population over age 25 had a B.A. or more. Seventy-one percent of the WSP women were suburb or city dwellers. The highest concentrations were in the East Central states, the West Coast, and the Midwest, with low participation in the Mountain states and the South. The WSPers were concentrated in the 25- to 44-year-old age bracket. Only 5 percent of the group were "never marrieds." Of the married women, 43 percent had from 1 to 4 children under 6; 49 percent had 1 to 4 or more children over 18. Sixty-one percent of the women involved in WSP were not, at the time of the questionnaire, employed outside the home. Nearly 70 percent of the husbands of the WSPers who responded to the survey were professionals. Only 4 percent of the WSPers were members of professional organizations.

Thirty-eight percent of the women who responded claimed to belong to no other organizations or, at least, did not record the names of any organizations in response to questions concerning community activities. Forty percent were active in a combination of civic, race relations, civil liberties, peace, and electoral political activity. Boulding concluded that many of the WSPers were nonjoiners.

As for their goals in joining WSP, the Boulding survey revealed that 55 percent gave abolition of war or multilateral disarmament as their primary goals, and 22 percent gave nonviolent solution to all conflicts, political and social. This indicated that the majority were not committed pacifists. The remainder chose as their goals a variety of proposals for world government or limited international controls such as a test ban treaty. As to their reasons for taking part in WSP activities, 28 percent of the women said they had joined the movement over concern about fallout, testing, and civil defense. Another 4 percent joined because of the Berlin Wall crisis, but 41 percent listed no specific event, just an increasing sense of urgency about the total world situation and a need to make a declaration of personal responsibility (Elise Boulding, *Who Are These Women?* (Ann Arbor, Mich.: Institute for Conflict Resolution, 1962).

37. Dorothy Dinnerstein, *The Mermaid and the Minotaur: Sexual Arrangements and Human Malaise* (New York: Harper Colophon Books, 1976), pp. 259–62.

38. It has been suggested that the WSPers subpoenaed by HUAC were more carefree and impudent because they did not need to worry about the economic reprisals that the professional and working-class witnesses had faced in the past. Actually this is not so. Several women were under extreme pressure. Anna Mackenzie, who took the First Amendment, faced not only jail but the loss of her job, and Dagmar Wilson has stated that her husband had been warned that he might be fired from his position in the British Embassy in Washington. Blanche Posner, who had retired from teaching and was married to a successful lawyer, had nothing to fear in terms of her own livelihood. However, she was extremely vulnerable because her son, who had recently graduated from Harvard Law School, was known to be serving as a clerk in the office of Supreme Court Justice William Brennan. His mother's notoriety could have led to reprisals for him in his law career.

39. "Testimony of Mrs. Phyllis Schlafly, Fairmont, Alton, Illinois," *Hearings Before the Committee on Foreign Relations, United States Senate*, 88th Cong., 1st sess. on "The Treaty Banning Nuclear Weapons Tests in the Atmosphere, in Outer Space, and Underwater, Signed at Moscow on August 4, 1963, on Behalf of the United States of America, the United Kingdom of Great Britain and Northern Ireland, and the Union of Soviet Socialist Republics, August 12, 13, 14, 15, 19, 20, 22, 23, 26, and 27, 1963" (Washington, D.C.: U.S. Government Printing Office, 1963), pp. 906–16.

40. Birmingham (England) History Group, "Feminism as Femininity in the Nineteen Fifties?" *Feminist Review* 3 (1979), pp. 48–65.

Comments

In the three decades spanning the activism of the Women's Strike for Peace in the early 1960s and Carol Cohn's participation in an MIT/Harvard Summer Program on Nuclear Weapons and Arms Control in 1984, the U.S. nuclear "experiment" had grown into a weapons establishment complete with its own language and metaphors.

A specialist in social and political thought, Cohn was one of forty-eight college teachers invited to that summer program. For the first time, she was immersed in an intensive study of the technology of nuclear weaponry and nuclear strategic doctrine. At the end of that program, she was invited to be a Visiting Scholar at MIT's Center for International Studies ("Center" in her narrative) and so spent a full year in the world of "defense intellectuals."

During that year she collected insightful anecdotes, many of which are detailed in this essay. Most interesting of all was the relationship between herself and the language of strategic thinking that began to evolve. First, she found the language distancing. She soon found that her own thinking was being altered by the specialized jargon she calls "techno-strategic" and by the aspects of gender and machismo inherent in its syntax and vocabulary.

Cohn's method, that of the participant-observer, develops what Clifford Geertz has called "thick description"—unpacking the webs of significance we spin for ourselves.[1] Cohn hits upon a fascinating and yet troubling phenomenon: the more we learn the language of some "other" (a group, a society, a discourse), the more we try to enter its world and

29

understand it, the more likely it is we will begin to see things through their eyes and in their terms. This happens because language is, as Wittgenstein insisted, a way of life.

It was this life of nuclear and defense intellectuals that Cohn entered, observed, and yet sought to retain her distance from. She demonstrates the ways in which strategic discourse, in Freeman Dyson's characterization, is a language promoting a style that is "deliberately cool, attempting to exclude overt emotion and rhetoric . . . emphasizing technical accuracy and objectivity,"[2] thereby structuring the way such analysts frame the world and locate themselves and their expertise within it. Through the use of metaphors and euphemisms, trafficking in what Jean Elshtain has called "pseudo-concrete universals," the nuclear priesthood sets about its work. Cohn resists easy condemnation of this discourse. Rather, she uses *their* rhetoric to form the basis of a reflective and distancing critique. She apprises us of how an ostensibly neutral language of scientific description is, in fact, a political and moral language of justification.

One question to consider is whether *all* this language is equally menacing and designed to obscure. Is there a difference between the terms "Peacekeeper" for the MX and "pacification" for the burning of villages and uprooting of peasants, and the acronyms ALCM, GLCM, and SLCM (for air-launched cruise missiles, ground-launched cruise missiles, and submarine-launched cruise missiles) that can be justified by simple economy? Are the former terms egregious attempts to mislead but the latter acronyms merely more innocent instances of a wide-spread practice? Thinking about these and other distinctions helps us to point to the use of language as it reveals the military mind-set and obscures the human suffering behind its jargon.

Another important question must be asked. Does the search for a parsimonious discourse as the preserve of experts, by definition available only to the initiated few, in itself disempower the vast majority of us and disallow us a voice in these matters? If we cannot enter the debate unless we speak "techno-strategically," what are the implications for democracy? These concerns are not new. The democratic theorists who emerged in the 1960s urged a return to a language of civic discourse as one feature of a revitalization of politics and as part of an attempt to stem the tide of policy science managerialism. Even before that, George Orwell, in his classic essay, "Politics and the English Language," urged upon us a language of representation that did not distance us from nor disguise that which it purports to describe.

Notes

1. See Clifford Geertz, *The Interpretation of Cultures* (New York: Basic Books, 1973).
2. Freeman Dyson, *Weapons and Hope* (New York: Harper and Row, 1984), p. 4.

2

"Clean Bombs" and Clean Language

Carol Cohn

Stage I: Listening

Entering the world of defense intellectuals was a bizarre experience, bizarre because it is a world where men spend their days matter-of-factly discussing nuclear weapons, nuclear strategy, and nuclear war. The discussions are carefully and intricately reasoned, occurring without any sense of horror, urgency, or moral outrage. In fact, there seems to be no graphic reality behind the words as the speakers talk of "first strikes," "counterforce exchanges," and "limited nuclear war," or as they debate the comparative values of a "minimum deterrent posture" versus a "nuclear war-fighting capability."

Yet, what is striking about the men themselves is not, as the content of their conversations might suggest, their cold-bloodedness. It is rather that they are men unusually well endowed with charm, humor, intelligence, concern, and decency. I liked many of them. My attempt to understand how such decent men could contribute to an endeavor that I see as fundamentally destructive became a continuing obsession for me, a lens through which I came to examine all of my experiences in their world.

In the early stage, I was gripped by the extraordinary language used to discuss nuclear war. I had, of course, previously encountered it in my reading, but hearing it spoken was a different experience. What hit me first was the elaborate use of abstraction and euphemism, the use of words so bland that they never forced the speaker or enabled the listener to touch the realities of nuclear holocaust.

Anyone who has seen pictures of Hiroshima burn victims, or tried to imagine the pain of hundreds of glass shards blasted into flesh, may at first find it perverse beyond imagination to hear a class of nuclear devices matter-of-factly referred to as "clean bombs." "Clean bombs" are nuclear devices that are detonated by fusion rather than fission; they release a higher proportion of energy as prompt radiation, but produce less radio-active fallout than fission bombs of the same yield.[1]

The term "clean bombs" provides the perfect metaphor for defense analysts and arms controllers. This sort of language shields us from the emotional reaction that would result if it were clear that one was talking about plans for mass murder, for mangled bodies. Defense analysts don't talk about incinerating cities; they talk about "countervalue attacks." Human death, in nuclear parlance, is most often referred to as "collateral damage"; for, as one defense analyst said with just the right touch of irony in his voice and twinkle in his eye, "the Air Force doesn't target people, it targets shoe factories."[2]

Some phrases are so sanitized as to invert meaning. For example, the MX missile will carry ten warheads, each with the explosive power of 300 to 475 kilotons of TNT—*one* missile is the bearer of destruction approximately 250 to 400 times that of the Hiroshima bombing.[3] Ronald Reagan has christened the MX missile the "Peacekeeper." This renaming was the object of considerable scorn in the community of defense analysts; some of these very same analysts refer to the MX as a "damage limitation weapon."[4]

Such phrases exemplify the astounding chasm between image and reality that characterizes techno-strategic language. They also hint at the terrifying way in which the existence of nuclear devices has distorted our perceptions and redefined the world. The phrase "clean bombs" tells us that radioactivity is the only "dirty" part of killing people.

But it is not only the existence of nuclear devices that changes the world. The endless discussion of scenarios for their use *itself* radically alters what is within the realm of human possibility. The very act of putting phrases like "20 million acceptable dead" into human consciousness cracks our conceptions of the limits of human suffering, and of men's willingness to violate all human values and social meaning.[5]

Men in Ties Discussing Missile Size

Feminists have often suggested that an important aspect of the arms race is phallic worship, that "missile envy" is a significant motivating force in the nuclear build-up.[6] I have always found this an uncomfortably reductionist explanation and hoped that my research at the Center would yield a more complex analysis. But I was curious about the extent to which I might find a sexual subtext in the defense professionals' discourse. I was not prepared for what I found.

I think I had naively imagined myself a feminist spy in the house of death—that I would need to sneak around and eavesdrop on what men said in unguarded moments, using all my subtlety and cunning to unearth the sexual imagery in how they thought and spoke. I had naively believed that these men, at least in public, would appear to be aware of feminist contexts. I thought that at some point at least, during a long talk about "penetration aids," someone would suddenly look up, slightly embarrassed to be caught in a blatant confirmation of feminist analyses of What's *Really* Going On Here.[7]

I was wrong. There was no evidence that feminist critiques had ever reached the ears, much less the minds, of these men. American military dependence on nuclear weapons was explained as "irresistible, because you get more bang for the buck." Another lecturer solemnly and scientifically announced, "to disarm is to get rid of all your stuff." (This may, in turn, explain why they see serious talk of nuclear disarmament as perfectly resistible, not to mention foolish. If disarmament is emasculation, how could any real man even consider it?) Other lectures were filled with discussion of vertical erector launchers, thrust-to-weight ratios, soft lay-downs, deep penetration, and the comparative advantages of protracted versus spasm attacks—or what one military adviser to the National Security Council has called "releasing 70 to 80 percent of our megatonnage in one orgasmic whump."[8] There was serious concern about the need to harden our missiles, and the need to "face it, the Russians are a little harder than we are."[9] Disbelieving glances would occasionally pass between me and my one ally—another woman—but no one else seemed to notice.

That defense intellectuals themselves use sexual imagery to such an extent does not seem especially surprising. Nor does it, by itself, constitute grounds for imputing motivation. For me, the interesting issue is not so much the imagery's psychodynamic origins as how it functions: how does it serve to make it possible for strategic planners and other defense intellectuals to do their macabre work? How does it function in their construction of a work-world that feels tenable? Several stories illustrate the complexity of the rhetoric.

During the summer program, a group of us visited the New London Navy base where nuclear submarines are homeported, and the General Dynamics Electric Boat boatyards where a new Trident submarine was being constructed. At one point during the trip, we took a tour of a nuclear-powered submarine. When we reached the part of the sub where the missiles are housed, the officer accompanying us turned with a grin, and asked if we wanted to stick our hands through a hole to "pat the missile." *Pat the missile?*

The image reappeared the next week when a lecturer scornfully declared that the only real reason for deploying cruise and Pershing II missiles in Western Europe was "so that our allies can pat them." Some months later, another group of us went to be briefed at NORAD (the North American Aerospace Defense Command). On the way back, word leaked out that our landing would be delayed because the new B-1 bomber was in the area. The plane was charged with a tangible excitement that increased as we flew in our holding pattern, people craned their necks to try to catch a glimpse of the B-1 in the skies, and the excitement climaxed as we touched down on the runway and hurtled past it. Later when I returned to the Center, I encountered a man who, unable to go on the trip, said to me enviously, "I hear you got to pat a B-1."

What is all this "patting"? What are men doing when they "pat" these high-tech phalluses? Patting is an assertion of intimacy, sexual possession, affectionate domination. The thrill and pleasure of "patting the missile" is an expression of that phallic power with the possibility of vicariously appropriating it as one's own.

But if the predilection for patting phallic objects indicates something of the homoerotic excitement suggested by the language, it also has another aspect. Patting is not just an act of sexual intimacy. It is also what one does to babies, small children, the pet dog. The creatures one pats are small, cute, harmless—not terrifyingly destructive. Patting removes the object's lethal purpose.

Much of the sexual imagery I heard was rife with the sort of ambiguity suggested by "patting the missiles." The imagery could be construed as a

36

deadly serious display of the connections between masculine sexuality and the arms race. But at the same time, it can also be interpreted as a way of minimizing the seriousness of militarist endeavors, of denying their deadly consequences. A former Pentagon target analyst, in telling me why he thought plans for "limited nuclear war" were ridiculous, said, "Look, you gotta understand that it's a pissing contest—you gotta expect them to use everything they've got." What does this imagery say? Most obviously, that this is all about competition for manhood. But at the same time, the imagery diminishes the contest and its outcomes by representing them as acts of boyish mischief rather than the dangerous and deadly possibilities that they really are.

Fathers, Sons, and Virgins

The word "virginity" made frequent, arresting appearances in nuclear discourse. One professor spoke of India's explosion of a nuclear bomb as "losing her virginity"; the question of how the United States should react was posed as "whether we should throw her away." Initiation into the nuclear world involves being deflowered, losing one's innocence, knowing sin. Although the manly United States is no virgin, and proud of it, the double standard raises its head in the question of whether a woman is still worth anything to a man once she's lost her virginity.

New Zealand's refusal to allow nuclear-armed or nuclear-powered warships into its ports prompted similar reflections on virginity. A good example is provided by (Ret.) United States Air Force General Ross Milton's angry column in *Air Force Magazine,* entitled, "Nuclear Virginity." His tone is that of a man whose advances have been spurned. He is contemptuous of the "woman's" protestations that she wants to remain pure, innocent of nuclear weapons; her moral reluctance is a quaint and ridiculous throwback. But beyond contempt, he also feels outraged— after all, this is a "woman" we've *paid* for, who *still* won't come across. He suggests that we withdraw our goods and services—and then we'll see just how long she tries to hold onto her virtue.[10]

The patriarchal bargain could not be laid out more clearly. We'll protect you (under our "nuclear umbrella" and the ANZUS Pact), and provide goods and services—but then you damn well better know what you must do—to provide other services in return. And you better not try to tell us how to protect you, or claim that you yourself know what's best for you. We are the ones in charge here. And if you're going to play coy with us, we'll prove it, and leave you defenseless.

Another striking metaphor of patriarchal power came early in the summer program, when one of the faculty was giving a lecture on deterrence. To give us a concrete example from outside the world of military strategy, he described having a seventeen-year-old son whose TV watching habits he disapproved of. He dealt with the situation by threatening to break his son's arm if he turned on the TV again "That's deterrence!" he said triumphantly.

This analogy is so striking because it at first seems so inappropriate. The popular understanding of nuclear deterrence is that it describes a relationship between two countries of almost equal strength, in which one is able to deter the other from a first strike by threatening to retaliate in kind. But in this case, the partners are unequal, and the stronger one uses his superior force, not to protect himself from grave injury, but to coerce.

But if the analogy seems to be a flawed expression of deterrence as we have been taught to view it, it is nonetheless extremely revealing about U.S. nuclear deterrence as an operational, rather than a rhetorical or declaratory policy. What it suggests is the speciousness of the rhetoric that surrounds deterrence—of the idea that we face an implacable enemy, and that we only stockpile nuclear weapons in an attempt to defend ourselves. Instead, what we see is the drive to superior power as a means to exercise one's will, and a readiness to threaten the disproportionate use of force in order to achieve one's own ends. There is no question of recognition of competing but legitimate needs here, no desire to negotiate, discuss, or compromise, and most important, no necessity for that recognition or desire, since the father carries the bigger stick.[11]

The United States frequently appears in international politics as a "father," sometimes coercive, sometimes benevolent, but always knowing best. The single time that any mention was made of countries other than the United States, our NATO allies, or the USSR was during a lecture on nuclear proliferation. The point was made that these other countries simply could not be trusted to know what was good for them, nor were they yet fully responsible, so nuclear weapons in their hands would be much more dangerous than in ours. The metaphor was that of parents setting limits for their children.

Domestic Bliss

Sanitized abstraction, sexual and patriarchal imagery, even if disturbing, seemed to fit easily into the masculinist world of nuclear war

38

planning. What did not fit, what surprised and puzzled me most when I first heard it, was another set of words, words that evoked images that can only be called domestic.

Nuclear missiles are based in "silos." On a Trident submarine, which carries twenty-four multiple warhead nuclear missiles, crew members call the part of the sub where the missiles are lined up in their silos ready for launching "the Christmas tree farm." What could be more bucolic—farms, silos, Christmas trees?

In the ever-friendly, even romantic world of nuclear weaponry, enemies "exchange" warheads; one missile "takes out" another; weapons systems can "marry up." "Coupling" is sometimes used to refer to the wiring between mechanisms of warning and response. It is also used to refer to the psychopolitical links between strategic (intercontinental) and theater (European-based) weapons.

The patterns in which a MIRVed missile's nuclear warheads land is known as a "footprint."[12] These nuclear explosives are not dropped; a "bus" "delivers" them. Nuclear bombs are not referred to as bombs or even warheads; they're referred to as "reentry vehicles," a term far more bland and benign, which is then shortened to "RVs," a term not only totally abstract and removed from the reality of a bomb behind it, but also resonant with the image of the "recreational vehicles" of the ideal family vacation.

Of course, I don't mean to say that this is the image intended by those who speak these words, but what is? What are the reasons they use these words? What are the effects of using them? How is one to interpret this whole phenomenon?

It seems clear that these images are more than simply one more form of distancing, one more way of removing oneself from the grisly reality behind the words, for plain, old-fashioned abstraction is adequate to that task. The fact that these words suggest the kind of imagery described previously suggests that something else, something very peculiar, is going on here. Calling the pattern in which bombs fall a "footprint" seems a willful distorting process, a playfully perverse refusal of accountability—because to be accountable to reality is to be unable to do this work. The images evoked by these words serve to domesticate, to *tame* the uncontrollable forces of nuclear destruction.

For example, PAL (permissive action links) is the acronym for the electronic system designed to prevent the unauthorized firing of nuclear warheads. BAMBI is the acronym for an early version of an antiballistic missile system (for Ballistic Missile Boost Intercept). The President's

Annual Nuclear Weapons Stockpile Memorandum, which outlines both short- and long-range plans for production of new nuclear weapons, is benignly referred to as "the shopping list." Carrying the culinary image farther, the National Command Authorities choose from a "menu of options" when deciding among different targeting plans. The "cookie cutter" is a phrase used to describe a particular model of nuclear attack. Apparently it is also used at the Department of Defense to refer to the neutron bomb.[13]

The imagery that domesticates, that humanizes insentient weapons, also serves, paradoxically, to make it all right to ignore sentient human bodies, human lives.[14] Perhaps it is possible to spend one's time thinking about scenarios for the use of massively destructive technology, and to have human bodies remain invisible in that technological world, precisely because that world itself now *includes* the domestic, the human, the warm and playful—the Christmas trees, the RVs, the affectionate pats. It is a world that is in some sense complete unto itself; it even includes death and loss. But it is weapons, not humans, that are "killed." "Fratricide" occurs when one of your warheads "kills" another one of your own warheads. There is much discussion of "vulnerability" and "survivability," but it is about the vulnerability and survival of weapons systems, not people.

Male Birth and Creation

There is one set of domestic images that demands separate attention— imagery that suggests men's desire to appropriate from women the power of giving life, and that combines creation and destruction.[15] The bomb project is rife with images of male birth.[16] In December 1942, Ernest Lawrence's telegram to the physicists at Chicago read, "Congratulations to the new parents. Can hardly wait to see the new arrival."[17] At Los Alamos, the atom bomb was referred to as "Oppenheimer's baby." At Lawrence Livermore, the hydrogen bomb was referred to as "Teller's baby," although those who wanted to disparage Teller's contribution claimed he was not the bomb's father, but its mother. They claimed that Stanislaw Ulam was the real father; he had the all important idea and inseminated Teller with it. Teller only "carried it" after that.[18]

Forty years later, this idea of male birth and its accompanying belittling of maternity—the denial of women's role in the process of creation and the reduction of "motherhood" to the provision of nurturance (apparently Teller did not need to provide an egg, only a womb)—seems thoroughly incorporated into the nuclear mentality, as I learned on a subsequent visit to the U.S. Space Command in Colorado Springs. One of the briefings I attended included discussion of a new satellite system, the not yet "on line" MILSTAR system.[19] The officer doing the briefing gave an excited recitation of its technical capabilities, and then an explanation of the new Unified Space Command's role in the system. Self-effacingly, he said, "We'll do the motherhood role—telemetry, tracking, and control— the maintenance."

In light of the imagery of male birth, the extraordinary names given to the bombs that reduced Hiroshima and Nagasaki to ash and rubble— "Little Boy" and "Fat Man"—at last become intelligible. These ultimate destroyers were the progeny of the atomic scientists—and emphatically not just any progeny, but male progeny. In early tests, before they were certain that the bombs would work, the scientists expressed their concern by saying that they hoped the baby was a boy, not a girl—i.e., not a dud.[20] General Grove's triumphant cable to Secretary of War Henry Stimson at the Potsdam conference, informing him that the first atomic bomb test was successful read, after decoding:

> Doctor had just returned most enthusiastic and confident that the little boy is as husky as his big brother. The light in his eyes discernible from here to Highhold and I could have heard his screams from here to my farm.[21]

In 1952, Edward Teller's exultant telegram to Los Alamos announcing the successful test of the hydrogen bomb, "Mike," at Eniwetok Atoll in the Marshall Islands, read, "It's a boy."[22]

The nuclear scientists gave birth to male progeny with the ultimate power of violent domination over "female" Nature. The defense intellectuals' project is the creation of abstract formulations to control the forces the scientists created—and to participate thereby in the scientists' world-creating/destroying power. The history of the bomb project is permeated with imagery that confounds man's overwhelming technological power to destroy nature with the power to create—imagery that inverts men's destruction, and asserts in its place the power to create new life and a new world, imagery that converts men's destruction into their rebirth.

William L. Laurence witnessed the Trinity test of the first atomic bomb, and wrote:

> The big boom came about a hundred seconds after the great flash—the first cry of a new-born world. . . . They clapped their hands as they leaped from the ground—earthbound man symbolising the birth of a new force.[23]

41

After watching "Fat Man" being assembled the day before it was dropped on Nagasaki, he described seeing the bomb as "being fashioned into a living thing."[24] Decades later, General Bruce K. Holloway, the Commander-in-Chief of the Strategic Air Command from 1968 to 1972, described a nuclear war as involving "a big bang, like the start of the universe."[25]

God and the Nuclear Priesthood

The possibility that the language reveals an attempt to appropriate ultimate creative power is evident in another striking aspect of the language of nuclear weaponry and doctrine—the religious imagery.

In a subculture of "hard-nosed realism" and hyper-"rationality," in a world that claims, as a sign of its superiority, its vigilant purging of all nonrational elements, and in which people carefully excise from their discourse every possible trace of sentimentality, as though purging dangerous nonsterile elements from a lab, the last thing one might expect to find is religious imagery, imagery of the forces that science often has been defined *as opposed to*. And yet, religious imagery permeates the nuclear world. The first atomic bomb test was called Trinity. Religious images are echoed in the language of the physicists who worked on the bomb, and witnessed the test: "It was as though we stood at the first day of creation." Robert Oppenheimer thought of Krishna's words to Arjuna in the *Bhagavad Gita*: "I am become Death, the shatterer of worlds."[26]

Defense intellectuals, when challenged on a particular assumption that underlies their paradigms, will often dismiss having to justify or support their assumptions with a wave of the hand and a casual "now you're talking about matters of theology." Perhaps most astonishing of all is the fact that the creators of strategic doctrine actually refer to members of their community as "the nuclear priesthood." It is hard to decide what is most extraordinary about this: the easy arrogance of their claim to the virtues and supernatural power of the priesthood; the tacit admission (*never* spoken directly) that rather than being unflinching, hard-nosed, objective, empirically-minded scientific describers of reality, they are really the creators of dogma; or the extraordinary statement about who, or rather what, has become God. If our new priesthood attains its status through an inspired knowledge of nuclear weapons, it gives a whole new meaning to the phrase "a mighty fortress is our God."

Stage II: Learning to Speak the Language

Although I was at first startled by the combination of abstraction and counter-intuitive imagery that characterizes the language of defense intellectuals, my attention and energy were quickly turned to decoding and learning to speak it. The first task was training the tongue in the articulation of acronyms. I had thought of them mainly as utilitarian. But, being at the Center, hearing the defense analysts use the acronyms, and then watching as I and others in the group started to fling acronyms around in our own conversation, revealed some additional, unexpected dimensions. At first many of these terms seemed very sexy. Submarine-launched cruise missiles are not referred to as "SLCMs," but "Slick'ems." Ground-launched cruise missiles are "Glick'ems." Air-launched cruise missiles are magical—Alchems (ALCMs). TACAMO, the acronym for the planes that provide communications links to submarines, stands for "take charge and move out." The image seems closely related to the nicknames given to the new guidance systems for "smart weapons"—"shoot and scoot," or "fire and forget."

Other acronyms work in other ways. The plane in which the President would supposedly be flying above a nuclear holocaust, receiving intelligence and issuing commands for the next bombing, is referred to as Kneecap (for NEACP—National Emergency Airborne Command Post). The edge of derision suggested in referring to this plane as Kneecap mirrors the edge of derision implicit when it is talked about at all, since few believe that the President really would have the time to carry out the plan or that the communications systems would be working at all. Some might even go so far as to question the usefulness of his being able to direct an extended nuclear war from his kneecap even if it were feasible. (I never heard the morality of this idea addressed.) But it seems to me that speaking about NEACP with that edge of derision is *exactly* what allows it to be spoken about and seriously discussed at all. It is the very ability to make fun of a concept that makes it possible to work with it rather than reject it outright.

In other words, what I learned at the program is that talking about nuclear weapons is fun. The words are racy, sexy, snappy. You can throw them around in rapid-fire succession. They're quick, clean, light; they trip off the tongue. You can reel off dozens of them in seconds, forgetting how one just might interfere with the next, not to mention with the lives beneath them.

A more subtle but perhaps more important element of learning the language is control. The experience of accomplishment, of mastering the words, infuses your relation to the material. Achieving mastery over the words gives a feeling of mastery over the thing—what I would call *cognitive mastery*—mastery over technology that was before *not* controllable, *not* masterable, but was powerful beyond human comprehension, powerful in a way that stretches and thrills the imagination.

I entered a world where people spoke what amounted to a foreign language, a language I had to learn if we were to communicate with one another. So I became engaged in the challenge of it—of decoding the acronyms and figuring out which were the proper verbs to use. My focus was on the task of solving the puzzles, developing language competency—not on the weapons and wars behind the words. Although my interest was in thinking about nuclear war and its prevention, my energy was deflected.

By the time I was through, I had learned far more than an alternate (if abstract) set of words to refer to familiar phenomena; for even when the ostensible *subjects* of a standard English and nukespeak description are the same, they are, in fact, about utterly different phenomena. Consider the following descriptions, in each of which the subject is the aftermath of a nuclear attack.

The passages differ not only in the vividness of their words, but in their *content:* the first describes the effects of a nuclear blast on human beings, the second describes the impact of a nuclear blast on technical systems designed to assure the "command and control" of nuclear weapons.

Everything was black, had vanished into the black dust, was destroyed. Only the flames that were beginning to lick their way up had any color. From the dust that was like a fog, figures began to loom up, black, hairless, faceless. They screamed with voices that were no longer human. Their screams drowned out the groans rising everywhere from the rubble, groans that seemed to rise from the very earth itself.[27]

[You have to have ways to maintain communications in a] nuclear environment, a situation bound to include EMP blackout, brute force damage to systems, a heavy jamming environment, and so on.[28]

There is no way to describe the phenomena represented in the first with the language of the second. These differences may stem in part from the difference of *perspective:* the speaker in the first account is a victim of nuclear weapons; the speaker in the second is a user. The speaker in the first is using language to try to name and contain the horror of human suffering all around her; the speaker in the second is using words to ensure the possibility of launching the next nuclear attack. Techno-strategic language can be used only to articulate the perspective of the users of nuclear weapons, not the victims.[29]

Thus, speaking the expert language not only offers distance, a feeling of control, and an alternative focus for one's energies, it also offers escape—escape from thinking of oneself as a victim of nuclear war. Even though defense analysts *know* they would die in a nuclear war, they are positionally allowed, even forced, to escape that awareness by virtue of their linguistic stance.

Stage III: Dialogue

It did not take very long to learn the language of nuclear war and much of the specialized information it contained. My focus quickly changed from mastering technical information and doctrinal arcana to attempting to understand more about how the dogma was rationalized. For example, instead of trying to find out why submarines are so hard to detect, or why, prior to the Trident II, submarine-based ballistic missiles were not considered counterforce weapons, I now wanted to know why we really "need" a strategic triad, given submarines' "invulnerability."[30] Or, why it is considered reasonable to base U.S. military planning on the Soviet Union's military *capabilities*, rather than seriously attempting to gauge what their *intentions* might be. This standard practice is one I found particularly troubling. Military analysts say that since we cannot know for certain what Soviet intentions are, we must plan our military forces and strategies *as if* we knew that the Soviets planned to use all of their weapons. While this appears to be prudent, it leads to a major problem: when we only ask what the Soviets *can* do, we quickly come to assume that that is what they *intend* to do. We base our planning on "worst-case scenarios" and then come to believe that we live in a world where vast resources must be committed to "preventing" them from happening.

Since underlying rationales are rarely discussed in the everyday business of defense planning, I had to start asking more questions. Although I was tempted to use my newly acquired proficiency in techno-strategic jargon, I vowed to speak English. I had long believed that one of the most important functions of an expert language is exclusion—the denial of a voice to those outside the professional community.[31] I wanted to see whether a well-informed person could speak English and still carry on a knowledgeable conversation.

What I found was that no matter how well-informed my questions were, no matter how complex an understanding they were based upon, if I spoke English rather than expert jargon, the men responded to me as though I were ignorant or simple-minded. A strong distaste for being patronized and dismissed made my experiment in English short-lived. I adapted my everyday speech to the vocabulary of strategic analysis. I spoke of "escalation dominance," "pre-emptive strikes," and one of my favorites, "sub-holocaust engagements." Using the right phrases opened my way into long, elaborate discussions that taught me a lot about techno-strategic reasoning and how to manipulate it.

But as I became better at engaging in this discourse, the more impossible it became for me to express my own ideas, my own values. To pick a bald example: the word "peace" is not a part of this discourse. As close as one can come is "strategic stability," a term that refers to a balance of numbers and types of weapons systems—not the political, social, economic, and psychological conditions implied by the word "peace." Not only is there no word signifying peace in this discourse, but the word "peace" itself cannot be used. To speak it is to immediately brand oneself as a soft-headed activist, instead of an expert, a professional to be taken seriously.

If I was unable to speak my concerns in this language, more disturbing still was that I also began to find it hard even to keep them in my own head. No matter how firm my own commitment to staying aware of the reality behind the words, over and over I found that I *couldn't* stay connected, couldn't keep human lives as my reference point. Soon I found I could go for days speaking about nuclear weapons without once thinking about the people who would be incinerated by them.

It is tempting to attribute this problem to qualities of the language, the words themselves—the abstractness, the euphemisms, the sanitized, friendly, sexy acronyms. Then all we would need to do is change the words, make them more vivid, get the military planners to say "mass murder" instead of "collateral damage," and their thinking would change.

The problem, however, is not only that defense intellectuals use abstract terminology that removes them from the realities of which they speak. There *is* no reality of which they speak. Or, rather, the "reality" of which they speak is itself a world of abstractions. Deterrence theory, and much of strategic doctrine altogether, was invented largely by mathematicians, economists, and a few political scientists. It was invented to hold together abstractly, its validity judged by its internal logic. These abstract systems were developed as a way to make it possible to "think about the unthinkable"—not as a way to describe or codify relations on the ground.[32]

The problem with the idea of "limited nuclear war," therefore, is not only that it is grotesque to refer to the death and suffering caused by *any* use of nuclear weapons as "limited." It is also that "limited nuclear war" is itself an abstract conceptual system, designed, embodied, and achieved by computer modeling. As such, there is no need to think about the concrete human realities behind the model; what counts is the internal logic of the system.[33]

The realization that the abstraction was not just in the words, but characterized the entire conceptual system itself, helped me make sense of my difficulty in staying connected to human lives. It also helped make sense of some of the bizarre and surreal quality of what people said. But there was still a piece missing. How is it possible, for example, to make sense of the following paragraph? It is taken from a discussion of a scenario ("regime A") in which the United States and the USSR have revised their offensive weaponry, banned MIRVs, and gone to a regime of single-warhead (Midgetman) missiles, with no "defensive shield" (familiarly known as "Star Wars," or SDI):

> The strategic stability of regime A is based on the fact that both sides are deprived of any incentive ever to strike first. Since it takes roughly two warheads to destroy one enemy silo, an attacker must expend two of his missiles to destroy one of the enemy's. A first strike disarms the attacker. The aggressor ends up worse off than the aggressed.[34]

"The aggressor ends up worse off than the aggressed"? The homeland of "the aggressed" has just been devastated by the explosions of a thousand nuclear bombs, each likely to be ten to one hundred times more powerful than the bomb dropped on Hiroshima, and the aggressor, whose homeland is still untouched, "ends up worse off"? What would make it possible to think such a thing? Abstract language and abstract thinking surely contribute, but they do not seem to be a sufficient explanation. To the uninitiated mind, this sentence remains insane.

I was only able to "make sense of it" when I finally asked myself the question that feminists have been asking about theories in every discipline: What is the reference point? Who (or what) is the *subject* here? In techno-strategic discourse, *the reference point is not human beings; it is*

47

the weapons themselves. The aggressor thus ends up worse off than the aggressed because he has fewer weapons left; human factors are irrelevant to the calculus of gain and loss.

If human lives are not the reference point, then it is not only impossible to talk about humans in this language, it also becomes in some sense *illegitimate* to ask the paradigm to reflect human concerns. Hence, questions that break through the numbing language of strategic analysis and raise issues in human terms can be easily dismissed. No one will claim that the questions are unimportant; but asking is inexpert, unprofessional, irrelevant to the business at hand. The outcome is that defense intellectuals can talk about the weapons that are supposed to protect particular political entities, particular peoples and their way of life, without actually asking if they *can* do it, or if they are the best *way* to do it, or whether they may even damage the entities you are supposedly protecting. It is not that the men I spoke with would say that these are invalid questions, rather that they are separate questions, questions that are outside what they do, outside their realm of expertise.

The problem is that this discourse has become virtually the only response to the question of how to achieve security that is recognized as legitimate. If the language of weaponry were one competing voice in the discussion, or one that was integrated with others, the fact that the referents of strategic paradigms are only weapons might be of less note. But when the only language and expertise is coextensive with weapons, the limits of this language and body of knowledge become staggering. And its entrapping qualities—the way in which, once you adopt it, it becomes so hard to stay connected to human concerns—become more comprehensible.

Stage IV: The Terror

As I learned to speak, my perspective changed. I no longer stood outside the impermeable wall of techno-strategic language, and once inside I could no longer see it. Speaking the language, I could no longer really hear it. And once inside its protective walls, I began to find it difficult to get out. The impermeability worked both ways.

I had not only learned to speak a language: I had started to think in it. Its questions became my questions, its concepts shaped my responses to new ideas. Its definitions of the parameters of reality became mine. Like the White Queen, I began to believe six impossible things before breakfast. Not because I consciously believed, for instance, that a "surgically clean counterforce strike" was really possible; but instead because some elaborate piece of doctrinal reasoning I used was already predicated on the possibility of those strikes, as well as on a host of other impossible things.[35]

My grasp on what *I* knew as reality seemed to slip. I might get very excited, for example, about a new strategic justification for a "no first use" policy, and spend time discussing the ways in which its implications for our force structure in Western Europe were superior to the older version.[36] And after a day or two of thinking and arguing about the different strategic rationalizations of a "no first use" policy, I would suddenly step back, aghast that I was so involved with the *military* justifications for not using nuclear weapons—as though the moral ones were not enough. What I was actually talking about—the mass incineration caused by nuclear attack—was no longer in my consciousness.

I began to feel that I had fallen down the rabbit hole—and it was a struggle to climb back out.

Conclusions

Learning to speak the language reveals something about how thinking can become more abstract, more focused on parts disembedded from their context, more attentive to the survival of weapons than the survival of human beings. In this instance, it reveals something about the process of the mind's militarization—and the way in which that process may be undergone by man or women, hawk or dove.

Most often, the act of learning techno-strategic language is conceived of as an additive process: you add a new set of vocabulary words; you add the reflex ability to decode and use endless numbers of acronyms; you add some new information that the specialized language contains; you add the conceptual tools that will allow you to "think strategically." This additive view appears to be held by defense intellectuals themselves; as one said to me, "Much of the debate is in technical terms—learn it, and decide whether it's relevant later."

This view also appears to be held by many in the opposition, be they critical scholars and professionals attempting to change the field from within, or public interest lobbyists and educational organizations, or some feminist anti-militarists.[37] They believe that learning and using the language can be a valuable political tool: some think that our nuclear

49

policies are so riddled with irrationality that there is room for well-reasoned, well-informed arguments to make a difference; others, even if they don't believe that the technical information is very important, see it as necessary to master the language simply because it is too difficult to attain public legitimacy without it. In either case, the idea is that you *add* the expert terms and information to your linguistic repertoire, and proceed from there.

However, I have been arguing throughout this essay that learning the defense language is a transformative rather than an additive process. When you choose to learn it you are not simply adding new information and vocabulary; you are entering into a particular mode of thinking about nuclear weapons, military and political power, and about the relationship between human ends and technological means.

Thus, those of us who find U.S. nuclear policy desperately misguided are in a quandary. If we refuse to learn the language, we are guaranteed that our voices will remain outside the "politically relevant" spectrum of opinion. If we do learn and speak it, we severely limit what we can say, and invite the transformation, the militarization, of our own thinking.

The question for those of us who do choose to learn is what use are we going to make of that knowledge? One thing we can do is to challenge the legitimacy of the defense intellectuals' dominance of the discourse on nuclear issues. When defense intellectuals are criticized for the cold-blooded inhumanity of the scenarios they plan, their response is that they are "objective and realistic." They portray those who are radically opposed to the nuclear status quo as irrational, unrealistic, emotional. But if the smooth, shiny surface of their discourse—its abstraction and technical jargon—appears at first to support these claims, a look just below the surface does not. There we find strong currents of homoerotic excitement, heterosexual domination, the drive toward competency and mastery, the pleasures of membership in an elite and privileged group, of the ultimate importance and meaning of membership in the priesthood, and the thrilling power of becoming Death, shatterer of worlds. Deconstructing techno-strategic discourse's claims to a monopoly on rationality is, then, in and of itself, an important way to challenge its hegemony as the sole legitimate language for public debate about nuclear policy.

Feminists and others who seek a more just and peaceful world have a two-fold task before us that is intimately linked.[38] Our deconstructive task requires paying close enough attention to techno-strategic discourse that we might begin to know how to dismantle it. The dominant voice of militarized masculinity and decontextualized rationality speaks so loudly in our culture, it will remain difficult for any other voices to be heard until that voice is muted. Our reconstructive task is to create alternative futures, alternative conceptions of rationality, alternative voices—diverse voices whose conversations with each other will invent those futures.

Notes

1. Fusion weapons' proportionally smaller yield of radioactive fallout led Atomic Energy Commission Chairman Lewis Strauss to announce in 1956 that hydrogen bomb tests were important "not only from a military point of view but from a humanitarian aspect." Although the bombs being tested were 1,000 times more powerful than those that devastated Hiroshima and Nagasaki, the proportional reduction of fallout apparently qualified them not only as "clean," but as "humanitarian." Lewis Strauss is quoted in Ralph Lapp, "The 'Humanitarian' H-Bomb," *Bulletin of Atomic Scientists*, vol. XII, no. 7, September 1956, p. 263.

2. I must point out that we cannot know whether to take this particular example literally: America's list of nuclear targets is, of course, classified. However, the defense analyst quoted is a man who has had access to that list for at least two decades. He is also a man whose thinking and speaking are careful and precise, so I think it is reasonable to assume that his statement is not a distortion, that "shoe factories," even if not themselves literally targeted, accurately represent a category of target. As such, they are worth thinking about. Shoe factories would be one among many "military targets" other than weapons systems themselves; they would be military targets because an army needs boots. The likelihood of a nuclear war lasting long enough for foot soliders to wear out their boots might seem to stretch the limits of credibility, but that is not a sufficient reason to assume that they are not nuclear targets. Nuclear targeting and nuclear strategic planning in general frequently suffer from "conventionalization"—the tendency of planners to think in the old, familiar terms of "conventional" warfare, rather than fully assimilating the ways in which nuclear weaponry has changed warfare.

In avoiding talking about murder, the "defense" community has long been ahead of the State Department. It wasn't until 1984 that the State Department announced it will no longer use the word "killing," much less "murder," in official reports on the status of human rights in allied countries. The new term is "unlawful or arbitrary deprivation of life." *The New York Times*, February 15, 1984, as cited in *Quarterly Review of Doublespeak*, vol. XI, no. 1 (October 1984), p. 3.

3. "Kiloton" (KT) is a measure of explosive power measured by the number of thousands of tons of TNT required to release an equivalent amount of energy.

The atomic bomb dropped on Hiroshima is estimated to have been 12 KT. An MX missile is designed to carry up to ten Mk 21 reentry vehicles, each with a W–87 warhead. The yield of W–87 warheads is 300 KT, but they are "upgradable" to 475 KT.

4. Since the MX would theoretically be able to "take out" Soviet land-based ICBMs in a "disarming first strike," the Soviets would have few ICBMs left for a retaliatory attack; thus, damage to the United States would theoretically be limited. However, to consider the damage that could be inflicted on the United States by the remaining ICBMs, not to mention Soviet bombers and sub-based missiles, "limited" is to act as though words have no meaning.

5. Conservative government assessments of the number of deaths resulting from a "surgically clean" counterforce attack vary widely. The Office of Technology Assessment projects 2 to 20 million immediate deaths (see James Fallows, *National Defense* [New York: Random House, 1981], p. 159). A 1975 Defense Department study estimated 18.3 million fatalities, while the U.S. Arms Control and Disarmament Agency, using different assumptions, arrived at a figure of 50 million (Desmond Ball, "Can Nuclear War Be Controlled?" Adelphi Paper No. 169 [London: The International Institute for Strategic Studies, 1981]).

6. The phrase is Helen Caldicott's. See *Missile Envy: The Arms Race and Nuclear War* (Toronto: Bantam Books, 1986).

7. For the uninitiated, "penetration aids" refers to devices that help bombers or missiles get past the "enemy's" defensive systems; e.g., stealth technology, chaff, or decoys. Within the defense intellectual community, they are also familiarly known as "penaids."

8. General William Odom, "C3I and Telecommunications at the Policy Level," in *Incidental Paper: Seminar on Command, Control, Communications and Intelligence* (Spring 1980), Center for Information Policy Research, Harvard University, p. 5.

9. This point has been amply documented by Brian Easlea, *Fathering the Unthinkable: Masculinity, Scientists and the Nuclear Arms Race* (London: Pluto Press, 1983).

10. General T. R. Milton, USAF (Ret.), "Nuclear Virginity," in *Air Force Magazine*, vol. 68, no. 5 (May 1980), p. 44.

11. I am grateful to Margaret Cerullo, a participant in the first Summer Program, for reporting the use of this analogy to me and sharing her thoughts about this and other events in the Program. The interpretation I give here draws strongly on hers.

12. MIRV stands for "multiple independently targetable re-entry vehicles." A MIRVed missile not only carries more than one warhead; its warheads can be aimed at different targets.

13. Henry T. Nash, "The Bureaucratization of Homicide," in *The Bulletin of Atomic Scientists* (April 1980), reprinted in E. P. Thompson and Dan Smith, eds., *Protest and Survive* (New York: Monthly Review Press, 1981), p. 159.

14. See Elaine Scarry, *The Body in Pain: The Making and Unmaking of the World* (New York: Oxford University Press, 1985), chap. 2, p. 67, for further discussion of language that reverses sentient and insentient matter, "th[at] exchange[s] idioms between weapons and bodies."

15. For further discussion of men's desire to appropriate from women the power of giving life and death, and its implications for men's war-making activities, see Dorothy Dinnerstein, *The Mermaid and the Minotaur* (New York: Harper and Row, 1977).

16. For further analysis of male birth imagery in the atomic bomb project, see Evelyn Fox Keller, "From Secrets of Life to Secrets of Death." Paper delivered at The Kansas Seminar, Yale University, November 20, 1986; and Easlea (note 9, this chapter).

17. Lawrence is quoted by Herbert Childs in *An American Genius: The Life of Ernest Orlando Lawrence* (New York: Dutton, 1968), p. 340.

18. Hans Bethe is quoted as saying that "Ulam was the father of the hydrogen bomb and Edward was the mother, because he carried the baby for quite a while," in J. Bernstein, *Hans Bethe: Prophet of Energy* (New York: Basic Books, 1980), p. 95.

19. The MILSTAR system is a communications satellite system that is jam-resistant and has as well an EMP-hardened capability. This means this is a system designed to enable the United States to fight a protracted nuclear war—the EMP-hardening is to allow it to act as a conduit for command and control of successive nuclear shots, long after the initial exchange.

20. Robert Jungk, *Brighter Than a Thousand Suns,* trans., James Cleugh (New York: Harcourt, Brace & Co., 1956), p. 197.

21. Richard E. Hewlett and Oscar E. Anderson, *The New World, 1939/46: A History of the United States Atomic Energy Commission,* 2 vols. (University Park: Pennsylvania State University Press, 1962), vol. 1, p. 386.

22. Quoted by Easlea, p. 130.

23. William L. Laurence, *Dawn Over Zero: The Story of the Atomic Bomb* (London: Museum Press, 1947), p. 10.

24. *Ibid.,* p. 188.

25. From a 1985 interview in which Holloway was explaining the logic of a "decapitating" strike against the Soviet leadership and command and control systems—and thus how nuclear war would be different from World War II, which was a "war of attrition," in which transportation, supply depots, and other targets were hit, rather than a "big bang." Daniel Ford, "The Button," Part II, *The New Yorker,* vol. 61, no. 7 (April 8, 1985), p. 49.

26. Jungk, p. 201.

27. Hisako Matsubara, *Cranes at Dusk* (Garden City, N.Y.: Dial Press, 1985). The author was a child in Kyoto at the time the atomic bomb was dropped. Her description is based on the memories of survivors.

28. General Robert Rosenberg, formerly on the National Security Council staff

during the Carter Administration, speaking at the Harvard Seminar on C3I. "The Influence of Policy Making on C3I," in *Incidental Paper: Seminar on Command, Control, Communications and Intelligence* (Spring 1980), Center for Information Policy Research, Harvard University, p. 59.

29. Two other writers who have remarked upon this division of languages between the "victims" and the professionals (variously named) are Freeman Dyson, *Weapons and Hope* (New York: Harper and Row, 1984), and Glenn D. Hook, "Making Nuclear Weapons Easier to Live With: The Political Role of Language of Nuclearization," *Journal of Peace Research*, vol. 22, no. 1 (1985), pp. 67–77. Dyson notes that there are two languages in the current discussion of nuclear weapons, which he calls the language of "the victims" and the language of "the warriors." He sees the resulting problem as being the difficulty the two groups have in communicating with each other and appreciating each other's valid concerns. His project is the search for a common language, and a good portion of the rest of the book is directed toward that end. Hook follows Camus in naming the two groups "the victims" and "the executioners." He is more explicit than Dyson about naming these as perspectives, as coming from positions of greater or lesser power, and points out that those with the most power are able to dominate and define the terms in which we speak about nuclear issues, so that no matter who we are, we find ourselves speaking as though we were the users, rather than the victims, of nuclear weapons. Although my analysis of perspectives and the ways in which language inscribes relations of power is similar to his, I differ from Hook in finding in this fact one of the sources of the experts' relative lack of fear of nuclear war.

30. The "strategic triad" refers to the three different modes of basing nuclear warheads: on land, on intercontinental ballistic missiles; at sea, on missiles housed in submarines; and "in the air," on the Strategic Air Command's bombers.

31. For an interesting discussion of the role of language in the creation of professional power, see JoAnne Brown, "Professional Language: Words That Succeed," *Radical History Review*, no. 34 (1986), pp. 33–51.

32. For the detailed accounts of the development of strategic doctrine, see Fred Kaplan, *The Wizards of Armageddon* (New York: Simon & Schuster, 1983), and Gregg F. Herken, *The Counsels of War* (New York: Knopf, 1985).

33. The work of Steven Kull provides thought-provoking data on the extent to which defense intellectuals are themselves actually aware of the disjunctions between their internally logical systems and the outside world. It would appear that, on some level, some of the time, some of these men are aware of this disjunction. Their justification for the continued use of these models is that "other people" (unnamed and, upon questioning, unnameable) believe in the models, thus giving them an important reality. See "Nuclear Nonsense," *Foreign Policy*, no. 58 (Spring 1985), pp. 28–52; and "Mind-Sets of Defense Policy-Makers," *The Psychohistory Review*, vol. 14, no. 3 (Spring 1986), pp. 21–37.

34. Charles Krauthammer, "Will Star Wars Kill Arms Control?" *The New Republic,* Issue 3,653 (January 21, 1985), pp. 12–16.

35. For an excellent discussion of the myriad uncertainties that make it ludicrous to assume the targeting accuracies posited in the notion of "surgically clean counterforce strikes," see Fallows, chap. 6.

36. "No first use" refers to the commitment to not be the first side to introduce nuclear weapons into a "conventional" war. The Soviet Union has a "no first use" policy, but the United States does not. In fact, it is NATO doctrine to use nuclear weapons in a conventional war in Western Europe as a way of overcoming the Warsaw Pact's supposed superiority in conventional weaponry and troop strength.

37. Perhaps the most prominent proponent of this strategy is Sheila Tobias. See, for example, "Demystifying Defense: Closing the Knowledge Gap," *Social Policy,* vol. 13, no. 3 (1983), pp. 29–32; and Sheila Tobias, Peter Goudinoff, Stefan Leader, and Shelah Leader, *What Kinds of Guns Are They Buying for Your Butter?* (New York: William Morrow & Co., 1982).

Comments

By 1984, American and Soviet strategic "deterrence" had increased the numbers of strategic nuclear weapons on both sides to 16,000 hydrogen bombs and warheads. Along with this vast increase in the nuclear arsenals went a transition in nuclear thinking culminating in scenarios for "limited" nuclear war. One response to these developments was the Nuclear Weapons Freeze. Another was the United States Catholic Bishops' Pastoral Letter, "The Challenge of Peace," a powerful document, as Segers explains, within the tradition of just war discourse. What the bishops did was to bring some of that tradition up to the present, applying the criteria of *jus ad bellum* (the legitimate grounds for going to war) and of *jus in bello* (the legitimate means by which war may be fought), to the dilemmas of the nuclear age.

As applied to nuclear war, the bishops have stated unequivocally that no purpose they can foresee could ever justify the use of nuclear weapons. Since it is immoral to *use* nuclear weapons, particularly against civilian populations, it is immoral to *threaten* to use them as well.

The possibilities for nuclear attack, if not nuclear extinction, have been with us for more than forty years. Pope Pius XII denounced the atomic attacks on Hiroshima and Nagasaki immediately and absolutely at the time that they took place. All the post–World War II popes have been unanimous in their condemnation of the possibility of nuclear war, the existence of nuclear weapons, and the nuclear arms race. The frequency of Pope John Paul II's denunciation of what he calls our "armed peace," helped to catalyze the United States Bishops' Conference and led to

57

several years of hearings, writings, and rewritings that finally culminated in the Pastoral Letter.

"Just war" is not synonymous with justifying the war one is currently fighting. That is a most cynical view. Instead, just war theory provides a powerful vocabulary for thinking about war. The roots of just war discourse lie in early Christian history when Christians, realizing that the Second Coming, and with it the end of History, was not imminent, concluded that they would have to adapt to life in an imperfect, indeed a very violent world. Christian thinkers began to raise questions that impinged on the survival of Christians and Christianity. Most importantly, they had to find survival strategies that could be justified in terms of their essentially pacifist beliefs. In a less than perfect world, what could Christians do to *limit* violence if they could not *eliminate* it?

There were other practical concerns. One had to do with armed service itself. Could Christians serve in the Roman Army, and if so might they kill? Some early Christians had been martyred, either because they would not bear arms, or because they would not take the oath of loyalty to the Emperor. Thus it would fall to Augustine of Hippo in the fourth century to develop criteria as to when and under what circumstances fighting could be justified and its violence limited. Augustine attempted to distinguish, among other things, the task of the soldier (war-fighting) and the task of the policeman (maintenance of the peace). Both would bear arms. Both might kill, as needed. But their purposes would distinguish them in a fundamental way.

Just war theory, then, revolves around the kinds of distinctions Christians needed to make in order to survive, even as they held their faith intact in an imperfect world. Augustine feared that the innocent, in the sense of purely pacifistic, would be destroyed. But most importantly, the Christian was limited in his license to kill even as he retained the right to survive. It is important to recall that Augustine is writing at the time of Rome's fall. Although Augustine condemns the horrors of Roman imperialism and, particularly, imperialistic wars, he also recognizes that the *Pax Romana* helped to bring order and a measure of safety and stability to the people within the Empire.

Augustine rests his just war doctrine in a single, very strongly grounded premise: that violence is always to be considered tragic, never celebrated, always abhorred, but sometimes resorted to because the alternative would be worse. Spelling out the legitimate reasons for initiating war (*jus ad bellum*) and standards of limiting violence during war (*jus in bello*),

Augustine set in motion the dialogue on the justice of war that would continue for centuries.

The just war tradition never died. It's been an ongoing enterprise, and not just among Catholics. Indeed, the most important contribution to just war doctrine in the early modern period was penned by Martin Luther. Just war thinking has continued to evolve into the modern era, particularly in regard to the increasing lethality of weapons.

Not all of those who will discuss and debate the American Bishops' statement will agree with it. Segers herself adopts a stance at once appreciative and critical. The important point is that when the Bishops write a pastoral letter, not everyone has to agree with it, but all Catholics are to talk about it. The strength and lasting significance of the Bishops' pastoral letter is the insistence that moral issues have to be part of the discussion of political questions.

How does Segers's interpretation relate to women? On the one hand, she is trying to make a link between the bishops' moral reasoning on nuclear war and on abortion. But, more subtly, she is making a case for the right of the amateur, the nonexpert, to participate in these debates over national security. At the time, the Pastoral Letter was promulgated in 1983, the bishops had to take a great deal of criticism, not so much on the merits of their position, but because they had ventured into a complex world of national security policy without being proven, trained experts in the field. That issue speaks to women who, in their concerns for peace, are just that: amateurs, not "experts" in the field.

Segers helps women to make the following kinds of claims: since we are among those who must live with these policies and we know how to listen and we know how to think, we belong in the middle of these discussions. We have a right to participate in these debates.

3

A Consistent Life Ethic: A Feminist Perspective on the Pro-Peace and Pro-Life Activities of the American Catholic Bishops

Mary C. Segers

The publication of the American Catholic Bishops' Pastoral Letter on war and peace was a major development in peace politics in the 1980s. It is now nearly six years since the bishops issued "The Challenge of Peace: God's Promise and Our Response." This important statement applies just war theory to issues of nuclear warfare, strategy, and deterrence. It is arguably one of the most important public statements ever made by the American bishops. Its significance derives in part from the timing of its

This essay was written during the 1985–86 academic year while I was Visiting Lecturer in Ethics and Women's Studies at the Harvard Divinity School. I wish to thank Judith Dwyer, S.S.J., Assistant Professor of Moral Theology at Weston School of Theology, and Gordon Zahn, Professor Emeritus of Sociology at Boston University, for conversations that helped me to clarify some of the points in this article. Needless to say, responsibility for the conclusions of the essay is mine.

publication as well as from the care taken in its drafting. The composition of this letter, from November 1981 to May 1983, coincided with growing public awareness of the dangers of nuclear warfare. In language and tone, the letter is magisterial and eloquent. In substance, its message is clear: we can ignore the moral dimensions and material implications of nuclear warfare only at grave risk to ourselves and our planet.

While it may be premature to draw any firm conclusions about the long-range impact of the bishops' letter, it is possible to offer a preliminary assessment of its general impact and contribution. This essay seeks to assess the influence of the peace pastoral on American public opinion and public policy. It does so through an examination of the bishops' attempts to pursue specific recommendations made in the letter. It may be difficult to chart cause-effect relations between the bishops' letter and public opinion, let alone the pastoral's impact upon defense and arms control policy. However, we can at least investigate the bishops' efforts to implement their own suggestions and to apply just war criteria to American military interventions and weapons policies since 1983. For the plain fact is that if the bishops do not follow through on their own recommendations, it is difficult to think anyone else will.

Thus, a central question is whether the pastoral letter on war and peace has become a dead letter for the bishops. Have they used it to monitor developments since 1983? Have the bishops themselves taken the peace pastoral seriously? Have they devoted the same amount of time, energy, and resources to peace programs as they have to another item on the pro-life agenda—namely, the campaign to reverse the 1973 Supreme Court decision legalizing abortion? This is a question of special interest to women in the peace movement.

In order to answer these questions, I have divided this essay into several sections. The first part briefly summarizes the major points of the 1983 peace pastoral. The second part then discusses the impact of the letter upon public opinion and public policy. In the third part, I shall examine what steps the bishops have taken to implement the letter's recommendations. This is followed by a fourth section discussing what the bishops have *not* done in following through on the pastoral letter. Finally, the fifth part is a comparison of the bishops' pro-peace and pro-life efforts. The essay concludes with a discussion of the implications of this comparison for women who are committed to both the peace movement and the struggle for gender equality.

I. The Substance of the Bishops' Letter: An Overview

The pastoral letter, "The Challenge of Peace," is divided into four parts: (1) theological, biblical, and moral perspectives on peacekeeping, including an assessment of the pacifist and just war traditions within Catholic social teaching; (2) the application of moral perspectives to problems of nuclear warfare and deterrence; (3) proposals and policies for promoting peace in the nuclear age; and, (4) a pastoral challenge to the church and selected constituencies. While each section of the letter is intrinsically important, the section that has probably received most attention is the section on nuclear warfare and deterrence, since these passages address most directly policy matters confronting the United States today.

The burden of the bishops' argument about nuclear warfare is that decisions about nuclear weapons involve fundamental moral choices. They maintain that "good ends (defending one's country, protecting freedom) cannot justify immoral means (the use of weapons which kill indiscriminately or threaten whole societies)."[1] According to the bishops, there are limits to what a nation can do, even in self-defense and for its own survival. These limits are suggested by the application of traditional just war theory to the nuclear dilemma.

Just war doctrine is the distillation of a long political-ethical tradition derived from Stoic and Patristic sources and developed in the works of St. Augustine, St. Thomas Aquinas, Francisco de Vitoria, Francisco Suarez, and Hugo Grotius, among others. It considers both the legitimacy of resort to war to settle disputes (*jus ad bellum*) and just conduct in the course of war (*jus in bello*). The initial presumption, of course, is always against resort to force. This presumption can be overridden only if a set of rigorous criteria are met. These include (1) just cause for war; (2) declaration by duly constituted authority; (3) right intention (e.g., to achieve peace, not vengeance); (4) resort to war as a last resort; (5) the principle of discrimination that holds that in war innocent noncombatants must not be the direct target of attack; (6) the principle of proportionality that requires that the destruction of attack, whether or not it is intentional, cannot be disproportionate to the good intended in applying force; and (7) probability of success: the notion that application of force must have a good chance of success, of resulting in the restitution of justice.

Now it seems obvious that nuclear warfare poses serious problems for just war doctrine. Nuclear weapons are fundamentally nondiscriminating, nonproportional instruments of mass destruction. Given these realities, the bishops conclude that just war criteria rule out most, if not all, types of nuclear use, including counter-population use, first use of nuclear weapons, and "limited" nuclear warfare (about which the bishops are profoundly skeptical). Concerning deterrence doctrine, the pastoral letter arrives at a "strictly conditional moral acceptance of deterrence." Such a policy, the bishops maintain, is inadequate as a long-term basis for peace, but is a transitional strategy justifiable only in conjunction with resolute determination to pursue arms control and disarmament. Note that this qualified acceptance of deterrence implicitly, if not explicitly, commits the bishops to periodically monitor disarmament and arms control policies in order to estimate progress or regression.

In addition to these general conclusions, the bishops make several specific policy recommendations. These include support for a bilateral nuclear freeze on testing, production, and deployment of new nuclear weapons systems; support for negotiated bilateral deep cuts in nuclear arsenals; support for a comprehensive test ban treaty; removal of nuclear weapons from areas most likely to be overrun in the early stages of regional conflict; and strengthening of command and control over nuclear weapons in order to avoid nuclear "accidents." The bishops characterize these policy recommendations as illustrative of the application of general, universally binding moral principles to specific, concrete policy choices. At the same time, they recognize the need for prudence in applying general moral principles to particular situations, and they acknowledge that, among persons of good will, there is room for legitimate disagreement with their policy recommendations (Sections 9–10, 282).

The pastoral's concluding sections cite the challenges posed to Catholic and non-Catholic Americans because the nation is so heavily armed with modern weapons, and recommend some responses for consideration. The letter calls for increased educational efforts in every diocese and parish, for prayerful living, for a return to the tradition among U.S. Catholics of fasting and abstinence every Friday. Catholics are reminded that "Peace-making is not an optional commitment. It is a requirement of our faith. We are called to be peacemakers, not by some movement of the moment, but by our Lord Jesus" (Sec. 333). The bishops stress that true peace can only be built on a foundation of reverence for life and call upon the millions who say "no" to nuclear war to say "no" also to abortion, which they consider direct, unjustifiable attack on innocent human life. They urge the American people and leaders to express profound sorrow for the nuclear attacks on Hiroshima and Nagasaki in 1945.

Finally, they address particular groups in society who are specially related to nuclear weapons production and possible use: scientists, military personnel, workers in defense industries, and public officials. Those in the military are reminded that even their own training and field manuals prohibit certain actions in the conduct of war and that "to refuse to take such actions is not an act of cowardice or treason but one of courage and patriotism" (Sec. 311). Catholics in defense industries are urged to use the moral principles of the pastoral to form their own consciences. Social scientists and public officials are encouraged to relate moral wisdom and political reality. All citizens are asked to exercise the virtue of patriotism by urging the nation "to live up to its full potential as an agent of peace with justice for all people" (Sec. 327).

II. The Influence of the Pastoral Letter on Public Opinion and Public Policy

While it is difficult to gage exactly what impact the bishops' letter had on public opinion and public policy, we can at least examine some preliminary data. Indications are that *The Challenge of Peace* caused a shift in public opinion about defense spending among American Catholics and also made a significant impact in scholarly circles of political scientists, international relations specialists, ethicists, and moral theologians. However, the letter seems to have had almost no impact upon governmental policy. If anything, the arms race has intensified since publication of the peace pastoral in May 1983.

According to sociologist Andrew Greeley, the pastoral was responsible for an "astonishing" shift against defense spending among Catholics.[2] Using the National Opinion Research Center's "General Social Survey," Greeley found that in 1983 before the pastoral was released, 32 percent of Americans—Protestants and Catholics alike—thought too much money was being spent on weapons. A year later, the percentage was still 32 percent for Protestants but 54 percent for Catholics, a change in attitude by perhaps 10 million Catholics. According to Greeley, the pastoral seems to be the only factor that could account for such a shift. He claims that release of the letter coincided with events in the early 1980s when many Americans became uneasy about the size of the Reagan Administration's military budget and the possibility of a nuclear arms race that could turn into a war. Astonishingly—and mostly as a matter of good fortune—the bishops "said the right thing at the right time." Moreover, release of the pastoral proved to be an effective use of the media by the bishops—

aided and abetted by the Reagan Administration, which tried openly and publicly to influence the bishops' deliberations.[3] As Greeley shows, many Catholics learned of the bishops' letter through the press and television, not through reading the pastoral or hearing about it in church (this, of course, speaks volumes about how churches might communicate with their congregations). It should be noted that, despite the opinion shift among American Catholics, a majority of Catholics voted for President Reagan's reelection in 1984.[4] At the 1984 annual conference of the American Political Science Association, five panels were devoted to analysis of the peace pastoral. The bishops have created space in the public debate for moral analysis and for renewed interest in just war doctrine as opposed to *raison d'état* thinking, which attributes absolute value to national security in international relations.[5]

Among moral philosophers, a particularly important event has been the publication of a special issue of the journal *Ethics* devoted entirely to the morality of nuclear deterrence.[6] The essay by Robert W. Tucker in this volume calls the bishops' letter an "impressive effort" to relate the just war tradition to nuclear realities.[7] And of course in theological circles the debate about the peace pastoral has been intense.[8]

Nevertheless, despite both the popular and scholarly debate about nuclear weapons occasioned by publication of *The Challenge of Peace*, the bishops' letter seems to have had little actual influence on U.S. policy. Since May 1983, the following developments in defense policy have occurred. The U.S. government plans to deploy a large number (21,000) of new nuclear weapons within the next decade at great cost. Research and development on first-strike nuclear weapons has proceeded with the MX and Pershing II missiles. Pershing II and cruise missiles have been deployed in Europe over the strong protests of the populations in the areas involved. The Strategic Defense Initiative (Star Wars) threatens a dangerous and costly new round in the arms race. Social welfare budgets continue to be reduced in order to finance the arms race. In view of these developments, some have concluded that, since release of the peace pastoral, there has been serious regression rather than progress in armscontrol.[9]

III. Steps Taken by the Bishops to Implement the Recommendations of the Peace Pastoral

The Articulation of a Consistent Life Ethic

The bishops have taken several measures to implement the initiatives of the peace pastoral. These include educational efforts (varying from diocese to diocese), testimony on defense policy by selected bishops before Congressional committees, a November 1985 decision of the National Conference of Catholic Bishops (NCCB) to reassess the 1983 "strictly conditional moral acceptance of deterrence," and some tentative efforts to think more concretely about selective conscientious objection. One of the more important initiatives stemming from the pastoral letter was the elaboration, beginning in 1983 and continuing through 1984 and 1985, by Joseph Cardinal Bernardin of Chicago of a "consistent life ethic," a theoretical construct designed to link together in coherent fashion the church's opposition to abortion and to most forms of nuclear warfare.[10] Since the development of this intellectual agenda is central to any understanding of current American Catholic attempts to shape public discourse, I shall explain this notion in some detail.

Cardinal Bernardin chaired the ad hoc committee that drafted the peace pastoral.[11] In December 1983, he addressed a convocation at Fordham University to mark his assumption of a new post within the American Catholic hierarchy, chairman of the NCCB's pro-life committee. Seeking to capitalize upon the momentum generated by the bishops' peace pastoral, Bernardin examined the possibilities for development that are latent in the various themes of the letter. In particular, he argued the case for a linkage (mentioned in the pastoral) between the issues of abortion and nuclear war.[12] Bernardin wished to use the letter "as a starting point for shaping a consistent ethic of life in our culture."[13]

> Certainly the serious, sustained interest manifested throughout American society in the bishops' letter on war and peace provides a unique pastoral opportunity for the church. Demonstrating how the teaching on war and peace is supported by a wider concern for all of life may bring others to see for the first time what our tradition has affirmed for a very long time: the linkage among the life issues.[14]

A consistent ethic of life is an outlook or attitude of respect for human life that undergirds activity on a variety of so-called life issues: nuclear war, abortion, capital punishment, euthanasia, even questions of social welfare and civil rights. Bernardin sees such an ethic implicit in the peace pastoral's basic norm of the sanctity and dignity of human life, and the personal and social responsibility of all to preserve, protect, and promote human life. A consistent life ethic emphasizes the ways in which rapidly changing technology—in both modern warfare and modern medicine—induces a sharper awareness of the fragility of human life. It calls attention to the moral aspects of every technological challenge and policy dilemma. In this way, a consistent life ethic addresses the essential questions posed by our ever-changing technology: in an age when we can do almost anything, how do we decide what we ought to do? The even more demanding question is: in a time when we can do anything technologically, how do we decide morally what we never should do?

A consistent life ethic is Bernardin's way of calling attention to the resources in the Catholic tradition for shaping a viable public ethic. Rather than depict the American Catholic church as a parochial, single-issue church concerned above all with public policy on abortion, Bernardin sees the role of the bishops as shaping public discourse on a wide range of issues.

> The spectrum of life cuts across the issues of genetics, abortion, capital punishment, modern warfare and the care of the terminally ill. These are all distinct problems, enormously complicated and deserving individual treatment. No single answer and no simple responses will solve them. My purpose, however, is to highlight the way in which we face new technological challenges in each one of these areas; this combination of challenges is what cries out for a consistent ethic of life. [15]

Bernardin cites as a basic issue the need in society for an elemental attitude or atmosphere "which is the precondition for sustaining a consistent ethic of life." Catholic opposition to abortion, nuclear war, and the death penalty are intended to be seen as specific applications of this broader attitude. The purpose of proposing a consistent ethic of life is to "argue that success on any one of the issues threatening life *requires* a concern for the broader attitude in society about respect for human life." [16]

In addition to a basic respect-life attitude in society, Bernardin cites a need for ethical principles to guide the actions of individuals and institutions. For example, the explicit connection or linkage between Catholic teaching on abortion and Catholic teaching on war in the peace pastoral is based on the moral principle that prohibits the directly intended taking of innocent human life. This principle is at the heart of Catholic teaching on abortion. The same principle yields the most stringent, binding, and radical conclusion of the pastoral letter: that directly intended attacks on civilian centers are always wrong—even in cases of retaliatory second strikes. And the same principle applies to care of the handicapped and the terminally ill, although not to the issue of capital punishment. [17]

Bernardin contends that the viability of the principle depends upon the consistency of its application. Moreover, he insists that the right to life of the unborn is intimately related to the quality of life of the already born.

> If one contends, as we do, that the right of every fetus to be born should be protected by civil law and supported by civil consensus, then our moral, political and economic responsibilities do not stop at the moment of birth. Those who defend the right to life of the weakest among us must be equally visible in support of the quality of life of the powerless among us: the old and the young, the hungry and the homeless, the undocumented immigrant and the unemployed worker. . . . Consistency means we cannot have it both ways: we cannot urge a compassionate society and vigorous public policy to protect the rights of the unborn and then argue that compassion and significant public programs on behalf of the needy undermine the moral fiber of society or are beyond the proper scope of governmental responsibility.[18]

Cardinal Bernardin's intentions in proposing a consistent life ethic seem obvious. Describing his position as "both morally correct and tactically necessary," Bernardin emphasizes consistency because he realizes that the anti-abortion stance of the bishops is unconvincing if the church restricts its concern only to the unborn. The church must demonstrate that the ethical vision that led the bishops to the conclusions of the peace pastoral also informs their position on abortion policy. In this way the church can respond to the challenge of a secular society: the challenge is "to state our case in nonreligious terms which others of different faith convictions might find morally persuasive."[19]

Cardinal Bernardin's formulation of a consistent life ethic sparked intense controversy and debate within the church. Pro-life advocates argued that his approach might dilute the thrust of the anti-abortion movement and ultimately betray the cause of those struggling to protect fetal life. Peace movement activists, who applauded the bishops' peace pastoral but criticized their position on abortion policy, argued that Bernardin's approach confused distinct, separate issues and did not address adequately the complexities and differences between the various life issues. Ethicists, especially those sympathetic to feminist concerns, lamented his failure to mention women in his lectures and addresses—either as agents in the abortion dilemma or as weak, vulnerable members of society who, like the hungry, the homeless, the unemployed, and the unborn, need special protection and support.[20]

We shall return to these criticisms of Bernardin's consistent life ethic in a later section of this essay. For now, I would like to emphasize how the formulation of a consistent life ethic affords a direct basis for comparing the pro-life and pro-peace efforts of the American bishops. Since they have linked these life issues together, we may properly (rightly) ask whether the bishops themselves have devoted as much time, effort, resources, and energies to activities on behalf of the born compared with the unborn. A consistent life ethic invites such a comparison. It also affords a basis for comparing the *process* through which the American Catholic bishops have engaged in moral reasoning and policy formulation on these two sets of issues.

Post-Pastoral Peace Activities of the American Bishops

The activities of the bishops in following through on peace pastoral recommendations include testimony to Congressional committees concerning weapons systems and the decision, in November 1985, to reassess their conditional acceptance of nuclear deterrence. In major testimony before the House Foreign Relations Committee on June 26, 1984, Cardinal Bernardin and John J. O'Connor, Archbishop of New York, summarized the pastoral letter and then elaborated two standards to assess new weapons systems: their impact on the arms race and the prospects for deterrence, and their cost. Using these criteria, they criticized development and deployment of the MX missile and of SDI (President Reagan's proposal for a space-based defense system) as both highly destabilizing and excessively expensive. They also criticized deployment of U.S. Pershing II and cruise missiles in Western Europe and called for "a new effort of political will and creative diplomacy" in superpower negotiations.[21]

On March 15, 1985, Bishop James Malone, president of the United States Catholic Conference (USCC), sent letters to members of Congress urging them to vote against funding the MX missile. Malone reiterated the criticism voiced earlier by Bernardin and O'Connor: the USCC's opposition, he wrote, "is based on two considerations: the potentially destabilizing impact of this weapons system on the nuclear arms race, and its cost, viewed in light of pressing human needs here and elsewhere in the world." Archbishop O'Connor had expressed similar views in testimony to a House subcommittee on housing development on March 7, 1985.[22] (The U.S. Senate subsequently voted 55–45 on March 19, 1985, to authorize release of $1.5 billion for 21 new MX missiles.)

The bishops justified their testimony and policy recommendations in terms of the pastoral letter's conditional acceptance of the strategy of deterrence. They pointed out that such acceptance requires ongoing scrutiny of weapons proposed for addition to the deterrent force. Six months later, Reagan Administration defense expenditures for destabilizing weapons systems had proceeded to the point that the NCCB and USCC felt compelled to undertake a new study reexamining their conditional acceptance in 1983 of nuclear deterrence strategy. At the November 1985 annual meeting of the NCCB, six bishops led by Thomas Gumbleton of Detroit requested a thorough study of whether the conditions for the moral acceptance of deterrence in the 1983 letter had been met. These bishops pointed to increased U.S. expenditures for SDI and for first-strike weapons (e.g., the MX, the Pershing II, and the Trident II submarine) as "evidence that our nation's policies are taking us far beyond a 'minimum' deterrence and giving no evidence of moving toward 'progressive disarmament.' " Moreover, they thought there had been no progress in arms control, citing "the persistent refusal to return to the Comprehensive Test Ban negotiations, the refusal to respond to the Soviet initiative for a moratorium on testing, and the U.S. decision to proceed with the test of an anti-satellite weapon, thus opening up an arms race in space."[23]

After discussion, Bishop Malone, as president of the NCCB, announced appointment of an ad hoc committee to assess whether the conditions of the pastoral letter are being met. This committee consists of six bishops (Cardinals Bernardin and O'Connor, Bishops Gumbleton of Detroit and Daniel Reilly of Norwich, Connecticut, and Archbishops John Roach of Minneapolis–St. Paul and Roger Mahony of Los Angeles) whose task is to make recommendations, based upon study and deliberation, to the NCCB for continuing, modifying, or repudiating the original position on deterrence. It should be noted that the bishops resisted earlier calls to reassess their position partly because it took so long for them to reach the strictly conditional acceptance of deterrence—obviously a compromise—espoused in the 1983 letter.[24] Knowledgeable observers speculate that the 1983 compromise was an effort by Cardinal Bernardin not to alienate Catholic churchgoers and to secure an almost unanimous vote of approval by the bishops for the peace pastoral.[25]

IV. What the Bishops Have Not Done

Any assessment of the bishops' efforts to implement the initiatives of the peace pastoral must take into account negative aspects as well as positive measures, that is, opportunities missed as well as steps taken to follow up on the important initial contributions of the letter. Three instances of failure to follow through come immediately to mind: sustained peace studies and educational programs, the U.S. invasion of Grenada and bombing of Libya, and the conduct of the bishops during the 1984 election.

First, to what extent have the bishops followed through on the educational intentions of the pastoral letter, which was meant to call the attention of Catholics and non-Catholics to the moral dimensions of public policy? The bishops' letter urged every diocese and parish to implement balanced and objective educational programs to help people at all age levels to understand better the issues of war and peace. However, according to a report in the *National Catholic Reporter*, educational implementation has been uneven, with significant progress being made in Catholic schools and institutions of higher education while efforts at parish and diocesan levels have lagged (following an initial burst of interest and enthusiasm). In the schools, organized projects were undertaken to integrate the pastoral's main themes into classes, curricula, textbooks, and nonacademic activities.[26] By contrast, barely one year after publication of the letter, the USCC closed its national Clearinghouse for the War and Peace Pastoral, a monitoring agency set up to report regularly on projects developed around the country in response to the letter. Parish and diocesan implementation of peace education programs has been very uneven,[27] and there seems to be a real fear that discussion of war and peace issues has been overtaken by developing interest in the bishops' pastoral letter on economic justice.[28]

Failure to implement peace education programs at the parish and diocesan level is serious because it is at this level that the bishops have potentially the greatest impact. While it is important for Catholic Church leaders to testify before committees and lobby in Congress, their influence is diffused because the voice of the NCCB/USCC is one among many such public interest groups seeking to influence Washington policymakers. By contrast, the far less glamorous task of communicating the message of the pastoral effectively among local parishes to Catholic churchgoers seems to be more properly the function of the bishops in their role as teachers. Sustained educational efforts and expanded peace studies programs seem perfectly consonant with the bishops' intention, in writing the letter, to shape public opinion and influence public debate about nuclear strategy. Indeed, as one analyst has commented, the drafting and publication of the peace pastoral reflected, expressed, and expanded intense public concern in the period 1980–1983 about the morality of nuclear policy. However, since 1983, the debate has somewhat subsided in the public arena, despite vigorous continuation among those elites concerned with policy formation and scholarly moral analysis. This commentator suggests that "the churches have an important continuing responsibility to keep the discussion alive among their members."[29] In American politics, churches are particularly well-positioned to ensure that debate about public policy on such important matters as the morality of nuclear deterrence is carried on at popular as well as elite levels of society.

A second area of concern is the application of just war doctrine to actual cases. Since publication of the pastoral letter in 1983, the United States has undertaken two military incursions, the invasion of Grenada in 1984 and the bombing of Libya in 1986.[30] Despite clear statements in the letter of the conditions to be met before any actual war can be regarded as "just," the bishops collectively said nothing about the government's invasion of Grenada. As Gordon Zahn noted, "Few voices were raised to question the proportionality of full-scale military action, including aerial bombings, to 'free' some medical students from factually unsubstantiated danger."[31]

Similarly the bishops did not apply just war theory to the government's bombing of Libya in 1986. No formal protest was made by the hierarchy of the bombing of innocent civilian members of Colonel Khaddafi's family. The USCC remained silent about the U.S. attack, but several bishops issued individual statements. Bishop Gumbleton condemned the U.S. action as "too macho and too vindictive and pragmatically not much use." He predicted the bombing would lead to "an escalation in violence that's going to result in loss of many more lives."[32]

Although the peace pastoral does not specifically address the problem of terrorism, it does intend just war doctrine to be applied to conventional as well as nuclear warfare. Ironically, according to a feature analysis in the *Boston Pilot* (the official newspaper of the Boston Archdiocese), William O'Brien, professor of government at Georgetown University and an expert who testified before the committee that wrote the letter, used just war theory to *justify* the Libyan raid. O'Brien claimed that administration policy-makers such as Secretary of Defense Caspar Weinberger and Secretary of State George Schultz had been influenced by the peace pastoral to use just war language in their official statements to the American people about the Libyan bombing.[33] The use of just war doctrine to arrive at contradictory conclusions about the morality of particular cases of military action has always been one of the problems with just war theory.

One glaring example of the bishops' failure to follow through on the pastoral letter is the 1984 presidential election campaign. That campaign was characterized by the forceful interventions of several prominent Catholic bishops on the abortion issue. Yet these same bishops were reticent in calling attention to the obligation of candidates to give due consideration to the moral aspects of nuclear weapons and arms control policies. Although Archbishop John O'Connor of New York and Archbishop Bernard Law of Boston criticized Democratic vice-presidential candidate Geraldine Ferraro for her support of legalized abortion, they steered clear of the choice voters had between Democrats, whose party platform agreed with the bishops' support of a nuclear freeze, and Republicans campaigning on a platform of continued escalation of the arms race through SDI and the MX missile. In their interventions in the 1984 campaign, leading American bishops antagonized numerous Catholic and non-Catholic voters who could not help but note the inconsistency between their partisan activism on abortion policy and their nonpartisan neutrality on defense policy. Although the NCCB specifically cautioned against a single-issue emphasis in the election campaign,[34] the behavior of some prominent American bishops suggested that the only issue leading members of the hierarchy really cared about was abortion.[35]

Coming barely a year after the issuance of the peace pastoral, the 1984 campaign offered an opportunity for the bishops to follow through on the moral principles and specific policy suggestions of the letter. Of course, the desire of the bishops to be nonpartisan in American elections is understandable, given first amendment strictures about church-state separation. What is not understandable is the willingness of some prominent bishops to abandon such restraint in matters of abortion policy while remaining silent about proper policy on nuclear weapons. While they showed leadership in writing the pastoral, they do not seem to follow through on real-world application of its conclusions.

V. Consistency in Pro-life Work: The Anti-abortion and Antiwar Efforts of the Bishops

When we apply Cardinal Bernardin's consistent life ethic to the peace activities of the bishops, the conclusion seems inescapable that the bishops have failed to follow through on the important initiatives of their pastoral letter. For the consistent life ethic invites comparison of the pro-peace and pro-life efforts of the American bishops. If we ask whether the bishops have devoted as much time, effort, and resources to promoting arms control and reduction as they have to promoting delegalization of abortion, the answer seems clear that church leaders do not apply the "seamless garment" metaphor equally to war and abortion.[36]

The first person to draw attention to the inconsistency between the bishops' qualified acceptance of some aspects of nuclear war and deterrence and their moral absolutism in opposing abortion was Sister Joan Chittester, O.S.B., prioress of the Benedictine Sisters of Erie, Pennsylvania, and a delegate to the White House Religious Conference on SALT II. Commenting on the first draft of the pastoral letter, she stated:

> The document undermines the credibility of other episcopal statements. The bishops claim that nuclear destruction and policy are repugnant to them but say it is impossible to be morally absolute in their repudiation of the manufacture or use of nuclear weapons because there is enough need for deterrence and enough doubt about their effects to command their toleration. It is troublesome to note that the bishops show no such hesitation or ambivalence about abortion. In that case from a given principle they draw universal and absolute implications with ease. Catholic hospitals may not permit abortions; Catholic doctors may not perform them; Catholic nurses may not assist at them; Catholic monies may not be used to sponsor abortion clinics. Nevertheless, the arguments for abortion are the same: the promotion of a greater good and the deterrence of evil for the parents or a handicapped child itself, for instance. What is a woman to think? That when life is in the hands of a woman, then to destroy it is always morally wrong, never to be condoned, always a grave and universal evil? But when life is in the hands of men, millions of lives at one time, all life at one time, then destruction can be theologized and some people's needs and lives can be made more important than other people's needs and lives? It is a theological imperative that we confront this dichotomy.[37]

Chittester's preferred method of resolving this inconsistency was to have the bishops say a clear, unqualified "no" to nuclear war and deterrence as well as to abortion. Failing that, it seemed to her unconscionable for the bishops to require heroism and sacrifice from women in the abortion dilemma but not from military men in decision-making situations.

Those who are skeptical about Cardinal Bernardin's consistent life ethic stress that the bishops are inconsistent in formulating and applying church teaching concerning *public policy* on abortion and war. At the level of *moral principle* Catholic teaching is consistent: the direct and deliberate killing of innocent human life in warfare and through abortion is morally impermissible. Inconsistency creeps in at the level of concrete application. Although the church imposes the extreme sanction of excommunication upon women who kill innocent life in abortion,[38] there are no religious sanctions for those who violate the principle of noncombatant immunity and destroy innocent life in war. In the age of total war, no soldiers, bomber pilots, or generals who order or carry out the destruction of towns and cities have been excommunicated or threatened with excommunication. Those passages of the pastoral letter that discuss the obligations of individual soldiers and officers are remarkable examples of instruction and persuasion rather than judgmental condemnation or heavy-handed coercion.[39] While women with the medical option of abortion are threatened with dire sanctions, men in the military are merely exhorted not to kill innocent life.

It may be argued, of course, that the reason the church imposes sanctions on women who kill innocent life in abortion and not on men who kill innocent life in war is that war is so complex that it is difficult to judge individual guilt. But Christine Gudorf points to the inadequacy of this reasoning.

> Is it so clear that the abortion decision is never complex? That women are not facing authorities with orders: employers who will fire them, men who will leave them, parents who will eject them from their homes? Are these never situations of self-defense?[40]

Studies of abortion decision-making, such as those of Carol Gilligan, Maryann Lamanna, and Judith Smetana, suggest how complex the abortion decision is and how numerous the factors that involuntarily pregnant women consider in their decision making.[41]

A second inconsistency in the church's approach concerns the complexity of nuclear strategy and deterrence. Recognition of this complexity led the bishops in their pastoral letter to enunciate a distinction between general moral principles that are universally binding and particular concrete applications about which there can be legitimate disagreement. This distinction had long been sound theological teaching, but the difficulty and delicacy of the nuclear issue compelled the bishops to emphasize it in the pastoral letter. The burden of the distinction is that Catholics might agree on general moral principles while loyally and even vigorously disagreeing on the many intervening factual and prudential judgments needed to translate these principles into public policy. Now for the bishops to emphasize this distinction in their pastoral letters on peace and economic justice is to raise the inevitable question of consistency: why should American Catholics not be any less free to disagree with the bishops on the human life amendment or the Hatch Amendment—both anti-abortion constitutional amendments—than on the nuclear freeze or welfare state policies?

Inconsistency also characterizes the *process* by which the bishops arrived at their policy recommendations on the issues of abortion and nuclear war. In the development of the church's moral position and political stance on abortion, women and those with opposing views were not consulted. By contrast, the elaboration by the bishops of their moral teaching and policy recommendations on nuclear warfare involved extensive interviewing and consultation, through a series of formal hearings, with moral theologians, policy analysts, military strategists, and government officials who often held opposing views. Whereas the bishops readily acknowledge that they are not experts in military strategy or economic policy and must therefore defer to secular specialists, there is no public acknowledgment by the bishops of insufficient expertise in the medical, legal, and political fields relevant to abortion policy. Above all, there seems to be no admission of any need to consult those most directly implicated in the abortion dilemma.

The tone as well as the substance of church teaching on these issues is inconsistent. As one writer has commented:

> When the church has spoken out against the arms race and economic inequality, it has not been in terms of the "mortal sins" of individuals, or of absolute moral norms. It has been in the context of encouraging mutual trust, respect, and cooperation, and with a view to collaboration in the discovery of practical avenues to moral ideals. I hope that this will come to be the case more frequently in discussions of sexual ethics and the roles of women in the church.[42]

A final inconsistency between the pro-peace and pro-life approach of the American bishops is the contrast between the time, energy, and resources devoted to the anti-abortion campaign and to the peace programs of the bishops. Anti-abortion efforts continue to have top priority, judging by the recent activities of the NCCB and the USCC. In March 1985, the USCC sought to attach an anti-abortion amendment to the proposed Civil Rights Restoration Act, a development that has stalled passage of this important piece of civil rights legislation.[43] The bishops don't miss a single development in abortion policy, whether on the state or national level; for example, *Origins* (the National Catholic documentary service) reprints state as well as federal court decisions on abortion and otherwise provides detailed coverage of the abortion controversy.[44] Less space is devoted to coverage of the arms race and weapons policies.

How are we to explain the inconsistent life ethic of the bishops on abortion and nuclear warfare? Why is so much effort expended on pro-life but not pro-peace activities? One reason is that, compared with the morality of nuclear war and deterrence, church teaching on the morality and legality of abortion *seems* simpler and clearer, involving as it does the individual actions of a single person. (We have seen how complex abortion decision-making actually can be.) A second reason undoubtedly involves the bishops' expectations of reactions from many churchgoers—"the people in the pews"—were the bishops to be more simple, direct, and consistent about nuclear policy. The bishops may fear that the laity as well as their own priests may simply not accept—or may even dismiss—any wholesale condemnation of nuclear warfare by the hierarchy. As well, a committed, well-organized, single-issue pro-life movement, which includes many Catholic members, is constantly pressuring the bishops to take a strong anti-abortion stand. By contrast, Pax Christi, the Catholic Worker, the Fellowship of Reconciliation, and other Catholic and non-Catholic peace organizations are perhaps less numerous and less single-minded in pressuring the bishops to support peacemaking initiatives.

VI. Conclusion

Comparison of the bishops' pro-peace and pro-life efforts carries certain implications for women who are committed to both the peace movement and the struggle for gender equality. Some have suggested that the methodological inconsistency of the bishops will not change without a strong dose of feminist historical consciousness. For at a profound level, perhaps a major reason that pro-life efforts continue to have priority over peace activities among the American Catholic bishops, is the historical separation of reality into two spheres, the public and the private, and the unconscious acceptance by the church at the end of the nineteenth century of the notion that religion belongs in the private realm of home and family, not in the public realm of business and politics. This public/

private dichotomy and the resultant feminization and privatization of religion is an historical legacy that the bishops are now struggling to overcome. As Gudorf suggests:

Only since Vatican II has the Church seen the public realm as an appropriate object of full-scale mission and begun regularly to address such issues as poverty, disarmament, human rights (other than religious), capital punishment, racism, and capitalism. In addressing these issues the Church still sees itself as a relative newcomer who must convince the principals of its right to participate and of the worth of its contribution. The Church speaks to persuade, because it cannot coerce. It uses reason and is careful to consult many other views. . . . In the private realm [by contrast], our Church feels it owns the turf, that moral principles are sufficient, that social analysis, while sometimes helpful, is not necessary because the principles are absolute and their practical application obvious.[45]

Gudorf maintains that the church uses an ethics of consequences in public-realm issues, and a deontological natural law approach (which emphasizes absolute moral obligations) in private realm issues. Thus the church employs consequentialist arguments regarding public issues such as nuclear deterrence and capital punishment and an absolutist morality in a private-realm issue such as abortion.

For this to change, the church would have to accept two basic premises of feminist thought: a conviction that the public-private distinction is artificial and can therefore be rethought and reshaped; and the feminist principle of women's moral agency and autonomy. Unless the church moves away from its apparent distrust of women as moral decision-makers, women with the medical option of abortion will continue to appear, in the bishops' eyes, to be a greater danger to life than men armed with tanks, missiles and bombs. The persistence of this misperception and misunderstanding of women will vitiate the inherent appeal and persuasiveness of Cardinal Bernardin's consistent life ethic.

Notes

1. National Conference of Catholic Bishops, *The Challenge of Peace: God's Promise and Our Response* (A Pastoral Letter on War and Peace), section 332, reprinted in Philip J. Murnion, ed., *Catholics and Nuclear War* (New York: Crossroad Publishers, 1983). Subsequent references to the pastoral letter will be to the text and the particular section; these references appear in parentheses in the text.

2. Andrew M. Greeley, "Why the Peace Pastoral Did Not Bomb," *National Catholic Reporter*, vol. 21, no. 24 (April 12, 1985), p. 11.

3. At its November 1982 general meeting to debate the second draft of the pastoral letter, the National Conference of Catholic Bishops (NCCB) was the object of open attempts by the Reagan administration to influence its deliberations. A letter was sent simultaneously to *The New York Times* and to Cardinal Bernardin, chair of the ad hoc committee of bishops drafting the letter, by William Clark, then national security adviser to the president. For a general historical account of the development and drafting of the peace pastoral, see Jim Castelli, *The Bishops and the Bomb* (Garden City, N.Y.: Doubleday and Company, 1983).

4. Paul R. Abramson, John H. Aldrich, and David W. Rohde, *Change and Continuity in the 1984 Elections* (Washington, D.C.: Congressional Quarterly Press, 1986), pp. 134–42. See also Gerald Pomper *et al.*, *The Election of 1984* (Chatham, N.J.: Chatham House Publishers, Inc., 1985).

5. For examples of analyses by political scientists who are sensitive to issues of just warfare in discussions of national security, see Susan Moller Okin, "Taking the Bishops Seriously," *World Politics*, vol. 36 (Summer 1984), pp. 527–54, and Zbigniew Brzezinski, "The Strategic Implications of Thou Shalt Not Kill," *America*, vol. 154, no. 21 (May 31, 1986), pp. 445–49.

6. *Ethics*, vol. 95 (1985).

7. R. W. Tucker, "Morality and Deterrence," *Ethics* 95 (1985), p. 461.

8. For reviews of this literature, see Richard McCormick, "Notes on Moral Theology: 1983," *Theological Studies*, vol. 45, no. 1 (March 1984), pp. 122–37; John Langan, S. J., "Pastoral on War and Peace: Reactions and New Directions," *Theological Studies*, vol. 46, no. 1 (March 1985), pp. 80–101; and David Hollenbach, S. J., "Whither Nuclear Deterrence? The Moral Debate Continues," *Theological Studies*, vol. 47, no. 1 (March 1986), pp. 117–33. Two excellent anthologies have been written about the peace pastoral by Judith A. Dwyer, S.S.J., ed., *The Catholic Bishops and Nuclear War* (Washington, D.C.: Georgetown University Press, 1984), and Philip J. Murnion, ed., *op. cit.*

9. The American branch of Pax Christi, the international Catholic peace organization, has published annual appraisals of the impact of the bishops' peace pastoral. See the 1984 assessment, "The Challenge of Peace: Its Promise and Impact—An Assessment," by Gordon C. Zahn (Pax Christi, 1984), and the 1985 appraisal, "Pax Christi USA—1985 Assessment Statement on The Challenge of Peace," by Francis X. Meehan (Pax Christi USA, 1985). Since this essay was written we have seen the signing of an Intermediate Nuclear Forces (INF) agreement between the superpowers. Any link to the pastoral letter is difficult to trace, but may be possible.

10. Cardinal Bernardin's major statements formulating a consistent life ethic are reprinted in *Origins*, the national documentary service of the National Conference of Catholic Bishops (NCCB) and the United States Catholic Confer-

ence (USCC). For Bernardin's address at Fordham University in New York on December 6, 1983, see *Origins*, vol. 13, no. 29 (Dec. 29, 1983), pp. 491–94. His address at St. Louis University on March 11, 1984, is reprinted in *Origins*, vol. 13, no. 43 (April 5, 1984), in Kansas City, Missouri, on June 7, 1984, see *Origins*, vol. 14, no. 8 (July 12, 1984), pp. 120–22.

11. The committee consisted of five bishops: Joseph Bernardin (Chicago), George Fulcher (Columbus), Thomas Gumbleton (Detroit), John J. O'Connor (military ordinariate, later archbishop of New York), and Daniel Reilly (Norwich, Connecticut). In addition, Father Richard Warner and Sister Julianna Casey were appointed to represent the Conference of Major Superiors of Men and the Leadership Conference of Women Religious, respectively. Bruce Martin Russett, professor of political science at Yale University, was engaged as the principal consultant for the letter. The committee's staff consisted of Father Bryan Hehir, Director of the Office of International Justice and Peace of the USCC, and Edward Doherty, adviser for political-military affairs in the same office.

12. *The Challenge of Peace: God's Promise and Our Response*, sections 284–89.

13. *Origins*, vol. 13, no. 29 (December 29, 1983), p. 491.

14. *Ibid.*, vol. 13, no. 43 (April 5, 1984), p. 709.

15. *Ibid.*, vol. 13, no. 29 (December 29, 1983), p. 493.

16. *Ibid.*

17. Some argue, against Bernardin, that abortion and capital punishment are not identical issues because the innocent unborn child may be distinguished from the convicted murderer. But Bernardin insists that there is a political psychological linkage among these life issues that we ignore at our own peril. He points out that while Catholic teaching still recognizes the theoretical right of the state to take life in defense of key social values, the use of the death penalty does not, in practice, deter future crimes. It is therefore questionable whether or not the state should exercise its right of execution. Adopting a consequentialist view, recent popes and the American bishops have argued that more humane methods of defending society exist and should be used.

18. *Origins*, vol. 13, no. 43 (April 5, 1984), p. 708. In Bernardin's view, a consistent life ethic does not equate the problem of taking life (e.g., through abortion and in war) with the problem of promoting human dignity (through humane programs of nutrition, health care, and housing). But a consistent ethic identifies both the protection of life and its promotion as moral questions.

19. *Ibid.*, vol. 13, no. 29 (December 29, 1983), p. 494.

20. See Christine E. Gudorf, "To Make a Seamless Garment, Use a Single Piece of Cloth," *Cross Currents*, vol. XXXIV, no. 4 (Winter, 1984–85), pp. 473–91.

21. *Ibid.*, vol. 14, no. 10 (August 9, 1984), pp. 154–58.

22. *Ibid.*, vol. 14, no. 41 (March 28, 1985), pp. 667–70.

23. *Ibid.*, vol. 15, no. 24 (November 28, 1985), pp. 399–400.

24. Vincent F. A. Golphin, "Peace Groups Want Pastoral Reassessed," *National Catholic Reporter,* October 18, 1985, pp. 13, 20. Earlier calls for reassessment were made at the 1983 general meeting of the NCCB by Bishop Maurice Dingman of Des Moines, Iowa, and at the 1984 general meeting by Auxiliary Bishop Peter Rosazza of Hartford, Conn.

25. Interview with Gordon C. Zahn, Pax Christi USA Center on Conscience and War, Cambridge, Mass., May 19, 1986.

26. A dissenting voice in the discussion of peace studies in Catholic colleges and universities is that of Gordon Zahn, who questioned the existence of ROTC in an article in *America,* vol. 153, no. 19 (December 21, 1985), pp. 439–41. A rejoinder by James Finn, defending the existence of ROTC on Catholic college campuses, is printed in the same issue of *America,* pp. 441–43.

27. Robert J. McClory, "Peace Pastoral Headed for Graveyard," *National Catholic Reporter,* vol. 21, no. 10 (December 28, 1984), pp. 1, 15. See also Gordon C. Zahn, "On Not Writing a Dead Letter," *Commonweal,* vol. CXII, no. 5 (March 8, 1985), pp. 141–43. Concerning the pastoral's provisions on conscientious objection, Zahn notes that "relatively few dioceses have established registries of prospective CO's, or have indicated a readiness to take even the most preliminary steps toward providing them with alternative service opportunities, should conscription be put into effect. It is important to note that the Selective Service System, for its part, is ready to go into full operation in a matter of hours."

28. See the essay by Harry A. Fagan, "Pastoral Possibilities: Conscience Formation, Education, and Conflict Resolution," in Murnion, ed., *Catholics and Nuclear War,* pp. 229–44.

29. Hollenbach, "Whither Nuclear Deterrence . . . ," *Theological Studies,* vol. 47, no. 1 (March 1986), p. 132.

30. The U.S. government has also aided Contra forces in Nicaragua and maintained a military presence in Central America during this time. Here the NCCB and USCC have regularly monitored developments in American foreign policy toward the region. A delegation of bishops visited Nicaragua and El Salvador in Spring 1985, and representatives of the bishops have testified before Congressional committees concerning U.S. policy in the region. See, for example, *Origins,* vol. 15, no. 45 (April 25, 1985).

31. Zahn, "On Not Writing a Dead Letter," p. 143.

32. "Franciscan Convent Hit in U.S. Attack: USCC Mute on Libya Bombing," *National Catholic Reporter,* vol. 22, no. 26 (April 25, 1986), p. 48.

33. Joe M. Feist, "U.S. Attack on Libya Meets Just War Principles, Scholar Says," *Boston Pilot,* May 9, 1986, p. 5.

34. USCC Administrative Board, "Political Responsibility: Choices for the 1980s," *Origins,* vol. 13, no. 44 (April 12, 1984), pp. 732–36.

35. For a detailed discussion of the behavior of the American Catholic bishops in the 1984 election campaign, see Segers, "Ferraro, the Bishops, and the 1984

Election," in vol. II of the Harvard Women's Studies in Religion Series, *Shaping New Vision: Gender and Values in American Culture*, edited by Clarissa Atkinson, Constance Buchanan, and Margaret Miles (Ann Arbor: UMI Research Press, 1987), pp. 143–67.

36. The metaphor, "seamless garment," was used by Cardinal Bernardin to symbolize the single attitude one should have toward life. The meaning of the term is familiar to everyone acquainted with the Gospel of St. John. As Cardinal Bernardin uses the term, it is intended to convey the idea that one should have a consistent ethic of life. Respect for life should include all human life. Thus, one should not draw a line, or put a seam in the garment, by making an exception where respect for human life is at stake. See John R. Connery, "A Seamless Garment in a Sinful World," *America*, July 14, 1984, pp. 5–8.

37. Sister Joan Chittester, O.S.B., "Stepping Tentatively Between Prophetism and Nationalism," *Commonweal*, vol. 109 (August 13, 1982), p. 428.

38. The sanction of excommunication is applied not only to women who decide, elect, or choose abortion, but also to Catholic women who serve as state-wide directors of planned parenthood organizations; see for example the case of Maryann Sorrentino, Director of Planned Parenthood for Rhode Island. See Matthew L. Wald, "Church Calls Excommunicated Catholic Abortion 'Accomplice'," *The New York Times*, January 25, 1986, p. 7. This may be compared with the number of times generals and other military decision-makers have been excommunicated for aiding in bombing attacks on population centers, saturation bombing, or even the bombing of Hiroshima and Nagasaki.

39. Gudorf, "To Make a Seamless Garment, Use a Single Piece of Cloth," p. 475.

40. *Ibid.*, p. 476.

41. See Carol Gilligan, *In a Different Voice: Psychological Theory and Women's Development* (Cambridge: Harvard University Press, 1982); Mary K. Zimmerman, *Passage Through Abortion: The Personal and Social Reality of Women's Experiences* (New York: Praeger, 1977); Judith Smetana, *Concepts of Self and Morality* (New York: Praeger, 1982); Magda Denes, *In Necessity and Sorrow: Life and Death in an Abortion Hospital* (New York: Penguin Books, 1977); and Louise Kapp Howe, *Moments on Maple Avenue: The Reality of Abortion* (New York: Warner Books, 1984).

42. Lisa Sowle Cahill, *Commonweal*, p. 2.

43. The Civil Rights Restoration Act (CRRA) was first introduced in Congress in April 1984 to counter the Supreme Court's ruling in *Grove City College* v. *Bell* 465 U.S. 555 (1984). In that decision, the Court sharply restricted the reach and sanctions of Title IX of the Education Amendments of 1982, which forbid sex discrimination at all colleges and universities receiving federal funds. The CRRA expressly states the congressional intent to bar discrimination throughout an institution, any of whose departments or branches receives federal funds. This bill, designed to overcome the limitations of *Grove City*, failed to pass in 1984 for

lack of time, and was reintroduced in the first weeks of the new congressional session in 1985. In March 1985, the United States Catholic Conference introduced an anti-abortion amendment to the bill, and this has blocked passage of the bill. See D. E. Anderson, "Is Abortion a Civil Right," *Christianity and Crisis*, April 7, 1986. See also Linda Greenhouse, "Abortion Issue Weaves an Intricate Web," *The New York Times*, April 22, 1986, p. A20.

44. See, for example, the reprint of a Pennsylvania Supreme Court decision on Medicaid funding of abortions and the Pennsylvania ERA, *Origins*, vol. 13, no. 42 (March 29, 1984), pp. 699–704.

45. Gudorf, "To Make a Seamless Garment, Use a Single Piece of Cloth," pp. 477–78. A similar point is made by James Carroll, "On Not Skipping the Sermon," *Commonweal*, November 2–16, 1984, pp. 604–5. See also Christine E. Gudorf, "Renewal or Repatriarchalization: Responses of the Roman Catholic Church to the Feminization of Religion," *Horizons*, vol. 10 (Fall 1983), pp. 231–51; and Jean Bethke Elshtain, *Public Man and Private Woman: Women in Political and Social Thought* (Princeton: Princeton University Press, 1981).

Part II

Citizenship and Soldiering, Then and Now

Comments

The question of who gets to be a citizen is a vital one. Linda Kerber, a respected student of American history and feminist scholar, helps us to understand how closely citizenship is tied to soldiering in our early history. Wars are periods of social change for women, but Kerber helps us raise the question as to whether these periods are also eras of progress. We can characterize the changes, but how are we to assess them? This is what her essay helps us to do.

Soldiering and citizenship, however, remain the nexus of her piece, and Kerber helps us to understand the power of the citizen-soldier attachment. Sometimes women considered themselves to be citizens and sometimes the nation referred to them as citizens in the same way as men, but not always. The notion that there are alternative forms of citizenship, not just the right to hold public office and to vote, but the right to engage in certain kinds of public activities, indicates a broadening of the definition of citizenship. What Kerber suggests, though, is that some forms of citizenship will always be more equal than others.

There are many residual examples of this phenomenon long after the American Revolutionary period. Any U.S. immigrant, whatever his status, who joins the American military, particularly during a period of crisis, is automatically awarded American citizenship upon discharge. There is no five-year wait, no need to pass a pro forma examination. It is the "wage" of his service. The way this nation thanks soldiers who are not mercenaries is to offer them citizenship.

At the same time, fighting is a privilege. During World War II many black Americans were inducted, put in uniform, and set to the task of loading and unloading ammunition. But when the ammunition exploded and they died, they were not awarded the Purple Heart because they hadn't been killed in combat (combat being narrowly defined as fighting the enemy on the battlefield). So there are hierarchies of military sacrifice, just as there are hierarchies of citizenship.

Kerber also details the complex case of *Martin* v. *Massachusetts*. Here, encoded in the law of the Revolutionary period, was the very radical notion that wives might be encouraged to leave their Tory husbands (if their husbands decided to leave the United States) by being offered the citizenship that their husbands had forgone in exchange for their loyalty to the young Republic.

4

May All Our Citizens Be Soldiers and All Our Soldiers Citizens: The Ambiguities of Female Citizenship in the New Nation

Linda K. Kerber

On September 3, 1783, Benjamin Franklin, John Adams, and John Jay made their way down the Rue Jacob in Paris to the lodgings of David Hartley, the British Commissioner charged with the negotiation of the Definitive Treaty of Peace between England and the newly established United States of America. The Peace of Paris they signed that day was a public triumph for the Americans and a personal triumph for Adams and Jay. They had not only negotiated firmly and effectively with their British enemy; they had, in addition, outwitted their French allies, their compatriots in Congress, and their own colleague Franklin by resolving the

---

An earlier version of this essay appeared originally in *The Work of Peace*, Joan R. Challinor and Robert Beisner, eds. (Westport, Conn.: Greenwood Press, 1982), pp. 1–22). Reprinted by permission of the author.

89

War of the Revolution in a way that resulted in wider boundaries for the United States than the French had bargained for. Preparing for a celebratory ball, John Jay's wife, Sarah Livingston Jay, drafted a list of toasts beginning: "The United States of America, may they be perpetual."

Standing at the threshold of peace, Sarah Jay thanked those who had made it possible: "The Congress, the King and Nation of France, the United Netherlands and all other Free States . . . , the Memory of the Patriots who have fallen . . ." and welcomed a new era: "Gratitude to our Friends and Moderation to our Enemies, Concord, Wisdom and Firmness to all American Council, Liberty and Happiness to all Mankind."

One toast, however, struck a discordant note, coming as it did from a woman: "May all our Citizens be Soldiers, and all our Soldiers Citizens." The words testified to the acceptance of a revitalized relationship between the military and the republican state. Read carefully, the toast also reminds us that generalizations often do not apply to men and to women in precisely the same degree. American men, listening to the toast, knew they were citizens and might be soldiers; for men, the two clauses were evenly balanced. American women, however, upon hearing the toast, knew they had fought for and supported the revolution in many ways but as yet were denied full rights as citizens. Consequently, they heard a rhetorical imbalance in which the gender of the listener made a difference. What did Sarah Jay mean by it? What did her audience hear in her words?[1]

On the face of it, the toast is primarily about *soldiers*. It refers to the military obligations of citizens. It also rests on the principle, important to the Founding Fathers and to the British tradition from which their thinking sprang, of no standing armies. The upheavals of the seventeenth century had established for liberals the rule, as Lois G. Schwoerer has recently put it, that "a standing army in peacetime was a threat to freedom and a menace to the English Constitution." It followed that a republic must rely on citizen-militias. The Declaration of Independence had explicitly complained of standing armies in peacetime and the quartering of soldiers in private homes. A few years after Sarah Jay's celebration, the Constitution would give Congress the power "to provide for organizing, arming, and disciplining the militia," and the Bill of Rights would limit the quartering of soldiers. Sarah Jay had in mind a future in which soldiers would be only temporarily recruited in rotation from the general population of citizens.[2]

The toast was also and obviously about *citizens*, a word that had particular resonance in the late eighteenth century. All but the youngest of Sarah Jay's American contemporaries had been born British subjects. But the concept of the *rebel subject* was an oxymoron, a contradiction in terms. The rebel had to find something else to become. Borrowing from the Roman Republic, the rebel subject was metamorphosed into an American *citizen*. However, now that their political identity had been transformed, were women and men both to be the same sort of citizen?

What it took to become a citizen was not fully clear when John Jay raised his glass. There was never a single, precise moment when the United States placed itself in a "state of nature" as the political metaphor of the time would have it, and asked its inhabitants explicitly whether they wanted to be part of the new polity. Even before the Declaration of Independence, a Congressional resolution of June 24, 1776, transformed subjects into *members* of the polity: "all persons residing within any of the United Colonies, and deriving protection from the laws of the same, owe allegiance to the said laws, and are *members* of such colony" [italics added]. This was done, James Kettner explains in his study of citizenship in the United States, in order to legitimize countermeasures against Tory espionage and counterfeiting. Since British law defined treason as opposition to the king, revolutionary leaders found it difficult to take stern measures against dissidents so long as the colonies technically remained in allegiance to George III. Therefore, the resolution had a second part that provided that "all persons, members of, or owing allegiance to any of the United Colonies . . . who shall levy war against any of the said colonies . . . or be adherents to the king of Great Britain . . . giving to him . . . aid and comfort, are guilty of treason against such colony."

By this law, both women and men who had been subjects of the King were transformed into members of the colonies; once independence was declared, by a short further step, the colonies became states and the "members," presumably, became citizens, whether they liked it or not.[3]

The refusal of citizenship, then, required explicit and physical removal of oneself—by emigrating, by enlisting with loyalist forces, or by going behind the British lines. In fact, Sarah Jay's aunt Margaret Livingston thought Loyalists had a point when they complained about a *fait accompli*. "I am not so unfeeling a patriot as not to Suffer exceedingly for the many families, who are now Leaving us, on their refusal to take the Oath to the State the tendering of which they Say, Should have been delay'd till we are, what we stile [*sic*] ourselves & which we have never yet been, our Independence to which they are to swear, being Still contested by a Large army in our Country."[4]

All were citizens, then, unless they had explicitly opted out. Were women also citizens? That depended on the meaning of the term. It might be used in a general way, to mean all permanent residents. But its roots in civic republicanism meant that the word carried with it the implication of political rights and privileges. J. G. A. Pocock has characterized the classical republican tradition in this way: civil action, carried out by *virtù*—the quality of being a man (vir)—seized upon the unshaped circumstances thrown up by fortune and shaped them, shaped Fortune herself, into the completed form of what human life should be: citizenship and the city it lived in.[5] Ancient Greece provided the model of the male citizen who made the city possible by taking up arms on its behalf. By the Renaissance, Pocock observes, military commitment was integral to civil identification. For example, Pocock cites the Florentine humanist Leonardo Bruni who thought of "arms as the *ultima ratio*, whereby the citizen exposes his life in defense of the state and, at the same time, ensures that the decision to expose it cannot be taken without him; it is the possession of arms that makes a man a full citizen.[6]

This mode of thinking, this way of relating men to the state, had no room in its conception of citizenship for women. According to Hanna Fenichel Pitkin, Machiavelli's sexual and familial imagery, meant to challenge men out of their concern with private, household matters of wealth and family into the more "manly" realm of political life, also has the opposite effect, arousing images of domination and submission and undermining that capacity for mutuality that citizenship requires. Men are not inherently more fit for citizenship than women and will appear so only in a society where women are denied access to public life.[7]

The assumptions of the classical republican tradition, summarized by Lawrence Cress, as the "association of propertied independence, political personality and military obligation with political stability," persisted into the American republic. If Liberty were to survive, male Americans would have to be willing to take up arms in her defense. In the eyes of revolutionaries, Charles Royster argues, war put to the trial military order and skill as well as the moral assumptions on which they based their hopes for American independence and liberty. To fail as defenders of ideals was to fail as Americans. In a formulation like this, the connection to the Republic of male patriots (who could enlist) was immediate; the connection of women, however patriotic they might feel themselves to be, was remote. Summarizing popular attitudes at the beginning of the Revolution, Royster writes: "The first anniversary of the Declaration of Independence was celebrated with the toast, 'May only those Americans enjoy freedom who are ready to die for its defense.' " To be free required a man to risk death.[8]

The definition of citizenship took a long time to stabilize in America. Although the obligation to bear arms on behalf of the King had once been central to the feudal understanding of the political order, it was not always explicitly articulated in pre-Revolutionary Britain or in America; the theme of *allegiance* was increasingly stressed in the revolutionary era. State constitutions usually spoke of free native-born inhabitants as citizens; the Articles of Confederation recognized "free inhabitants." By 1828, Noah Webster's dictionary offered a definition that did not include military obligation and that stressed civil rights: a citizen was simply "an inhabitant who enjoys the freedom and privileges of the city in which he resides. . . . In the United States, a person, native or naturalized, who has the privilege of exercising the elective franchise, or the qualifications which entitle him to vote for rulers and to purchase and hold real estate."[9]

If a citizen had to possess civic rights, then women were not citizens, for they did not vote except briefly in New Jersey. But unmarried women could hold property, and women, whether married or unmarried, could be naturalized. Citizenship awaited precise definition.

For Sarah Jay, even the framing of the toast was unusual; women were normally not expected to deliver themselves of political expressions. It had been the common sense of eighteenth-century political theory that women had less patriotism than men. The idea that women ought to have no politics is older than classical Athens. Because women were excluded from honors and offices, the usual methods of attaching subjects' self-interest to the outcome of national policy, women's relationship to their nation seemed to be vicarious. They were thought to experience politics only through husbands, fathers, and sons.[10]

But the prewar crises and the war of the revolution brought what Margaret Livingston called the "dreadful fruits of Liberty"—violence, uncertainty, disruption—to every dinner table. Even as they continued to write self-conscious variations on the theme that politics is not my province, it was impossible for many women, like male civilians, to ignore the highly charged political atmosphere in which they lived.[11] In many areas, the Revolution was a guerrilla war, and soldiers moved through civilian property, marching through one's corn, or quartering themselves in one's home, or raping one's neighbors. So it is not at all surprising to find political expression by women not so much as a radical challenge to the mores of the time but, rather, as the commonsensical response to the reality that surrounded them all.

For example, Helen Kortright Brasher of New York at first resented her husband Abraham's political commitment. "All our domestick happiness appeared at an end," she wrote in a private memoir years later. "He would often say, my country first and then my family. In this we differed. I thought a man's family should and ought to be his first Objekt . . . My politics were the same as his." She felt hurt because he was "every evening out at some meeting or other harranguing his fellow citizens, writing for the public prints." Although Brasher spoke first of her family and resented what she took to be excessive political involvement by her husband, she also took care to locate herself politically: her politics were the same as his.[12]

Sarah Jay herself came from a highly political family. Her father, William Livingston, was wartime governor of New Jersey. John Jay called Sarah's sister Catharine his best correspondent, and Catharine, acknowledging her interests, once observed to her prospective husband, "I . . . fancy I hear'd you exclaiming what a rage this girl has for politics." Sarah Livingston Jay, born into one political family and married into another, may have been better informed and more sophisticated in her political interests than most of her contemporaries, but she shared with many of her generation a "rage for politics" engendered by the intensity of the prewar crises and the war itself. Playing unaccustomed roles during the war would inevitably affect how women approached the peace that followed.[13] "The various emotions that must have been excited in the different Parties by the Articles of Peace presents indeed a true picture of human happiness which rarely exists without its shades as well as its brighter colors," Sarah Jay observed shortly after the Peace of Paris was signed.[14]

As the twentieth-century experiences of China, Algeria, Cuba, and Israel have suggested, wars of national liberation seek the support of women. Certainly the war of the American Revolution drew many women from the role of political observer into that of actor. Patriot women redefined their political boundaries. Some of these changed perceptions would persist into the postwar years as explicit claims; others would remain unspoken. Yet, whether in peace or in war, women had their own form of a revolutionary inheritance.[15]

First, the consumer boycotts of the prewar years had been predicated on the support of women, both as consumers who would make distinctions on whether they purchased British imports or goods of domestic origin, and as manufacturers who would voluntarily increase their level of household production. Women who had thought of themselves as exempt from political choices now found that they had to make these choices, most especially within their own homes. After the war, control of their family's consumption patterns remained their most effective political weapon. For example, in 1787 the "Patriotic and Economic Association of Ladies of Hartford" announced that they would eschew conspicuous consumption as a way of redistributing scarce goods and helping to pay off the national debt. An anonymous columnist (it is impossible to tell whether male or female) offered their reasoning: "The sheep's wool that grows in this state is not sufficient for stockings for its inhabitants; what then must be the wretched situation, particularly of the poor in this town in the approaching winter, when the wool which might cover the legs of hundreds, is diverted from that use to form fashionable dresses and petticoats and bustlers which deform the shape."[16] Consumption boycotts were used during the quasi-war in the 1790s and persisted into the nineteenth century. When, in the 1830s and 1840s, women's abolitionist societies searched for a strategy to bring pressure on the slave economy, a boycott of slave-made goods was organized.

Second, the most radical of the revolutionaries included women in the mobilized "Body of the People." When the Sons of Liberty called meetings of the Body of the People in 1770, they were explicitly inviting everyone, "male or female, franchised or not, free or bound," and when, in 1772, the Boston Committee of Correspondence circulated the Solemn League and Covenant, establishing a boycott of British goods, they demanded that both men and women sign it. Thus, for the first time during the revolutionary crisis, an organized secular group mobilized women for political purposes.[17]

Third, the war itself created many occasions for direct displays of political will. Women were encouraged to display their patriotism by sending husbands and sons off cheerfully; that is, women's behavior was expected to ease the problems of general mobilization. Some women displayed their commitment directly, taking advantage of old expectations that women didn't make political choices by serving the side of their choice in secret ways. Thus, Washington suspected that women who got permission to cross from American lines into British-held territory were often smugglers, and Henry Livingston complained that women communicated to the British "everything that passed among us." There were women who helped prisoners escape. For example, the British placed a bounty on the head of Elizabeth Burgin for helping two-hundred American prisoners escape in New York in 1779.[18]

Finally, there was the informal quartermaster corps popularly known as the "Women of the Army." As Barton Hacker has recently pointed out, the American Revolution was one of the last of what might be called the early modern wars in the West. Thousands of women and children traveled with the armies, functioning as nurses, laundresses, and cooks. Amazingly little attention has been paid to these women. They were not prostitutes, who were dealt with severely; not traditional camp followers like Brecht's "Mother Courage," who sold goods to soldiers. Often, they were married to waggoners or sutlers, and worked alongside their husbands. These women drew rations in the American army, and, in imitation of British practice, a limited number of them could be attached to each company. They often brought children with them, who drew half-rations (American regulations took care to insist that "suckling babes" could draw no rations at all since they couldn't eat). "The very rules that denied a place in the army to all women sanctioned a place for some," Hacker remarks. Washington was constantly issuing contradictory orders—whether the women of the army were to ride in the wagons so as not to slow down the troops, or walk so as not to fill important space. But he knew he needed them.[19]

It is true that cooking, laundering, and nursing were considered "female skills" and that the Women of the Army were doing, in a military environment, what they would normally do in a domestic one. But we ought not discount these services for that reason or visualize them as taking place in a context of softness and luxury. One observer of American troops attributed their ragged and unkempt bearing to the insufficient number of women to do their washing and mending. "The Americans, not being used to doing things of this sort, choose rather to let their linen, etc. rot upon their backs than to be at the trouble of cleaning 'em themselves." Washington was particularly shocked at the demeanor of the troops at Bunker Hill, some of whom apparently were so sure that washing clothes was women's work that "they wore what they had until it crusted over and fell apart."[20] A friend of Mercy Otis Warren wrote a description of the women who followed the Hessians after the surrender of Burgoyne: "Great numbers of women who seemed to be the beasts of burthen, having a bushel basket on their back by which they were bent double, the contents seemed to be Pots and Kettles, various sorts of Furniture, children peeping thro' gridirons and other utensils, some very young Infants who were born on the road, the women's bare feet clothed in dirty raggs, such effluvia filled the air while they were passing, had they not been smoking all the time, I should have been apprehensive of being contaminated by them."[21] Susannah Rowson's fictional "Charlotte

Temple," at the end of her rope, is bitterly advised to "go to the barracks and wash for a morsel of bread; wash and mend the soldiers' cloaths, and cook their victuals . . . work hard and eat little."[22]

Women who served such troops were performing tasks of the utmost necessity if the army was to continue functioning. They did not live in gentle surroundings in either army, and the conditions of their lives were not pleasant. Although they were impoverished, they were not inarticulate. The most touching account of Yorktown I know is furnished by Sarah Osborn, who cooked for Washington's troops and delivered food to them under fire because, as she told Washington himself, "it was not fair that the poor fellows should fight and go hungry, too." At the end, she watched the British soldiers stack their arms and go off to meet their destiny."[23]

Historians face a real problem in finding out what these women thought they were doing. We have some testimony, like Sarah Osborn's at Yorktown. We also know of the women of Philadelphia, who raised $300,000 and refused to merge it into the general fund. They used it to buy fabric to make shirts so that each soldier would know that he had received something special from the ladies of Philadelphia. We have Elizabeth Burgin's petition, in which she asks for a pension for war-time services. We have large numbers of widows' petitions asking for financial support from state legislatures and the Continental Congress (which rarely responded), and we have the stunning petition of Rachel Wells of Bordentown, New Jersey, asking, in horrible spelling but with intellectual clarity, for full payment on her war bonds: "I have Don as much to Carrey on the war as maney that Sett Now at the healm of government . . . say of me if She did not fight She threw in all her mite which bought the Sogers food & Clothing & Let them have Blankets."[24]

By the war's end, many women's self-perception had changed, but mechanisms for collective action by women had not been developed. Rachel Wells's petition was tabled; Burgin did not get the pension to which she felt entitled. (She did, however, get a charitable handout from George Washington, which she had not wanted.) Political theory was not modified to take into account what it might mean to perceive women's will as part of the general will. Without a strategy of collective behavior, without political theorists of their own, women did not immediately develop a mode of forcing the political community to take account of their distinctive interests. Nor had they begun to grapple with the implications of variants of citizenship that bore—for free blacks and Indians as well as white women—only limited responsibilities and obligations. As Edward

Countryman recently put it, the radicalism of the Revolution was, in some ways, parochial and, in many ways, selfish. It was to artisans, white laborers, small farmers, and expectant small capitalists that the policies of the 1780s appealed, and it was their support that was vital if the new order was to stand.[25]

It would be for succeeding generations of American women to invent the mechanisms to promote their political identity. The Revolutionary generation only began the process by articulating their sense of resentment. Typical was Charles Brockden Brown's fictional Mrs. Carter who fumes, "I am tired of explaining this charming system of equality and independence," or Sarah Jay's aunt, Margaret Livingston, who did not expect women to have "such romantic notions" of the Goddess of Liberty as men have because "Our sex are doomed to be obedient in every stage of life so that *we* shan't be great gainers by this contest."[26]

In the traditional governments of Europe, all men and women had been subjects of their rulers, but only some men had civic responsibilities and obligations. In the new American republic, an ideologically radical revolution had transformed all free adults—men and women—into "citizens," but had not yet clearly defined their rights and responsibilities. Some male citizens, those who could meet state age and property requirements, exercised the franchise; others did not. Rarely did anyone attempt to evaluate the precise boundaries of female citizenship.

One of the few occasions in which the nature of the relationship of women to the new republic came to be publicly analyzed, occurred with the case of *Martin* v. *Massachusetts*, a lawsuit involving the property claims of the son of an absentee Tory. In 1779, in the midst of the Revolutionary War, the General Court of Massachusetts had passed a confiscation law to govern the property left behind by fleeing loyalists. The statute explicitly encouraged wives of Tory absentees to break from their husbands, declare their own loyalty to the revolutionary state, to set themselves at risk for the republic, and in so doing to protect their property from confiscation. Specifically, the statute provided that when the wife or widow of a loyalist absentee "shall have remained within the jurisdiction of the United States, she shall be entitled to the improvement and income of one-third part of her husband's real and personal estate . . . , and her dower shall be set off to her by the Judges of probate wills, in like manner as it might have been, if her husband had died intestate."

By this statute, the wife of an absentee would not be treated as the wife of a traitor (who traditionally had their dower reserved to them). Rather, the Commonwealth of Massachusetts promised to protect the

wife's property only if she remained in America, dissociated herself from
her husband, and in effect declared her own political allegiance. The
statute, perhaps the most radical of the time, was eventually tested not
by a wife but by a son of an absentee loyalist, James Martin, whose
parents, William and Anna Martin, had fled Boston with the British only
ten days before his birth, leaving their property in Braintree and in
Boston to be confiscated. James Martin was twenty-five years old in 1801
when he sued to claim his property.

Daniel Davis, the solicitor-general for the Commonwealth, defended
the statute as written. He argued that all inhabitants of the state were
members of the political community. If a married woman, "covered" in
contemporary usage by her husband's legal identity, could levy war and
commit treason, Davis was confident that she should also be expected to
declare her own political allegiance. Since a wife could have elected to
stay with the rebel Americans, Mrs. Martin's departure was tantamount
to a political choice and the rebel state owed her and her heirs nothing.
To argue this way was to protect the Commonwealth but to undercut
couverture; it was to establish the principle that a married woman could
be held responsible and even punished for her political will.

Two attorneys argued for the plaintiff. George Blake and Theophilus
Parsons took the position, which the court eventually upheld: Martin
deserved the return of his property because it had been unfairly seized
from his mother. Blake argued that as a married woman, Anna Martin
had "no political relation to the state any more than an alien." (Years
later, the abolitionist Sarah Grimke would ask plaintively, "Are we aliens
because we are women?") Blake distinguished between inhabitants and
members of the state. He pointed out that married women were not
required to take an oath of allegiance. He asked a string of rhetorical
questions: "How much physical force is retained by retaining married
women? What are the personal services they are to render in opposing
by force an actual invasion? What aid can they give to an enemy?" Women
were not of service in defense of a country; in fact, they were an
impediment to that defense. Parsons, in his turn, added that the "statute
extends to persons who have *freely* renounced their relation to the state.
Infants, insane, *femes covert,* all of whom the law considers as having no
will, cannot act *freely.* Can they freely renounce?"

The court upheld Martin. In his decision, Judge Theodore Sedgwick
made the point that the married woman traditionally was not held to be
guilty of actions performed jointly with her husband except of the most
aggravated nature because "she is viewed in such a state of subjection

and so under the control of her husband that she acts merely as his instrument." This subjection was implicit in the vow of obedience a woman took at marriage. "Was she to be considered as criminal because she permitted her husband to elect his own place of residence? Because she did not, in violation of her marriage vows, rebel against the will of her husband?"[27]

The court ruled for James Martin. The judges concluded three to one that the revolutionary legislatures had not intended that women should be forced to choose between disobeying husband and losing property. Thus, retrospectively, the second-generation Federalists chose to establish as policy the more narrow interpretation of the statute.

It is the common sense of the matter that no group can expect specific benefits from a revolution unless it has been—as a collective body—a force in making the revolution. Women had served in and supported the American Revolution, but as individuals, not as collectivities. As a result, in 1783 they were not in a strong position to make demands. Nor did male politicians demand for women what women did not demand for themselves. Before a distinctively female republicanism could be devised, certain preconditions had to be met: either married women had to be able to manipulate property of their own or property requirements for voting would have to be eliminated. Both trends would establish themselves in the half century that followed the Peace of Paris. The one, which I have elsewhere called "Republican Motherhood," would enable women to understand their domestic roles in a political context.[28] The other would come with the movement for women's rights.

Perhaps it is enough to say that the Revolutionary generation embarked on a great debate over the implications of the republican experiment, a debate that would persist into our own time. However hesitantly, Sarah Livingston Jay expressed the politicization of her female compatriots. Mercy Otis Warren, a woman older than Sarah Jay, said it in verse. In 1784, a year after the Peace of Paris, Mercy Warren wrote a play called *The Ladies of Castille*.[29] The play is about two women of contrasting temperaments caught up in a revolutionary civil war in the Spain of Charles V, according to the play, but meant quite obviously to be a metaphor for the recently ended American revolutionary war. One woman is the soft, delicate Louisa; the other is Maria, who scorns to "live upon ignoble terms." The message of *The Ladies of Castille* is simple and obvious. Even in the exigencies of war, women must keep control of themselves and of their options. The Louisas of the world do not survive revolutions; the Marias, who take political positions, come to their own judgments, risk their lives, and emerge stronger and in control. "A soul, inspir'd by freedom's genial warmth," says Maria, "Expands, grows firm, and by resistance, strong."

So, in time, would the daughters of America's Revolution grow firm, and by resistance, strong.

Notes

1. Sarah Livingston Jay, Paris [After 3 September 1783], in Richard B. Morris, ed., *John Jay: The Winning of the Peace—Unpublished Papers 1780–1784* (New York: Harper & Row, 1980), p. 581. See also Sarah Livingston Jay to Catharine W. Livingston, December 14, 1782: "I was telling young Franklin the other day that he must aid me in contriving a Ball when Peace is concluded," p. 590.

2. *No Standing Armies: The Antiarmy Ideology in Seventeenth-Century England* (Baltimore: Johns Hopkins University Press, 1974), p. 188. For the debate over standing armies in America, see Lawrence Delbert Cress, *Citizens in Arms: The Army and the Militia in American Society to the War of 1812* (Chapel Hill: University of North Carolina Press, 1982), and "An Armed Community: The Origins and Meaning of the Right to Bear Arms," *Journal of American History*, 71 (1984), pp. 22–42.

3. *Journals of the Continental Congress* V (June 24, 1776), pp. 475–76, quoted in James H. Kettner, *The Development of American Citizenship, 1608 1870* (Chapel Hill: University of North Carolina Press, 1978), pp. 178–79.

4. Margaret Livingston to Susan Livingston, July 1778, Ridley Papers, Massachusetts Historical Society, Boston. For disputed status of Loyalists, see Kettner, pp. 183–84.

5. J. G. A. Pocock, *The Machiavellian Moment: Florentine Political Thought and the Atlantic Republican Tradition* (Princeton: Princeton University Press, 1975), p. 41. For insightful comments on the contrast between *fortuna* and *virtù*, see Hannal Fenichel Pitkin, *Fortune Is a Woman: Gender and Politics in the Thought of Niccolo Machiavelli* (Berkeley: University of California Press, 1984), pp. 138–39.

6. Pocock, p. 90.

7. Pitkin, p. 306.

8. Cress, *Citizens in Arms*, p. 17; Charles Royster, *A Revolutionary People at War: The Continental Army and American Character, 1775–1783* (Chapel Hill: University of North Carolina Press, 1979), pp. 3–4, 32. See also pp. 39–40.

9. For comment on the concepts of inhabitant and citizen as they appear in early state constitutions, see Mary-Jo Kline and Joanne Wood Ryan, eds., *Political Correspondence and Public Papers of Aaron Burr* (Princeton: Princeton University Press, 1983) vol. I, pp. 170–72, nn. 1–16. The *Oxford English Dictionary*

(Oxford, U.K.: Oxford University Press, 1933) also links citizenship with privilege but not necessarily with military obligation: "1. An inhabitant of a city or (often) of a town; esp[ecially] one possessing civic rights and privileges, a burger or freeman of a city. 2. A member of a state, an enfranchised inhabitant of a country, as opposed to an alien; in U.S. a person, native or naturalized, who has the privilege of voting for public offices, and is entitled to full protection in the exercise of private rights." The sources on which definition 1 is based range from 1314 to 1848; definition 2 from 1538 to 1884.

10. Abigail Adams observed that women had every reason to be *indifferent* to the public welfare; that when they displayed "patriotick virtue" the fact ought to be noted as especially heroic. Abigail Adams to John Adams, June 17, 1782, in L. H. Butterfield *et al.*, eds., *Adams Family Correspondence* (Cambridge, Mass.: Harvard University Press, 1963) IV, p. 328. I have discussed this point at length in *Women of the Republic: Intellect and Ideology in Revolutionary America* (Chapel Hill: University of North Carolina Press, 1980), chap. 2.

11. Margaret Livingston to Catharine W. Livingston, October 20, 1776, Ridley Papers, Massachusetts Historical Society, Boston.

12. When the British occupied New York City, Abraham Brasher joined the Assembly in Esopus, after first making sure Helen and the children were settled in Paramus, well back, he hoped, from the fighting. At this point, in 1776, Helen Brasher made her peace with the situation, telling Abraham, "Go my dear and serve your country. I will find the means to provide for the family." "Narrative of Mrs. Abraham Brasher," manuscript, New York Historical Society.

13. John Jay to Catharine Livingston, April 6, 1783. Box 2, Ridley Papers; Catharine Livingston to Matthew Ridley, May 1783, Box 3, Ridley Papers, Massachusetts Historical Society, Boston.

14. Sarah Jay to Susannah Livingston, November 22, 1783, Jay Papers, Columbia University.

15. I have discussed the following themes in *Women of the Republic*, chapters 2 and 3. See also Mary Beth Norton, *Liberty's Daughters: The Revolutionary Experience of American Women* (Boston: Little Brown, 1980).

16. *American Museum and Repository* II, August 1787, November 1787.

17. Gary B. Nash, *The Urban Crucible: Social Change, Political Consciousness and the Origins of the American Revolution* (Cambridge, Mass.: Harvard University Press, 1979), p. 356. See also "The Resolves of the Inhabitants of the Town of Gorham [Mass.] on the Port Bill," June 1774, signed by 220 men and 6 women, [5 of whom identified themselves as widows], in L. Kivin Wroth, *et al.*, eds., *Province in Rebellion: A Documentary History of the Founding of the Commonwealth of Massachusetts* (Cambridge, Mass: Harvard University Press, 1975), microfiche document 224.

18. Kerber, *Women of the Republic*, pp. 48–55.

19. Barton C. Hacker, "Women and Military Institutions in Early Modern Europe: A Reconnaissance," *Signs* VI (Summer 1981), pp. 643–71.

20. Royster, pp. 59–60; Hacker, pp. 660–61.

21. Hannah Winthrop to Mercy Otis Warren, November 11, 1777, in *Warren-Adams Letters*, vol. II, *Collections of the Massachusetts Historical Society*, vol. 73 (1925), p. 451.

22. Susannah Rowson, *Charlotte Temple*, [1794] eds. Clara M. and Rudolph Kirk (New York: Twayne Publishers, 1964), chap. XXIX.

23. Sarah Osborn, in John C. Dann, ed., *The Revolution Remembered: Eyewitness Accounts of the War for Independence* (Chicago: University of Chicago Press, 1980), pp. 240–50.

24. Petition of Rachel Wells, May 18, 1786, *Papers of the Continental Congress*, National Archives Microfilm no. 247, roll 56, item 42, vol. VIII, 354–55.

25. Edward Countryman, *A People in Revolution: The American Revolution and Political Society in New York, 1760–1790* (Baltimore: Johns Hopkins University Press, 1981), pp. 288–89.

26. Charles Brockden Brown, *Alcuin: A Dialogue*, Lee Edwards, ed. (New York: Grossman Publishers, 1971), p. 33; Margaret Livingston to Catharine Livingston, October 20, 1776, Ridley Papers, Massachusetts Historical Society, Boston.

27. *Martin* v. *Commonwealth of Massachusetts* (1805), vol. I *Mass. Reports*, pp. 347–97. I have discussed this issue at length in *Women of the Republic*, chap. 4.

A few years later, in *Kempe's Lessee* v. *Kennedy et al.*, February 1809, *U.S. Supreme Court Reports* V (Cranch) pp. 173–86, Richard Stockton, arguing on behalf of a Loyalist widow, tossed off the opinion that a *feme covert* "cannot properly be called an inhabitant of a state: the husband is the inhabitant. By the Constitution of New Jersey, all inhabitants are entitled to vote; but it has never been supposed that a *feme covert* was a legal voter. Single women have been allowed to vote, because the law supposes them to have wills of their own" (p. 177).

28. "The Republican Mother—Women and the Enlightenment: The American Perspective," *American Quarterly* XXVIII (1976), pp. 187–205; and "Daughters of Columbia: Educating Women for the Republic," in Stanley Elkins and Eric McKitrick, eds., *The Hofstadter Aegis: A Memorial* (New York: Knopf, 1974), pp. 36–59.

29. Mercy Otis Warren, "The Ladies of Castile," in *Poems: Dramatic and Miscellaneous* (Boston: I. Thomas, 1790).

Comments

More than one hundred and fifty years separate the American Revolution from World War II. Yet, as some historians suggest, "the more things change, the more they stay the same." D'Ann Campbell posits that soldiering and citizenship went hand in hand in the America of the Second World War. During this time, women's auxiliary roles continued to reflect their second-class status as citizens.

Women never comprised more than 2 percent of the military during the Second World War—at peak strength, 271,600 women served in some branch of the military—but most women did not sign up. The army was man-made. A staggering 99 percent of American women led private lives; about one-fourth engaged in volunteer activity; many planted victory gardens. Despite the popular appeal of Rosie the Riveter, during the war years, nine out of ten mothers with children were *not* in the labor force. For the first time, women entered heavy industry only to find themselves squeezed out at war's end; in all other forms of manufacturing, their numbers did not decline.

Despite a barrage of government propaganda extolling the femininity of women in overalls who carried wrenches and wore sprightly bandannas 'round their curls, factory work, according to recent studies, was considered an "ideal work plan" for only one woman in eight in 1943. Most women were housewives but, as D'Ann Campbell has written in her book, *Women at War with America*, the "entire logic of full wartime mobilization depended heavily on the behavior of housewives" who had to comply with rationing, price and wage controls, frustrating scarcities, and add-on work like growing vegetables, finding substitutes for meat, canning, and learning new ways to cook. Housewives *complied*. Their civic virtue was secure enough to sustain them through these restrictions and frustrations. If housewives in sufficient numbers had jettisoned government policies by turning to the black market, fomenting food riots, or encouraging tax evasion, the war effort might have been jeopardized. "Make do" was the housewives' slogan.

Campbell is one of the leading historians of the women of this epoch. In her essay, she continues to expand our knowledge of World War II by taking up the case of "regimented women," that minority that was actually drawn into the armed services. She shows how the war years did not even begin to change prevailing stereotypes of the "proper" social identities of men and women.

5

The Regimented Women
of World War II

D'Ann Campbell

The decision to introduce large numbers of women into the armed services during World War II constituted a radical—arguably the most radical—break in the history of gender. Women have, in fact, participated in warfare in one way or another throughout much of history.[1] Women have even donned uniforms.[2] But not always as women. The American experiment during World War II challenged prevailing norms on practical and symbolic levels. Women in uniform filled roles that had previously been reserved for men, and crossed gender lines. Perhaps more importantly, women in uniform directly challenged the centuries-old association of men with warfare, that is, challenged the most deeply anchored preconceptions of gender identity.

A close look at the history of American women's military participation in the WACs (Army), WAVEs (Navy), Women Marines, and SPARs (Coast Guard) reveals the depth and strength of men's and women's ingrained

Support for the research was provided by grant HRO-20660-84 from the National Endowment for the Humanities, Research Division.

attitudes towards the intimate association between the military and the male gender—and their no less deeply ingrained attitudes towards appropriate roles, behavior, and status for members of the female gender.[3] In fact, many women found military service a valuable and even agreeable experience on the day-to-day level. Some did experience harassment, denigration, and exclusion. But more found that their years of military service broadened their horizons, improved their skills, and above all, increased their self-confidence.[4] Nonetheless, the positive aspects of that experience rarely proved transferable to civilian life where entrenched attitudes towards gender roles held firm. Nor did the success of women's military participation have any recognizable or abiding impact on the military's view of itself as the bastion of masculinity at the symbolic level.

Most women recruits had never traveled beyond their state borders before boarding the train to boot camp. In some cases the crowded trains arrived at 5:30 A.M. and reveille was blown at 0600. Muster here. Muster there. On the double. Boot camps began in earnest. The new recruits found some surprises. Few were prepared for the lack of privacy. Even in large gym classes, women had always tried to protect their modesty. Imagine the shock for many to walk into the women's latrine and discover a row of toilets with no doors or seats, some urinals still in place, and no shower curtains. As a new WAAC explained, "How can you sit? Oh no! I can't learn to squat (But I did)."[5] Women with a college background were better prepared. "It was harder for us who hadn't been to college to realize that in many ways our barracks life was bound to be beset by some of the traditional 'hardships' of dormitory life." Such hardships included "rules about closing hours, lockouts from the dining room if we were late, roast pork and dressing for dinner when we felt like a light salad, fire drills at the most inconvenient times."[6]

The next major hurdle was a cultural shock: the hierarchy of rank and the niceties of its associated protocol. Young women, who had not grown up playing war games, did not know the difference between an officer and an enlisted person, let alone the gradations within these categories. Consequently, overzealous recruits saluted anything in uniform, including fire chiefs and airline pilots. One WAC gave her first military salute with her left hand when she was on break from her first class on Military Courtesies (she had a lit cigarette in her right hand).[7] Others forgot to salute the top brass, much to the annoyance of many high-ranking officers. Stories abound of the problems caused by these neophytes. Some officers refrained from giving a rebuff. When Admiral King came to dinner, a WAVE fresh from the boot camp asked him his name so she could help him find his seat. "I think he might have chewed out a boy who did this, but Betty was so nice and so innocent and so polite," explained a WAVE officer.[8] As Captain Mildred McAfee, Director of the WAVEs, summarized the problem, "We came to do a job and we didn't know enough to know that rank would make any difference."[9]

The language barrier created additional problems for the new recruits. They were forced to learn a foreign language, on the double. The Coast Guard administered the same examination to men and women to determine job assignments. One question asked:

> Five cutters are at anchor in a horizontal row. Cutter A is beside and to the port of Cutter B. Cutter C is beside and to the starboard of Cutter B. Cutter D is beside and to the port of Cutter A. Cutter C is beside and on Cutter E's starboard. Which of the Cutters is not facing the same direction as the others?[10]

Some potential recruits wondered what a "cutter" was, others puzzled what "port" and "starboard" meant. However, soon SPAR recruits went "topside" by way of "ladders." Walls became "bulkheads" and they lived on "decks."[11] A WAVE added, "We receive 'sugar reports' and spread 'scuttlebutt,' we know the 'pill peddlers' and do not believe the 'snow jobs.' We drink our 'joe' and hit the 'sack.' "[12]

The jargon would continue to plague women when they began their job assignments. One SPAR assigned to Vessel Control was asked, "What is the weather outside?" The SPAR snapped back, "It's raining, can't you look out the window and see?" The caller wanted to know what the weather was "outside the harbor."[13]

Women soldiers also found themselves in trouble because their training did not cover the basics of survival in a war zone. The Pentagon had assumed that women would not need such information since women were not being sent into combat. Policy officials forgot that nurses and nurses' aides were often sent to hospitals near the front lines and that women soldiers overseas were often in areas that were not completely secure. One WAC on General Eisenhower's staff in Tunisia relates:

> [I] ducked under the single strand of wire and walked through a stubble field down to the bottom of the slope. Here I found all sorts of Army equipment—American, British, French, and German tanks. I strolled about for at least half an hour and then angled back up the slope to the farmhouse. As I ducked under the wire, my eyes fell on a pair of polished military

boots. . . . [Eisenhower] helped me get out from under the wire and asked, "Did you have a nice stroll, Scottie? I'm glad you're back. Do you know what those little red tapes mean hanging on the wire?"[14]

The tapes meant that the area had not been cleared of mines.

While the women had trouble learning the ropes in some areas, they excelled in others. Much to the surprise of the men, these women loved to drill. "I guess most of us get a tingling sensation when we hear martial music. Weekly regimental review was a high spot in the week for me, and in spite of the usual heat and strain, I always enjoyed it." The SPAR continued, "It's really something to watch regiments of girls in blue, their white gloves swinging and their heads held high and proud."[15] A WAAC recalled,

All eight hundred of us marched out on the Parade Ground to be reviewed by Colonel Faith. We certainly put our hearts into column left and by the right flank, and when we went by the reviewing stand, our heads snapped around so energetically that I'm surprised a few didn't go bowling off down the field. Being out there, with all those trim, eager women moving perfectly in ranks, and the band playing, and the sun on the colors, was the most tremendous experience I've had yet. There is nothing that can equal the feeling of being part of something infinitely larger than yourself.[16]

Other women fondly associated marching with the flag-raising ceremonies. "There I stood at attention saluting with a lump in my throat and wondering how I was going to help win the war!"[17] Drilling had the effect of solidifying the boot camp experience. Captain McAfee described the review of 2,500 WAVEs at the Washington Monument to celebrate the WAVEs' first birthday.

I'll never forget the actual effect of this—the scene of it—as we stood at the Monument and saw these women coming from all over the city of Washington, marching, and forming a regular pattern of company marching. Well, this is the kind of thing that made them know they were a part of the Navy, and it was a very dramatic and exciting kind of thing, which you couldn't do if you hadn't been trained to do it.[18]

So concerned were the women about learning to drill correctly, that it was not atypical for recruits to form small groups and practice drills during their breaks. Thrill and drill were synonymous for most recruits.[19]

Learning to drill was not an easy task. The language barrier contributed to the problem. The male sergeant yelled, "Har" or "Haw," not "forward march" and "halt." Instead of counting cadence, "He made weird sounds like 'hup, hoop, heep, ho,' and [often] . . . slipped in a phrase or two that the girls up front would not repeat."[20] When an instructor yelled at a WAVE, "pick up your dress," she began to cry. Later she learned that he meant for her to dress up the lines.[21] At officer's training camp at Mt. Holyoke, confusion over drilling reached a new height when there were just enough WAVEs and women Marines left over to form one combined platoon. A Marine described the problem of the "Goon Platoon":

> The Marines were used to swinging along smartly to a . . . chant [that was something like], "Wah, tup, threep, fo, reep-bo-yo-lelf" while the Navy, at a slightly slower tempo, would chant, "Hu-up, two, three, four, hu-up, two three, four. . . ." Worst difference of all, the WAVES were encouraged to sing in ranks, while the Marines were told their ears would be cut off if they EVER sang in ranks! So the pitiful little platoon would straggle across campus, half of it singing and half of it marching in stonyfaced silence.[22]

Trouble developed as the women assumed drill instruction. One woman told to "take over" asked, "take them over where, sir?"[23] Quick thinking sometimes replaced Navy protocol. A visiting WAVE officer was ordered to march the WAVEs down main street in front of all the male drill instructors. This WAVE, a member of the first class of officers, had undergone a crash course in indoctrination, which had not included drill instruction. When she began marching the women, she spotted a parked car in the way. Not knowing the proper command for getting the women to march around it, she turned and said (out of the earshot of the watching men), "Ladies, use your judgment."[24] They did.

Legends soon grew up around the women drillers. Apparently the road-building program around Ft. Des Moines went faster than expected because the road crews dumped gravel along the way of the new road and then asked the WAACs to practice drilling there. Apparently they were "WAACs-ing the roads."[25] At Mt. Holyoke, a training base for WAVE officers, the superintendent of buildings and grounds came to the commanding officer very concerned. "We're finding that the old buildings are being threatened by this marching in unison, so will you ask your women to break step when they come into the buildings."[26] The WACs received a similar request from the town mayor when they were housed at the Chamberlain Hotel. "The shop keepers felt like their places of business were like the Walls of Jericho getting ready to tumble down." The WAC continued, "The most difficult task for us during the next ten and a half weeks was learning to stay out of step. It wasn't easy."[27]

Women recruits took everything seriously at boot camp. As one WAC explained, "I've never concentrated on anything . . . the way I did on getting my underwear folded and arranged just right in the footlocker and my canteen and mess kit on the top shelf of the wall-locker. . . . It practically becomes an obsession."[28] Male instructors were often surprised by how conscientious the women were. At Ft. Des Moines, the commanding officer officially requested that the officer candidates not study more than two hours a night. Similarly it was reported that an enlisted WAC was going "outside after lights out and studies under the lamp post. . . . No wonder our instructors look a little dazed at such industry. . . . We are simply *determined* to set the world on fire."[29] Navy women were as determined to succeed in the military as the Army women. In describing Northampton, the training center for WAVE officers, Captain Joy Bright Hancock concluded:

> Without fear of denial, I can state that the morale prevailing at the school was unsurpassed anywhere in the naval establishment. Every officer candidate was determined to prove that she was equal to the extremely high standard of effort and accomplishment demanded by the staff and to the opportunity for service to her country.[30]

Instead of disliking regimentation and resisting discipline, these women soldiers and sailors excelled. Morale soared. Of 350 women veterans who were asked how proud they were of their women's corps or women's reserve, 94 percent said *very* proud.[31] When asked how military life compared with what they had thought it would be like before they joined, 4 in 10 of these women claimed they liked it better, and 29 percent thought it was about what they expected. Fear of military life had not discouraged these women from volunteering. One third had not even thought about what it would be like before they joined. When asked how they liked military life, 79 percent said "very much." Over half recalled, "wonderful" in evaluating what sort of time had they had in the service.[32]

After boot camp and, for some, advanced training, the women reported for their service jobs. Most found their male co-workers skeptical about their abilities to perform well. As one WAC explained, "They thought that all women were dumb."[33] It took male leaders a while to realize that having women as co-workers required some adjustment. "A lot of the commanding officers were just genuinely surprised because they'd never seen women in this kind of action. . . . Obviously the boys, many of them, had no interest in being yeomen from the point of view of running a typewriter."[34] Over half of the women in the military served in clerical roles. Soon it was clear that they were very skillful in such positions. A WAC explained, "The colonel under whom I worked did not think that a WAC would work out and made the fact known to our company commander, who was determined to prove him wrong." She continued, "Five WACs were able to replace the nine men in the office. After a few months, the colonel told me that he was pleased with our work."[35] Actually these women were filling positions that were considered women's work in civilian life. Other women filled less traditional positions.

One WAC reported: "A captain started the interview by asking if I could say 'No' to a man. . . . The problem was that a male G.I. was unable to refuse a direct order from, let us say, a major who demanded a billet assigned to a light colonel." He continued to question her, "Could I do that tactfully? I told the captain that it would be no problem, and it never was."[36] Even in positions that required great physical strength some women sometimes could perform well. Two WAVEs assigned to a warehouse were told by a couple of strapping men, "Look, the job that you've got to do is to get these truck tires stowed away up in that loft," and they knew they couldn't do it. And they went off gleefully, chuckling to themselves. When the men returned they found the tires up in the loft. When asked "How on earth did you do it? one WAVE replied, 'We rigged a pulley, of course.' "[37] Yet in some instances, women were not even given a chance to see if they could do a job because of the effect their presence could have on the men. One colonel told a WAC that she had passed the airplane mechanics examination with the highest marks in the class. Yet he refused to let her enter the all-male advanced training course, explaining that, "My classroom would be in shambles, as those guys would either be looking at you or chasing you."[38]

Little by little, as the women proved themselves, the climate began to change.[39] "Commanders who in 1942 had cried, 'Over my dead body will I take military women,' were soon asking for their 'fair share.' "[40] One army report showed that the negative comments dropped from 90 percent to 28 percent after the WACs had been in the field for a few months. The correspondence by American soldiers stationed in Australia also reflected the increase in positive feelings towards the WACs once male and female soldiers worked side by side. By the end of the first year of WACs in Australia, the American soldiers' favorable comments increased from 30 percent to 70 percent.[41] Our survey of 350 women veterans revealed that

113

86 percent believed that their male supervisor had a favorable attitude toward the women's units. While 76 percent of the women felt that they had worked well with the men, 83 percent recalled that they had worked better with women co-workers.[42]

Being taught by a woman could even become a status symbol. When women were first made Link Trainers, the pilots trained by them concealed this information from their peers. Eventually it was clear that many of the best pilots had been trained by women so men began to brag about their training.[43] Some commanding officers who were assigned women when they ran short of men said, "Well, get me some girls and I'll train them to do it."[44] The women did well because they became a project of their male supervisor. "It was just part of the whole Navy psychology that once they belonged, they were all right."[45] When it was *their* post or *their* base, then *their* women were accepted. One WAVE argued that what happened to her the day before her discharge symbolized the rapport she had achieved with her male co-workers. The men dunked her, "clothes and all, into a gigantic vat of water."[46]

Yet it was also true that some women experienced severe problems, including sexual harassment and the abuse of command position.[47] A WAVE explained that she wound up in a captain's mast (court martial) because her commanding officer consistently ordered his WAVEs to "paint the tower (no less), clean garbage cans, and any other difficult or menial jobs he could think of."[48] Finally two WAVEs refused to take it any longer. When they described their working conditions, the charges of insubordination against them were dropped, but the women were admonished for not complaining before rebelling. An Army nurse could have been court-martialed had it not been for the testimony of a WAC enlistee when the nurse reached down to tie a patient's shoe and the patient "reached out and grabbed her by the waist, pulled her on to his lap, and began spanking her. At that moment in walked the commanding officer of the post."[49] Another WAC had to rescue a co-worker when she was attacked by a "war weary soldier" while they were making hospital rounds.[50] Other women felt compelled to take precautions. A WAVE explained that her boss seldom played "footsies" under the desk while she took dictation because she made a point of keeping the office door slightly ajar.[51] Another WAC clerk's boss finally installed a "Dutch door" with a counter top which locked securely when it dropped down to keep off "those friendly wolves from pestering Alice."[52]

The general hazing that these women experienced was intensified for blacks. At Lowell General Hospital, Fort Devens, Massachusetts, black

114

WACs protested that their co-workers were racist; blacks were only given menial jobs. Sixty blacks launched a protest; four refused to go back to work and were court-martialed. These four blacks were sentenced to one year of hard labor and a dishonorable discharge. Later the Army nullified the trial on a technicality after receiving a barrage of pressure from the national black newspapers. [53]

For a long time, the WAVEs did not have a "race" problem because there were no black WAVEs. Black Navy men were cooks and bakers, and more black men wanted these jobs than were needed. Since WAVEs were recruited literally to free a man to fight, there was no reason to recruit black WAVEs. [54] President Roosevelt finally informed the Navy that they had to form a company of 250 black WAVEs. However, the black community staged a boycott of the Navy and only 25 black women were recruited. Since there were not enough blacks to form a viable unit, the Secretary of the Navy and two admirals then met with Captain McAfee and decided to allow the black WAVEs to serve in integrated units. [55]

Through all of this hostility and harassment, the women's morale often remained high. "We were told we were in the men's Army and would be treated that way. We were. Even in those conditions, our morale was high." [56] Two-thirds of our sample said that their morale was very high and 38 percent said that it was fairly high. The morale of their units was slightly lower: 43 percent said that it was very high, and 53 percent more said that it was fairly high. [57]

In 1943, morale for women in the Armed Forces suffered a blow from which it never recovered. The problem was a slander campaign that was concocted and spread by the rank and file men. As Brigadier General Jeanne Holm recalled, "In the machismo world of barracks humor, where women and sex are a primary topic, military women had become fair game. Having joined what was a masculine domain, the women were 'asking for it.' "[58] As one WAC leader explained the underlying motive, "Men have for centuries used slander against morals as a weapon to keep women out of public life."[59] The rumor spread that all women in the service were whores or prostitutes. Two WAVEs discovered that some sailors actually believed the WAVEs were government-issue concubines. When they politely refused the advances of two sailors, "one of them sought out the MP riding the train and demanded that we be forceably compelled to carry out our military assignment."[60] Such an interpretation was popular among the men who felt the need to prove themselves "real men" while fighting for "motherhood and family." It was important to them that the "real" women whom they fought to protect back home stayed back home. A June 1945 survey revealed that Army men had firm notions about the place of women. When asked if they would advise their girl friends to join the WAC, 64 percent definitely would not, and 20 percent probably would not. Almost half of the soldiers felt that women could do more for their country working in a war industry; only 18 percent thought they could do more in the WAC. One-third of the soldiers felt it was "pretty bad" for a girl's reputation to be a WAC; one-fifth thought it was very bad. Almost half concluded that the WAC was no place for a woman to be.[61]

Consequently, even though individual women were accepted by their male co-workers, the tension between the sexes remained apparent. For many, men and manhood were both threatened in basic ways by having women in the service. Army men who sang these verses reflected this underlying tension:

> The WACs and WAVEs are winning the war, parley vous/ The WACs and WAVEs are winning the war, parley vous/ The WACs and WAVEs are winning the war/ So what the hell are we?[62]

Recruiters worked in vain to keep enlistments up but the rumors about the loose morals of women warriors spread around the countryside and overseas. Rear Admiral Ross T. McIntire, Surgeon General of the U.S. Navy, explained in an open letter to the young women of America. "In the hospital corps you can fill a man's job and still do a woman's work."[63] That is, women soldiers were to perform stereotypical female tasks such as nursing or clerical work so that the men could get down to the business of war, the fighting. Some men feared that the arrival of women meant they would be sent to the front. Hostility to women's joining the services remained high throughout the war, so recruitment of women into the services became harder and harder to accept.

The slander campaign meant that no one—not even generals and admirals during a war—could issue a command that went against the basic foundations of the community. The rank and file simply would not follow the orders if these orders countermanded existing cultural norms. However, the presence of women in the armed forces during the war demonstrated that women could indeed perform well in a man's world. These women were very pleased with the rapport they established with their superiors and co-workers as well as with their own personal growth and maturity. Half of the 350 women veterans surveyed ranked the war years 9 or 10 in terms of the most important events in their life (with 1 =

116

worst, 10 = best). Two-thirds of them ranked their service during the war years as an 8, 9, or 10. Almost all, 95 percent, had mainly positive memories of their military experience, and 91 percent would do it all over again if given the opportunity. When asked about the positive legacies of the war, women claimed that it gave them a broader perspective, made them more independent, and provided them with rewarding memories and lifelong friends. The negative legacies were caused by the problems that the service presented for their families.[64]

Military women learned a way of life that had been reserved for men. Many women believed that they made better dates and wives because their fiancés and husbands could reminisce about their military service and not stop every few seconds to explain the terminology. A third met their husbands in the service, and 87 percent of those surveyed who married had husbands who had served in the military during the war.[65] Whether they ever married or not, most argued that they had learned a great deal by operating in a man's world. Such experience proved invaluable when these women went to apply for middle-management positions in business after the war. The military provided opportunities for women officers that the civilian world did not. Officers were trained for leadership positions and were paid more than an average college-educated woman could earn in the private sector.

Unfortunately, women veterans also experienced discrimination after the war. If they were trained in nontraditional jobs, some civilian employers were reluctant to hire them or train them further. Army psychologists worried about the woman veteran's fitting back into civilian life because, "Even more than men, these women have become unsuited to their former civilian environment because the change in their pattern of life was more radical. . . . Most of them have matured, have broader interests and a new and finer sense of values."[66] Potential employers did not always recognize women as having veterans' status and as thereby being eligible for preferential treatment in securing jobs. Nor was such discrimination always unintentional. The Veterans of Foreign Wars, for example, adopted new by-laws after the war to ban women from membership.[67] Worst of all, many women found that civilians—men and women—had heard, even believed, the rumors of sexual promiscuity of the women in uniform. Demoralized, some women never mentioned wartime service. Only now, forty years later, are they willing to talk about their participation in the war effort. Others will talk enthusiastically about their wartime experience but stop abruptly when asked about the slander campaign.

The wartime experience did not change American women in a basic way—in their attitude toward war. From the first public opinion polls to the present, the major difference in attitudes between men and women centers on the issues of war and violence. Even when you control for the same socio-economic background, women are 10 to 20 percent more dovish than men. The generation gap between the women veterans of World War II and young women today is reflected in *how* they demonstrate their pacifism. While antiwar protests are popular with young women today, the overwhelming majority of World War II women veterans believe that the antiwar protests are harmful to the best interests of the nation.[68]

Even women with wartime military experience reflect this male-female dichotomy. Some women veterans began their answers to open-ended questions by explaining that they didn't approve of war but felt that they had no choice but to serve when Pearl Harbor was attacked. Others prefaced their comments by explaining that it was an unfortunate time for our country but it was the best of times for them. Half the women veterans surveyed believed that the real enemy is no longer communism, but rather war itself.[69]

Paradoxically, then, military service was often a rewarding and broadening experience for individual women but a disaster for women as a gender. Women mastered military language and customs, thrived at marching, accepted the discipline, excelled at their jobs, and enjoyed the experience, all to the amazement of military leaders who had stereotyped visions of what men and women could and could not do. Even though the male rank and file could rattle off the names of women they worked with and respected, and male officers could point with pride to the accomplishments of their women, most of these men still believed that women did not belong in the armed forces. Putting women in uniform was simply too radical a step for most Americans. A handful of war years could not erase deeply ingrained norms and stereotypes. The result was symbolized by the comment of a sailor who, when asked what the initials WAVEs meant, replied, "Women Are Very Essential Sometimes."[70]

Notes

1. Barton C. Hacker, "Women and Military Institutions in Early Modern Europe: A Reconnaissance," *Signs* VI (Summer 1981), pp. 643–71; Linda Grant De Pauw, *Seafaring Women* (Boston: Houghton Mifflin, 1982).

2. There were Army and Navy nurses and over 11,000 Yeomen (F) (female), and Marinettes who served in World War I. These Navy and Marine women were primarily telephone operators. For a discussion of one Yeoman (F)'s experiences, see Joy Bright Hancock, *Lady in the Navy: A Personal Reminiscence* (Annapolis, Md.: U.S. Naval Institute, 1972).

3. The peak wartime enrollments were 100,000 WACs (Army), 86,000 WAVEs (Navy), 17,600 Marines, 10,000 SPARs (Coast Guard), 47,000 Army Nurse Corps, and 11,000 Navy Nurse Corps. The total number of women who served at one time or another during the war was 140,000 in the WAAC/WAC, 100,000 WAVEs, 23,000 Marines, 13,000 SPARs, 60,000 Army Nurse Corps, and 14,000 Navy Nurse Corps. Estimates calculated from data provided by Mattie E. Treadwell, *The United States Army in World War II, Special Studies, The Women's Army Corps* (Washington, D.C.: Office of the Chief of Military History, Dept. of the Army, 1954), pp. 765–69, and Ruth Chenery Street, "History of the Marine Corps Women's Reserve: A Critical Analysis of Its Development and Operation, 1943–1945," December 5, 1945, pp. 99, 100, 126, Schlesinger Library, Radcliffe College, Cambridge, Mass. The Women's Airforce Service Pilots (WASP), the 1,074 women who ferried the planes, were classified as a civilian group and did not receive military status and privileges until 1977, after a long struggle. Their story is very different from the WACs, WAVEs, Women Marines, and SPARs, and thus will not be included in this paper. See Sally Van Wegener Keil, *Those Wonderful Women in Their Flying Machines: The Unknown Heroines of World War II* (New York: Rawson, Wade Publishers, 1979) and Jacqueline Cochran, *The Stars at Noon* (Boston: Little, Brown & Co., 1954).

4. The experiences of the Army and Navy nurses were radically different from those of the other women in uniform during the war and must, because of space limitations, be discussed in another essay. For a preliminary survey of the experiences of nurses, see D'Ann Campbell, *Women at War with America: Private Lives in a Patriotic Era* (Cambridge: Harvard University Press, 1986), chap. 2.

5. Sara Ann Allen, ed., *Daughters of Pallas Athene: Cameo Recollections of Women's Army Corps Veterans* (Kansas City, Mo.: Aero Graphics Inc., 1983), p. 117, contributed by Esther Shapiro Herz; Elizabeth R. Pollock, *Yes, Ma'am: The Personal Papers of a WAAC Private* (Philadelphia: J. B. Lippincott Co., 1943), p. 125.

6. Mary C. Lyne and Kay Arthur, *Three Years Behind the Mast: The Story of the United States Coast Guard, SPARs* (Washington, D.C.: U.S. Naval Office, 1946), p. 85.

7. Allen, *Daughters of Pallas Athene*, pp. 68, 118, contributed by Esther Shapiro Herz and Aneida (Gonzie) Fortmayer.

8. Mildred McAfee Horton, "Recollections of Captain Mildred McAfee [Horton], USNR (Ret.)," 1971, p. 113, Oral History Collection, U.S. Naval Institute, Annapolis, Md.

9. Horton, "Recollections," p. 9.

10. Lyne and Arthur, *Three Years Behind the Mast*, p. 19.

11. *Ibid.*, p. 29.

12. Marie Bennett Alsmeyer, *The Way of the WAVEs* (Conway, Ark.: Hamba, Books, 1981), p. 24.

13. Lyne and Arthur, *Three Years Behind the Mast*, p. 69.

14. Allen, *Daughters of Pallas Athene*, p. 104, contributed by Inez G. Scott.

15. Lyne and Arthur, *Three Years Behind the Mast*, p. 31.

16. Pollock, *Yes, Ma'am*, p. 31.

17. Allen, *Daughters of Pallas Athene*, p. 53, contributed by Marian Smith Jacot.

18. Horton, "Recollections," p. 66.

19. Allen, *Daughters of Pallas Athene*, pp. 48, 49, 118, contributed by Esther Shapiro Herz, Virginia H. Warren, and Esther Lukon; Pollock, *Yes, Ma'am*, p. 86. Lyne and Arthur, *Three Years Behind the Mast*, p. 23.

20. Alsmeyer, *The Way of the WAVEs*, p. 15.

21. *Ibid.*, p. 15.

22. Barbara A. White, *Lady Leatherneck* (New York: Dodd, Mead and Co., 1945), p. 26.

23. Alsmeyer, *The Way of the WAVEs*, p. 15.

24. Horton, "Recollections," p. 67.

25. Pollock, *Yes, Ma'am*, p. 149.

26. Horton, "Recollections," p. 63.

27. Allen, *Daughters of Pallas Athene*, p. 13, contributed by Juanita Farrell Martin.

28. Pollock, *Yes, Ma'am*, p. 22.

29. *Ibid.*, p. 86.

30. Hancock, *Lady in the Navy*, p. 77.

31. The 350 women veterans answered a thirteen-page self-administered questionnaire that covered 100 topics. Many questions were borrowed from surveys done by Stouffer's research teams during the war or from questionnaires administered in the 1980s to veterans so that I could test my results with other scholars' findings. These questionnaires were passed out during the fortieth reunions of the WACs, WAVEs, Women Marines, and SPARs and sent additional questionnaires to friends of these women who were also veterans. Thus a snowball sample was formed. A similar questionnaire was administered to several hundred nurses. A comprehensive analysis of these results will be the subject of another paper. The question "How proud were you of your corps?" was question 41. Henceforth I will refer to this survey as Campbell Survey, 1984.

32. Campbell Survey, 1984, questions 28, 45, 38.

33. Allen, *Daughters of Pallas Athene*, p. 77, contributed by Bonnie L. Tourat.

34. Horton, "Recollections," p. 18.

35. Allen, *Daughters of Pallas Athene*, p. 281, contributed by Lena A. Keller.

36. Allen, *Daughters of Pallas Athene*, p. 149, contributed by Lucille M. Hall.

37. Horton, "Recollections," p. 73.

38. Allen, *Daughters of Pallas Athene*, pp. 38–49, contributed by Betty Richardson.

39. Alsmeyer, *The Way of the WAVEs*, p. 29.

40. Jeanne Holm, *Women in the Military* (Novato, Cal.: Presidio Press, 1982), p. 50.

41. Treadwell, *Women's Army Corps*, p. 448.

42. Campbell Survey, 1984, questions 24, 25.

43. Horton, "Recollections," p. 87.

44. *Ibid.*, p. 89.

45. *Ibid.*, p. 27.

46. Thelma Beaton and Harriet Conn, eds., "Through the Looking Glass . . . with the Anchorettes. Unit Two of WAVEs National Corporation (Covina, Cal., n.d.) p. 28, interview with Dories Shannon Seevers by Harriet Conn, August 1982.

47. June A. Willenz, *Women Veterans: America's Forgotten Heroines* (New York: Continuum, 1983), p. 45. Chapter 3 is devoted entirely to profiles of women veterans.

48. *Ibid.*, pp. 41, 42, interview with Phyllis Borland Wrigley by Harriet Conn, January 1983.

49. Allen, *Daughters of Pallas Athene*, p. 269, contributed by Neva Stark Buckley Nunes.

50. *Ibid.*, p. 243, contributed by Florence Land.

51. Alsmeyer, *The Way of the WAVEs*, p. 46.

52. Allen, *Daughters of Pallas Athene*, p. 30, contributed by Alice I. Conlon.

53. *Time*, April 2, 1945, p. 20, and April 16, 1945, p. 24; Treadwell, *Women's Army Corps*, pp. 598–99.

54. Horton, "Recollections," p. 44.

55. *Ibid.*, pp. 45–48.

56. Allen, *Daughters of Pallas Athene*, p. 276, Georgia Jensen Frazier.

57. Campbell Survey, 1984, questions 39, 40.

58. Holm, *Women in the Military*, p. 52.

59. *Ibid.*

60. Treadwell, *Women's Army Corps*, pp. 211–14; Lyne and Arthur, *Three Years Behind the Mast*, p. 70.

61. Samuel Stouffer, "The American Soldier in World War II," Survey S-215, Methodological Study, June 1945, Roper Center, Williams College, Williamstown, Mass., and University of Connecticut, Storrs, Conn.

62. Allen, *Daughters of Pallas Athene*, p. 220, contributed by Elizabeth A. Reilly.

63. Quoted in E. G. Dennis, "Each Hospital Corps Wave Frees a Fighting Sailor 'And Helps 100 Men,' " *Hospitals* 18 (March 1944), p. 38.

64. Campbell Survey, 1984, questions 46, 85, 124, 127, 48A, 48B.

121

65. Campbell Survey, 1984, questions 69, 70, 72.

66. *The Women Veteran,* Research Studies MPR-2, 31 April 1946, Reports Control Symbol PAB-7-S, by Research Service, Va., quoted in Treadwell, *Women's Army Corps,* p. 738.

67. *Ibid.,* p. 739. See also Willenz, *Women Veterans: America's Forgotten Heroines.*

68. See Tom W. Smith, "The Polls: Gender and Attitudes Toward Violence," *Public Opinion Quarterly* 48, pp. 384–96. See also John M. Benson, "The Polls: U.S. Military Intervention," *Public Opinion Quarterly* 46 (Winter 1982), pp. 592–98; Sandra Baxter and Marjorie Lansing, *Women and Politics* (Ann Arbor: University of Michigan Press, 1983), pp. 56–60; and Campbell Survey, 1984, question 118 on antiwar protests.

69. Campbell Survey, 1984, question 115.

70. Horton, "Recollections," p. 19. For background information on women in uniform in World War II, Mattie Treadwell's *Women's Army Corps* cited previously is excellent. See also Campbell, *Women at War with America,* chap. 1; Susan M. Hartmann, "Women in the Military Service," in Mabel E. Deutrich and Virginia C. Purdy, eds., *Clio Was a Woman: Studies in the History of American Women* (Washington, D.C.: Howard University Press, 1980), and Hartmann, *The Home Front and Beyond* (New York: G. K. Hall, 1982), chap. 3; Susan H. Godson, "The Waves in World War II," *Naval Institute Proceedings* 107 (December 1981), p. 46; Bureau of Naval Personnel, Historical Section, "Women's Reserve," Washington, D.C., 1946, in Navy Department Library, Washington, D.C.; and Pat Meid, "Marine Corps Women's Reserve in World War II," 1964, Historical Branch, G-3 Division Headquarters, U.S. Marine Corps, Washington, D.C.

Comments

The idea of conscription for women is not new in America. Kathy Jones, a political scientist at San Diego State University, takes up the recent debate in her essay. Eleanor Roosevelt, a strong proponent for peace, saw the need and the desirability of conscripting women as long ago as the Second World War. Conscription of women has always been a controversial topic. The issues revolve around two questions: Why are men and not women subject to the draft? What does this tell us about the way our culture views women and citizenship?

On the one hand, men are dominant; on the other, they are expendable in large numbers in time of war. Women have not been expendable in the same way. Can it or should it be a goal of feminism to break that distinction by assimilating the bodies of defenders with the bodies of those who historically have been "protected"? Is it essential for women to be drafted to gain first-class citizenship?

Insofar as the National Organization for Women's (NOW) brief *amicus curiae* on conscription favors drafting women (1981), the organization reinforces the connection between citizen and soldier and does not challenge it. NOW, founded by Betty Friedan in 1966, has not always been of one voice on this and other issues. Early in its history, NOW established task forces on various issues, during whose deliberations policy was to be forged. Divisions occurred on issues differentially affecting white women and women of color; middle-class and working-class women. The issue of the draft was an extremely divisive one. But

123

finally, the organization took its position in the *amicus* brief referred to in this article and has never wavered from it.

Under what circumstances could and should feminists of different political persuasions resort to the draft? Feminist-pacifists would say "never." Radical feminists would resist the draft because the army, even if women are in it, is a male-dominated institution. But those feminists indebted to the liberal, civic-republican, and just war traditions must pose this question to themselves. They cannot simply evade it. Do women have an obligation to protect their country if it is in peril? Must that duty take the form of involuntary conscription?

One of the arguments in favor of male conscription has been that the values and virtues embodied in notions of "home" and "country" can sometimes only be preserved by resort to collective violence. Does that argument hold for women? An underlying theme here is whether it is preferable, overall, apart from considerations of women's role, to have an all-volunteer force (AVF) in place of a drafted army. On the one hand, the "career" in the military distorts the notion of civic duty. On the other, conscription historically has presaged war. There are no easy answers to any of these questions.

6

Dividing the Ranks: Women and the Draft

Kathleen Jones

The controversy surrounding the conscription of women for military service has divided United States feminist ranks over questions of principle and strategy. The significance of the debate that has ensued extends beyond the issue of the coherence of feminism as a political movement. Its ultimate value lies in the opportunity to determine how to reconcile the immediate demand for equality of opportunity with the recognition of the need for systematic elimination of the structural roots of inequality. At stake is the larger question of the role of reform in programs calling for structural change.[1]

Liberal feminists traditionally have advocated fully extending the current civil rights and responsibilities of citizenship to women. Consequently, the position they have taken on the draft issue is that the best way to insure women's equal treatment with men is to render them equally vulnerable with men to the political will of the state. The elimination of exclusions based on gender in the area of conscription and,

Reprinted courtesy of *Women and Politics* (Winter 1984), vol. 4, no. 4, pp. 75–87.

ultimately, in the criteria used to recruit for combat-related positions has been held necessary as a means of establishing full political rights for women.

It is my intention to examine the necessary connections between the principles and strategies entailed in the liberal feminist defense of the drafting of women, to criticize the grounds of that defense, and to provide a radical argument for reform of the military. I have narrowed the analysis to a critique of the liberal position because the unresolved contradictions of that position's definition of citizenship and democratic authority particularly limit the effectiveness of feminism as social criticism. The National Organization for Women (NOW) is taken to be the organization most paradigmatic of liberal feminism.[2]

Although opposed to a draft in principle, NOW's reaction to the question of registering women in the event a draft became inevitable was strongly affirmative.[3] To exclude women would be detrimental to the military, NOW argued, since it would reduce the pool of qualified, technically trained personnel at precisely the point when the supply of men willing to serve had dwindled and was likely to continue to do so. Given their exclusion from combat and combat-related positions, women would continue to be denied equal opportunity to reap the rewards of medical care, housing, education, career training, retirement and other benefits, which the military provides. However, the ultimate damage, NOW held, would be the reduction of women to the status of second-class citizens—the result of having denied them the chance to fulfill that "unique political responsibility" of risking one's life for the state.[4]

Three recurrent themes typify the liberal position. These are: (1) the utilitarian argument that the defense needs of the United States depend upon getting the most skilled personnel regardless of sex; (2) the contention that the nonregistration of women contradicts liberal principles of equality of opportunity; and (3) the stand that the elimination of women from the draft is an arbitrary restriction of their citizenship.

Acceptance of these principles confronts feminists with a dilemma not easily resolved. On the one hand, a system of sex segregation in the military *is* economically and politically costly. For instance, as of 1984, roughly 80 percent of current positions in the military were logistical, clerical, administrative, and medical, and are thus not combat-related, though this is now changing. Nearly 20 percent more enlisted women than enlisted men are found in the four lowest pay grades, and the percent of enlisted men in the four highest pay grades exceeds that of enlisted women many times.[5] Finally, the combat exclusion limits the increase of women in the officer ranks, which not only prevents all but a small percentage of women from holding military decision-making positions, but also narrows significantly the availability of higher pay scales, academic scholarships, and the many specialized programs that provide training ultimately useful in procuring lucrative civilian positions.[6]

The ultimate effect of such restrictions is costly to women. Their ability to take advantage of the chance for the upward social mobility that military life affords for many of the nation's disadvantaged is limited by prevailing policies.[7] Clearly, there is a lack of correspondence between the skills and dedication that women bring to the military, and the opportunities for promotion within the military ranks with which the armed forces reward their female recruits. By being denied equal access to privileged and powerful military positions, women are undercompensated for the net value of their defense contribution. To ignore the economic and political liabilities for women of existing sexually discriminatory policies in the military would be to assume a posture of "cynical indifference to the immediate plight of women."[8]

True, but the reduction of demands for a new system of public policy priorities to demands for an agenda of nondiscriminatory opportunities *within* the existing framework bears all the markings of co-optation. Women's "liberation" comes to be measured by standards of the male-dominated status quo. The assumption is that access to the state's legitimate use of force is necessary in order to redefine the values in defense of which that force is currently employed.[9]

This argument is flawed for several reasons. First, access to the use of legitimate force is important if one essentially agrees with the ends toward which that force is applied. But, if there is marked disagreement with the *purposes* of state power, then the challenge to eliminate the male monopoly of power shades over into challenge to the authority of the state itself. In the latter instance, access to the state's power is not necessary to accomplish the goal of redefined priorities. What is necessary is to create new sources of power.[10]

Second, in modern warfare the principle of civilian control of the military, at least in the Western democracies, has been accepted. It is to the state's institution of political authority—the government—that the task of designing what Clausewitz called "grand strategy" has evolved.[11] Grand strategy is the determination of the nature, direction, and intensity of the state's defense and intervention policies. The power of the military, as a number of the U.S. military elite noted with regret during the Vietnam years, is a function of political decisions. The military employs force on behalf of the state's interests in directions determined by political authorities. To the extent women have equal access to positions of political authority, their power to influence the use of legitimate force is secured, although whether this would mean the development of different strategies is debatable. However, removing the barriers to women's recruitment into the higher circles of the military's hierarchy cannot compensate for women's unequal recruitment into those governmental positions, the duties of which include responsibility for the formulation of U.S. military strategy.[12] Criticisms should be levied against the inequitable distribution of these latter positions of authority if the concern is to equalize access to power for women.

Given this dilemma, the crucial issue can be summarized as follows: how can women's demand for equality be made the compelling basis for a fundamental reconstruction of social norms? The problem with feminist critiques of inequality has been the tendency to define justice as the objective distribution of existing "public goods" and responsibilities on a nonexclusionary basis. This is an important aspect of any theory of justice; but the question of *what* is to be distributed—the nature of a society's values—demands equal attention. It is by addressing the latter question especially that feminist theory can make a unique and profound contribution to the dialogue on equality. This contribution depends upon the ability of feminists to challenge not only the lopsided definition of woman's nature, which has legitimated the exclusion of women from certain activities because they are presumed to be "naturally" ill-suited for them. It also entails a critical understanding of the values implicit in the activities themselves. The inadequacy of the liberal feminist response can be demonstrated by considering the arguments and evidence offered in support of the drafting of women.

Given these recognitions, let us return to the NOW *amicus* brief. NOW's representatives argued forcefully that several facts made a compelling case for the inclusion of women in any draft. First, projected demographic patterns suggested that the pool of draft-age males would continue to diminish through the 1990s.[13] Women, as the armed forces have recognized, would have to be relied upon to meet the personnel needs of the military. Indeed, until fairly recently, each branch of the service had projected a net increase in the number of female inductees and had even proposed a revision of statutory law in order to modify combat classifications, and to increase the percentage of women who would be recruited to service. Second, most military personnel experts had testified that the overall quality of women volunteers, when assessed in terms of educational achievement, skills performance, retention rates, and self-discipline, measured up to and, in some cases, exceeded the quality of male recruits.[14] Consequently, if the military was concerned with the quality of its recruits, its own experience with women warranted their inclusion in a draft. As NOW argued, "discrimination against women in the military costs this nation literally billions of dollars a year because better qualified women are not recruited while less qualified males are and at much higher enlistment bonuses and costs."[15] Third, a draft that excluded women would not only solidify the inequities that women face in the military; it might even exacerbate them. Fourth, the exclusion of women from a draft seemingly contradicts the more stringent review standards for sex-based discrimination established by the U.S. Supreme Court in 1976. These standards required that "classifications by gender must serve important governmental objectives and must be substantially related to achievement of those objectives."[16] Fifth, the inclusion of women in the draft would insure the treatment of women as full citizens for two significant reasons. It would remove the final obstacle to women's rightful claim to equal privileges of citizenship because they would share the responsibilities of full citizens. Sexual integration in the military would also contribute to the erosion of sexual stereotypes just as racial contact in the military was alleged to result in a greater acceptance of each race by the other.

Although each of these points contains a partial truth, the extent to which, even in combination, they contribute meaningfully to the debate about equality and citizenship needs to be assessed. The first two arguments concern military personnel needs and attempt to demonstrate the inevitable link between adequate defense and reform of military policies and statutory restrictions on the use of women in the military. While the evidence is strong that the quality of women military personnel contributes in significant, positive ways to U.S. defense preparedness, whether this evidence supports the drafting of women is moot. At best it is a good argument for removing the obstacles to women's full access to the military by repealing the policies that discriminate in the assignment of positions on the basis of sex alone.[17]

Moreover, the critical issue in need of consistent recognition is the character of the strategic context warranting a radical change from volunteer recruitment policies to a draft. As Bella Abzug noted, excessive focusing on the issue of registering women diverts attention from the real debate about what circumstances would warrant the drafting of anyone.[18] Little evidence was offered in the Senate and House hearings on registration that the strategic scenario had shifted significantly enough to justify such a move. Even more ironic is the fact that the very policies to which some feminists were subscribing would entail expenditures whose negative consequences would be borne by women disproportionately. Extended military programs are purchased at the price of reduced spending in the general areas of social services that women, especially those with young children, have come to depend upon increasingly.[19] There is no guarantee that the women who would benefit from extended opportunities in the military would be recruited, or drafted, from the same economic strata as those who would be hurt by reductions in social spending.

The arguments related to citizenship remain the most problematic. The point has been made that a draft is intrinsically fairer than an all volunteer force insofar as it distributes the burdens of citizenship throughout the population. Nevertheless, in his study of the draft, Michael Useem suggested that anything short of a full-scale mobilization effort, which would tend to push conscription to near universal levels, results in a class-biased system. For instance, despite the fact that conscription was a major source of troops during both the Korean and Vietnamese wars, the "limited" nature of U.S. commitments of military forces maximized the opportunity for social class criteria to enter the selection process. During the Vietnam period, "the heaviest conscription rates fell on children of blue-collar and lower-echelon white-collar workers.[20] Consequently, the introduction of women into the pool of potential draftees would not equalize distribution of liabilities since class is an important variable in the distribution process. In addition, as Selective Service System witnesses testified, if current combat exclusions remained intact, the drafting of women would actually increase a male's chances of going into combat, in proportion to the number of women drafted and excluded from combat.[21] Such difficult issues as these have yet to be confronted by those who subscribe to the view that conscription institutionalizes equality. What many fail to recognize is that if all alike, regardless of social or economic class, were inducted, this would be "a doctrine of equality, but it is equality of slavery, not liberty," according to Thomas Reaves and Karl Hess.[22] This is not to suggest that there would never be just cause for the use of universal conscription. The difficulty with any critique of the concept of mandatory military service, based abstractly on either libertarian or pacifist premises, is that it denies the historical context that alone ought to determine military policy.

But, are there characteristics specific to the relationship of the individual to the political system entailed in obligatory military service that correlate intrinsically with the concept and quality of citizenship? Jill Laurie Goodman argues that historical evidence demonstrates the extent to which ideas of citizenship and military service have always been intertwined.[23] As ideas of political privilege changed in a more democratic direction, the concept of the citizen soldier emerged. The connection made between the obligation to defend the state and the right to share in the exercise of sovereignty was stated forcefully in the *Dred Scott* decision of 1856. In his opinion, Chief Justice Taney argued that the exclusion of blacks from military service was indicative of the fact that, although blacks were born in the state, they were "not by the institutions and laws of the State numbered among its people." He also asserted that citizenship was not coterminous with military service. The latter is symbolic of citizenship, but, as the black troops in World War I learned, symbols do not guarantee equal protection before the law.

The real limitations of the liberal notion of citizenship and sovereignty can best be grasped by contrasting it with a social-democratic one. In classical liberal theory, political rights are a necessary corollary to the concept of sovereignty, delineating the proper relationship between the individual and the state. The people can only be sovereign insofar as their "natural" freedom and equality—defined as the equal right of each individual to be free from arbitrarily coercive authority—are secured by a set of legal arrangements that guarantee the integrity of each individual and stabilize the individual's relationship to the state. The implication of liberal theory is that sovereignty does not exist primarily in the relation of individuals to one another, but in the relation of each citizen to the state. These relations, and the inclusion of classes of people within them, are established by the institutions and laws of the state. Consequently, sovereignty and citizenship are only accidentally social; essentially, they are juridical.

Socialist theory inverts this perspective. Sovereignty exists as a function of fully developed *social* relationships. Citizenship is an inclusive and extensive relation to others, rather than an exclusive and intensive relation to the state. As against the liberal notion of "natural" freedom, socialist theory posits social freedom and diversity. Both citizenship and sovereignty emerge historically not as a function of the simple granting of political rights, but as the result of the development of activities that contribute to the substantive democratization of choices and responsibilities in everyday reality, economically and socially as well as politically.

The contrast between these two views is stark. In the first instance,

131

the substance of available opportunities secured by political rights is virtually irrelevant. That opportunities are equally available is the point. In the second instance, the equality of opportunities becomes virtually insignificant if their substance contributes to a narrowing of choices in the long run.

If we relate these notions to the demand for full and equal citizenship raised by feminist critiques of discriminatory norms, we discover that meeting this demand can signal real social transformation only if it is linked, theoretically and practically, to the restructuring of those institutions and activities that currently exclude women to one extent or another. It is not enough, Susan Sontag wrote several years ago, to change the laws that discriminate against women in specific situations. The situations themselves must be changed.[24] If women content themselves with petitioning for entry into certain quarters, leaving the institutions arranged as they find them, women will discover the existing characteristics and values of society unscathed, if not strengthened. As C. B. MacPherson noted about the effects of democratizing the liberal state, when the competitive political system was opened to include all those who had been created by the competitive market system, the liberal state was fulfilling its own logic. Indeed, the ultimate effect of these democratic reforms was to strengthen the liberal state and the market society upon which it was founded.[25]

None of which is to suggest that democratic reforms are not needed. Rather, it is to remind ourselves that a mere enlargement or expansion does not constitute a real change in values.[26] Many of those who have argued for an end to discrimination in the military simply have failed to recognize this distinction. At best, their claim has been that the self-contained, "closed" world of the military might make the breakdown of sexual stereotypes a relatively easy task to accomplish. Such changes could then spill over into civilian life.[27] But even this argument begs the question of how to define stereotypes broadly enough so as not to "portray the 'new woman' as the 'old man,' battle cry and all."[28]

The ultimate difficulty with accepting the policy choice as structured—either support the drafting of women, or mortgage women's full citizenship and equality—is that it diverts attention and energy from tasks that have become imperatives. These include a critical analysis of those institutions and policies whose very structures preclude the full development of some individuals. Sexual discrimination in the labor market, both civilian and military, is only part of the mechanism whereby work is hierarchically organized. The elimination of sexual barriers, although a

132

necessary step, can be fully effective only if linked to the struggle to redefine the meaning and structure of work. The exclusion of any group from positions of political leverage and power is an injustice that deserves to be criticized since it arbitrarily impedes the ability of the excluded group to further its interest within the terms laid down by the market structure. But since inequality is endemic to those terms themselves, the attempt to eradicate inequality by affirmative action ultimately must confront its limits in the distributive mechanism of the market itself.

It is not enough to claim that women can do anything that men do. Feminists should demand access to the military only as a means to acquire the power base from which to redefine the range of responsibilities included in the concept of citizenship. This means that while feminists should attempt to eradicate all arbitrarily exclusionary criteria for distributing the privileges and obligations of citizenship, the real task of feminism is to enrich the meaning of citizenship. Jean Elshtain summarized well the challenge that the draft poses to feminist politics when she argued that "feminist thinkers must conceptually appropriate those aspects of traditional definitions of femininity and feminism that would help create ways of seeing the world, America's role in it and the responsibilities of American citizens that are powerfully and unsentimentally against war in our post-Holocaust, nuclear epoch."[29]

Notes

1. For a general discussion of this issue, see Sandra G. Harding, "Feminism: Reform of Revolution?" in *Women and Philosophy: Toward a Theory of Liberation*, Carol C. Gould and Marx Wartofsky, eds. (New York: G. P. Putnam's Sons, 1976), pp. 271–84.

2. The testimony given by other individuals and groups generally identified with liberalism during the Senate and House hearings on the reinstitution of registration procedures confirms that NOW's position is typical of a liberal defense of the inclusion of women in the draft. See especially the statement of David E. Landau, staff counsel for the American Civil Liberties Union in *Hearing Before the Subcommittee on Manpower and Personnel of the Committee on Armed Services, Reinstitution of Procedures for Registration Under the Military Selective Service Act*, U.S. Senate, 96th Cong., 1st sess., Mar. 13, May 21, July 10, 1979, pp. 92–107.

3. "The Registration and Drafting of Women in 1980," *National NOW Times* 14 (March 1980), p. 1.

4. Jill Laurie Goodman, "Women, War and Equality: An Examination of Sex

Discrimination in the Military," *Women's Rights Law Reporter* (Summer 1979), p. 243.

5. "Prepared Statement of Judy Goldsmith on Behalf of the National Organization for Women, Inc." in *Hearing Before the Task Force on Defense and International Affairs of the Committee on the Budget, Selective Service Registration*, House of Representatives, 96th Cong., 2nd sess., Feb. 20, 1980, pp. 45, 61 (hereafter referred to as *Selective Service Registration*).

6. Vice Admiral James D. Watkins testified that, as a result of existing statutes, there had not been an increase in female line officers proportionate to an increase in enlisted Navy women, because "many officer billets ashore require warfare specialties which women are restricted from obtaining." The same is true of the Air Force and the Army. *Hearings Before the Subcommittee on Priorities and Economy in Government of the Joint Economic Committee, the Role of Women in the Military*, 9th Cong., 1st sess., July 22, Sept. 1, 1977, pp. 59, 65 (hereafter referred to as *The Role of Women in the Military*). General Kingston, Assistant Deputy Chief of Staff for Personnel in the Army, reported that Army policy regarding the awarding of ROTC scholarships is affected also by combat requirements. Consequently, although women get their "fair share of scholarships based on non-combat arms requirements," of the 2,200 scholarships awarded in 1976–77, only 200 went to women because the majority were slated for the combat officer corps. A similar situation prevails in the Navy and Air Force ROTC program (*ibid.*, pp. 46, 55, 65).

7. It is interesting to note that the current exclusion of women from combat-related positions in the army is solely a function of Army policy. The Assistant Secretary of the Army (1977), Robert Nelson, testified that should the Department of Defense choose to change that policy, it did not require an Act of Congress to do so (*ibid.*, p. 28).

8. Goodman, "Women and Equality," p. 246.

9. Similar distinctions are made in the literature on political disobedience. The catalogue of forms of dissent ranges from those that simply challenge the application of a particular law to those that challenge the social system itself. See Leslie J. MacFarlane, *Political Disobedience* (London: The Macmillan Press, Ltd., 1971). I have maintained that access to the use of the state's power is not sufficient to secure the ends to which the women's movement has been committed, if these ends are defined as the full institutionalization of principles of equality, regardless of sex. This does not mean that such access is not expedient. MacFarlane notes that revolutionary groups have often used the tactic of seizing establishment power "as a focus for further operations by those who have become radicalized through the experience of seeing and holding a citadel of the establishement" (p. 38). A good recent example of the employment of these tactics in the Women's Movement is the British women's encampment at Greenham Common, and the American parallel at the Seneca Falls Army Depot.

10. The necessity to maintain political control of the army is all the more

imperative, if more problematic, in a nuclear age. Deference to the expertise of both civilian and military scientists and engineers, who design and operate the technological armaments of modern warfare, is as characteristic of defense policy making as of other technically complicated policy areas, such as energy planning, genetic engineering, and environmental protection. Nevertheless, acknowledging the fact that policy-making trends are drifting in the direction of the "rule of the experts" ought to lead to the demand for a renewal of politics and an infusion of new principles in policy making, instead of capitulation and adaptation.

11. Karl von Clausewitz, *On War*, ed. and trans. M. Howard and P. Paret (New Jersey: Princeton University Press, 1976).

12. An argument could be made that, given the heavy recruitment of key policy makers and other defense strategists from within the upper ranks of the military, it is important for women to be represented adequately in those ranks. One could counter this argument with the response that the pattern of recruitment itself should be altered since it weakens the ability of the government to retain autonomous control of strategic planning.

13. In January 1977, the Congressional Budget Office calculated that there would be a significant gap between the supply and demand of male recruits even if unemployment in the civilian sector remained critical. If unemployment were as low as 4 percent, the availability of male recruits could decline drastically to as much as 40 percent below recruiting goals. See *The Role of Women in the Military*, p. 17.

14. *Ibid.*, pp. 25–27. See also *Selective Service Registration*, pp. 48–55.

15. *Ibid.*, p. 65.

16. *Craig* v. *Boren*, 429 U.S. 190 (1976), p. 199. The most recent Supreme Court decision left standing an interpretation of a male-only registration as consistent with constitutional principles. The court argued that Congress was correct in deferring to the military's historical policy of excluding women from the draft. This policy, the court claimed, was based on the military's judgment of how best to structure the tactics of combat situations. Congress had allowed the military to determine such policies independently in the past, and there was no constitutional reason to alter the state of affairs now. Since sex-based discrimination was not subject to strict scrutiny, the court ruled that the only thing that needed to be demonstrated was a rational basis for the exclusion of women. This the military had provided, according to the court. See *Rostker* v. *Goldberg*, 453 U.S. 57 (1981).

17. In many ways this depends upon the removal of the combat restriction. The resolution of this issue is complicated by political as well as the moral dimensions of the debate. In no country that conscripts both men and women are women permitted in combat positions. See the testimony of Bernard Rostker, Director of Selective Service, *Hearings Before the Committee on Armed Services, Department of Defense Authorization for Appropriations for Fiscal Year 1981*, U.S. Senate, 96th Cong., 2nd sess., Part 3 Manpower and Personnel, Feb. 19;

Mar. 6, 10, 12, 17, 18, 19, 21; Apr. 2, 1980, pp. 1671–72. For a discussion of the ironies involved in women's combat capabilities, see Jean Elshtain, "Women, War and Feminism," *The Nation* 230 (June 14, 1980).

18. Bella Abzug's testimony in *Selective Service Registration*, p. 8.

19. See Women's International League for Peace and Freedom, *Women, Taxes and Federal Spending* (Philadelphia: June 1983).

20. Michael Useem, *Conscription, Protest and Social Conflict: The Life and Death of a Draft Resistance Movement* (New York: Wiley, 1973), pp. 81, 83.

21. *Defense Appropriations for Fiscal Year 1981*, p. 1689.

22. Thomas Reeves and Karl Hess, *The End of the Draft* (New York: Random House, 1970), p. 123.

23. Goodman, "Women, War and Equality," p. 247.

24. Susan Sontag, "The Third World of Women," *Partisan Review* 60 (1973), p. 186.

25. C. B. MacPherson, *The Real World of Democracy* (New York: Oxford University Press, 1972), p. 11.

26. For a sometimes misguided analysis of the dangers of cooperation implicit in some feminist theories, see Jesse Bier, "NOW . . . and Then: Bringing a Man's Theories, Hints, Entertainments, and Nuances to the Woman's Movement," *Virginia Quarterly Review* 55 (Autumn 1979), pp. 630–43.

27. Goodman, "Women, War and Equality," pp. 242–43.

28. Elshtain, "Women, War and Feminism," p. 724.

29. *Ibid.*, p. 724.

Part III

Wars, Militarism, and Feminist Politics

Comments

Joyce Berkman is a feminist historian. Her narrative reminds us that peace movements are not monolithic. The women who participate in peace movements differ in their views of what peace politics is and how to combat war. They frequently have sharply dissimilar assumptions about why wars occur. When reading Berkman's essay, look for diversities, conflicts, and internal debates.

Berkman's essay helps us to understand what is going on now, given our divergent assumptions and the politics that flow from them. We are invited to reflect on whether or not a prenuclear-age history is useful as a model. The reader might be tempted to speculate as to whether current issues render the peace politics of yesterday obsolete. Perhaps most important, Berkman delineates the conflicts between feminism and pacifism, showing that it would be a mistake to conflate the two. There have always been feminists who want nothing to do with pacifism, and pacifists who do not support feminist politics.

One feature of her essay is the emphasis on the enormous trauma of World War I, not only in its human cost, but in the rapid and total abandonment of peace politics by pacifists, socialists, and feminists on all sides. For example, social theorist and reformer Jane Addams did not support our participation in World War I. But even she had doubts about going against the majority of American citizens, who supported the war effort.

Berkman's essay is necessarily compressed. She writes primarily about individuals, some of whom are not well known. She pays little attention to the organization of peace movements, as that is not her central focus. But it should be noted that organization is always important to peace politics and that those who work for peace tend not to have the access to government and professional services that the military have.

This treatment of World War I and the sudden death of pacifism leaves one with the chilling thought that pacifism may do very well, but not in time of war.

7

Feminism, War, and Peace Politics: The Case of World War I

Joyce Berkman

A gender-focused discourse on peace has long been a subtheme of a more general inquiry into the nature and causes of war. The question is whether women have a special interest in and propensity for nonviolence; whether their gender, rooted as it is in their potential or actual maternal experience, makes a distinctive contribution toward promoting peace.

On the one hand, women's "peaceable" nature is claimed to be universal. Yet women's attitudes toward and willingness to participate in war varies substantially from one historic period to another, and from culture to culture. At certain moments, behavior surfaces that challenges the too easy assumptions made about gender and politics. Our current generation inhabits one such moment. The World War I generation lived through another. The subject of this essay is the unsettling and divisive effect that World War I had on feminism and pacifism. To come to any understanding of those issues, we need to weigh both the pacifist and feminist contexts in which this apparent reversal occurred, and weigh its meaning for the future.

Two Images

The image of woman as peacemaker, held by Europeans and Americans in the decades preceding World War I, was relatively new. In earlier human history, woman's image might equally well incorporate two roles: that of warrior and that of mother or fertility goddess—giver of life. The redoubtable Ashanti, Australian aborigines, Plutarch's Spartan mothers, Norse and Germanic folk heroines—these are the symbolic and actual foremothers of Joan of Arc. History and myth blur in the accounts of Amazons, of the biblical Deborah who led the Israelites in victory against the army of Siserand, and of Chinese military heroines, such as the woman hauntingly portrayed in Maxine Hong Kinston's novel, *The Woman Warrior*.

Sometimes the two contrasting images are assigned to different folk heroines. Other times they merge into one. In the Ibo tradition, the Great Mother Ala simultaneously wields a sword and nurtures the harvest, the sword signifying her willingness to use violence to protect the harvest and her people.[1] A contemporary equivalent might reside in the notion of "combative motherhood," a term describing women of modern revolutions who hold a rifle on one arm, a baby on the other, to show that if they are to care for their children, their country's "liberation" must come first.[2]

Anthropologists attribute this dual symbolism to men's fear, envy, and admiration for women's reproductive powers (powers manifest not only in the act of giving birth but also in menstruation and breast-feeding).[3] The seemingly magical powers of women have cast them nearly universally as good/evil, angel/whore, witch/wise woman. Prior to the nineteenth century, we do not have much evidence as to whether or not women played any role at all in shaping these archtypes (men usually wield power over symbol-making); nor do we know how women responded to these projections of themselves.

In Europe and America, the woman warrior has played a lesser role than in some other cultures. Yet there are shared symbols that even European women invoke. During the first French Revolution, for example, when a female militia formed in Paris, the group took the name of "Amazons."[4] And the history of European women in the early modern period documents women's participation in the hunt and in urban riots, as well as their willingness to practice infanticide.[5] Still, when Joan of Arc attempted to participate in *organized* military activity, she had to dress as a male. The symbols are there, but in European and American culture

142

they tend to shift meaning as situations change in which women dwell, and sex roles follow suit.[6]

Sex Roles and Peace

What distinguish the nineteenth century in Europe from the nineteenth century in America are both the exaggeration of sex differences demanded by Victorian morality, and the increase in the number and breadth of pro-peace organizations in which women could play a prominent part.

Victorian strictures can be quickly reviewed: women as potential and actual mothers enjoyed reproductive power at the expense of physical and intellectual prowess. As mothers, they belonged in the home, away from the hurly-burly of the market place, no less the battlefield. Further, since woman was delicate, it would not be appropriate for her to resolve any conflicts—even within her own family—in a combative manner. Rather, her obligation was to create a harmonious family life, to promote her children's growth and her spouse's success. Armed with an innate empathic ("female") sensitivity, she would develop a repertoire of nonviolent strategies with which to function in this world, a repertoire that would give her appropriate authority over her children and servants yet subordinate her to her husband's will for which she could expect economic and physical protection.

Male responsibilities were no less "natural" and conveniently complementary. Geddes and Thompson, not particularly "sexist" physiopsychologists writing at the end of the nineteenth century, traced male roles back to cell metabolism. Male cells, wrote the authors, were "katabolic"— active, aggressive, exuding energy; women's cells were "anabolic"— quiescent, conserving of energy, stabilizing.[7] Indeed, nineteenth-century gender constructs were rooted in complementarity. Since "maleness" might sometimes turn destructive, women must exercise their inborn taming skills to temper men's behavior. Yet, since masculine pugnacity was also essential to community safety, the proper mother (daughter, sister) must support male kin in physical and military contests. Role socialization was thus central to Victorian moral precepts: fathers were charged with developing bravery, patriotism, and physical prowess in their sons; mothers were charged to support them in these endeavors. Twenty-five centuries after Sparta, a young French woman could tell researchers engaged in an attitude survey on the eve of World War I

143

(1914): "A patriotic girl will want to found a French family and give her country good soldiers."[8]

Sex Roles and Women's Pacifism

Women sometimes took the ideology out of the home. In the nineteenth century, middle-class women spearheaded an array of humanitarian movements to abolish slavery, duelling, public hanging, and flogging in the military. They organized to end the abuse of animals, to modify cruel and inhuman treatment of criminals and the mentally ill, and brought the issues of wife- and child-abuse to the fore. In the same spirit, women's temperance groups, peace, and suffrage associations were founded.

There is a considerable difference, one could argue, between the do-goodism inherent in caring about prisoners or the mentally ill and the presumption that women could and should work for their own enfranchisement and for international peace. But so long as all these interests were couched within acceptable Victorian precepts, women might become more politically active. Some recognized right away that women's entry into "peace politics" represented an element of amateurism that diplomacy dare not tolerate, and tried to keep women from influencing national security policy with their peace advocacy. The "harmonizing traits hallowed in the home" were believed to be inappropriate for a world beset by national and imperial rivalries.

Not every nineteenth-century woman (or feminist) forsook the warrior tradition. Elizabeth Cady Stanton regards Deborah, the woman warrior in the Old Testament, very favorably in her version of the testament she called *The Woman's Bible*.[9] Deborah dispensed justice directly, proclaimed war, led her men to victory, and glorified the deeds of her army in immortal song, writes Stanton of her heroine. Deborah, Stanton concluded, was a "woman of genius and power." The popularity, too, of such folk heroines as Calamity Jane and Annie Oakley, and the stories told of Carrie Nation, the indomitable saloon-destroyer, bespoke some continuing regard for lively if not violent women's images in the nineteenth century, at least on the American frontier.

Finally, there was the Church, as an inspiration and outlet for women's moral energies. Solitary women, as members of historic peace churches, were protesting against war and working for alternate methods of resolving conflicts between nations long before peace politics emerged center

144

stage in the mid-nineteenth century. Some of them joined their husbands in refusing to pay for their countries' militias. The first peace societies appearing in the United States and England were rooted in religious affiliations. Not surprisingly, women were present in them from the beginning.

Women and Organized Pacifism

Probably the first person to conceptualize an alliance of women-*only* dedicated to peace was Swedish feminist, Frederika Bremer. She promulgated her idea in 1854, and nearly fourteen years later, in 1868, it was realized by Marie Geogg, a Swiss woman, as the Association Internationale des Femmes. Two wars influenced this peace activity: the Crimean War (Europe's first since the Napoleon era), and the most life-costly war ever fought till then—the American Civil War.

Some of the inspiration for late nineteenth-century peace activity can also be traced to the book, *Waffen Nieder* (Lay Down Your Arms), an enormous best-seller by Bertha Von Suttner, a Viennese feminist, published in 1889. Like Harriet Beecher Stowe's *Uncle Tom's Cabin*, which is credited with teaching America that slavery could never be humane, Von Suttner's book became a clarion call to action. After 1889, peace organizations in general and separate alliances of women began to proliferate. One of the first of the women's organizations was the Ligue Internationale de la Paix et de la Liberté founded in Geneva in 1867 by Eugenie Niboyet, a Saint Simonian, who viewed the struggle for international peace as inseparable from economic and social justice. Later, there was the Union Internationale des Femmes pour la Paix, a product of a joint effort of two French women and one English woman, a socialist, a feminist, and a pacifist, respectively; L'Alliance Universelles des Femmes pour la Paix, sometimes called Ligue des Femmes pour le Désarmement Internationale, and L'Association la Paix et le Désarmement par les Femmes—were others. As founders of all female peace societies and as active members of peace groups including men, women enjoyed more presence and influence on the peace movement in the nineteenth century than on any other reform movement, save perhaps Abolition.[10]

Of course, women were no more than men of one mind as to how to wrest peace from the tendencies toward war. Some were absolute pacifists, renouncing all warfare. Others allowed for purely defensive wars and wars of liberation. Still others took capitalism to be the cause of all wars

145

in contrast to those who were quite comfortable with free enterprise in the economic sphere at home but who expected international law and international bureaucracies to arbitrate and resolve conflicts among nations. Von Suttner, for one, had great faith in the arbitration process; Niboyet, of the Ligue Internationale, would not suffer peace without economic justice. By and large, French women were more socially radical than other women. But the point is that there were divisions among women peace activists even before the outbreak of World War I.

Feminism and Pacifism

While not all pacifists were feminists and not all feminists were pacifists, the two movements overlapped in theory and in membership. In the recently published historic *Dictionary of Modern Peace Leaders*, only one of the six hundred women listed was, at the time of the First World War, opposed to women's suffrage.[11] The peace movement and feminism were yoked together more closely than any other feminist nongender struggle (again with the possible exception of Abolitionism). Indeed, in France, pacifist beliefs became *the* criterion for screening membership in the mainstream, liberal-feminist movement. In 1909, the National Council of French Women expelled Jeanne Oddo-Deflore's French Feminist Studies Group for its unwillingness to commit itself to a pacifist position.[12]

Peace was quite straightforwardly a priority for active women. The first standing committee established by the International Council of Women was the Committee for Peace and International Relations. This spirit is epitomized by the South African writer, Olive Schreiner, who described herself, in the years immediately prior to World War I, as a "citizen of the world." Other women, notably Séverine (pseudonym of Caroline Rémy), declared that all Europe was "*ma patrie*," and Marie Goegg put it this way: "Woman has a unique ability to catalyze the love of the human race and friendship among neighboring nations."[13]

The rhetorical linkage had been there from the beginning of the nineteenth century: feminism and pacifism were braided together in Mary Wollstonecraft's earliest writing. Her opposition to war emerged not out of any squeamishness or feminine reluctance to kill but from a feminist-*political* opposition to hierarchical politics and unquestioning obedience to authority. Militarism, Wollstonecraft wrote, was inimical to critical thought and to intellectual freedom, "for the strong wind of

146

authority tends to push the crowd of subalterns forward (they rarely know or care why) with headlong fury." Further, "Every military corps is a chain of male despots crawling for rank and power."[14] Thus, while threatening social and moral progress in general, militarism, in Wollstonecraft's view, threatens women in particular by reinforcing masculine habits of authority.

It is no mere coincidence that the peak of prewar peace activism coincided with the crest of the first wave of the women's movement. Each movement fed the other. Peace continued to be viewed primarily as a woman's concern—a consensus reflecting the established gender conventions among white Americans and Europeans. Some feminists rejected those conventions but attached themselves to "peace" just the same. The power of this alliance was in evidence when 15,000 women marched along Fifth Avenue in New York City on August 29, 1914, as part of a Women's Peace March convened just as the troops were being mobilized in Europe.[15] As one observer wrote at the time: "Men were preparing to march to war, while women were marching for peace."[16]

Yet, within *months*, for European women whose *"patries"* rapidly declared war on one another in 1914, and *years* for American women whose nation stayed out of World War I until 1917, most feminists and pacifists, and most feminist-pacifists, would fairly quickly exchange their peace politics for patriotism and allow themselves, in some instances, to indulge in frenzied patriotic rhetoric. How was it possible for them to lose those long-held notions that women are naturally antiwar? Did women in fact shed these ideas, or were they coopted? If they remained pacifists, how did they fare during World War I? And finally, how did World War I change the principles of feminist-pacifism?

With the outbreak of World War I, European and American peace advocates split broadly into pro and antiwar camps. By far the majority of peace women abandoned their antiwar agitation once their country declared war. The organizational history of women's suffrage groups and feminist and female socialist organizations in three countries—England, France, and the United States—reveals the severity of the schism. By 1915 in England, the National Union of Women's Suffrage Societies, with more than 50,000 members, the largest and most encompassing suffrage association, split. The antiwar forces, although the majority of the executive committee, represented the minority will of the members. These executive committee members resigned. The remaining prowar rump continued to steer the organization.

The antiwar group of NUWSS leaders and supporters joined various peace groups. They also organized the British Committee of the International Women's Congress, which eventually became the British section of the Women's International League for Peace and Freedom. Similarly, the majority of the members of the rival suffrage group to the NUWSS, the Women's Social and Political Union, supported the war. The minority defected and formed the Independent WSPU and the United Suffragettes. Allied to neither of the two major suffrage associations were such small, fringe groups as the East London Federation, which adopted a vigorous feminist and socialist antiwar position.

Prior to America's entry into the war, the principal suffrage group, the National American Women's Suffrage Association, supported the Women's Peace Party, which had formed in 1914 as the rallying point for antiwar women. When on April 2, 1917, America entered the war, the Executive Committee of NAWSA, however, in contrast to its kindred organization in England, NUWSS, voted overwhelmingly to offer the organization's services to President Wilson. As a result, the Women's Peace Party ruptured, with the leadership of the WPP opposed to NAWSA's decision. Membership in the WPP rapidly declined.

In uncertain contrast, the Congressional Union (which became in June 1916 the National Woman's Party, representing a more militant approach to suffrage akin to the WSPU in England) did not follow English suffragettes in supporting the war. Composed as it was of many Quakers, including its leader, Alice Paul, it took an equivocal stance short of active opposition.

In the prewar years, socialist women in America, as elsewhere, waged an energetic antiwar campaign. In May 1914, the Women's National Committee, the coordinating committee of women in the American Socialist Party, urged women throughout the United States to form antiwar movements in their home towns. With the outbreak of war, the WNC continued to press for peace, but for a variety of reasons independent of the war, the WNC dissolved. New York socialist women continued nationwide antiwar efforts, but with America's entry into fighting, socialist feminist women divided.[17]

In contrast to England and the United States, French antiwar efforts were almost exclusively socialist and anarchist-feminist in political character. Most of the prominent late nineteenth-century liberal feminist peace organizers and campaigners had died before the outbreak of World War I. Only a tiny contingent of liberal feminists deviated from the majority who rallied to the support of the French government. These few organized the French section of the Women's International League for Permanent Peace, launched by the Hague Conference.[18]

The French socialist feminist response to the war showed striking parallels to those in England and the United States. The precursor of the wartime socialist women's groups was the *Groupe Feministe Socialiste*, begun in 1899 with a fairly autonomous status, until it merged in 1905 into the French socialist party, the *Section Français de l'Internationale Ouvrière* (SFIO), forming anew in January 1913 as the *Groupe des Femmes Socialistes*. Following the lead of the SFIO, the vast majority of French socialist feminists became prowar patriots. Those few who did not formed the *Comité d'Action Feminine Socialiste pour la Paix contre le Chauvinisme* (CAFSPC), which served as a base for their international peace efforts. Eventually, CAFSPC integrated with a gender-mixed socialist antiwar group, the *Comité d'Action Internationale*, soon re-formed as *Comité pour la Réprise des Relations Internationales*.[19]

Within these antiwar and prowar camps themselves, in Europe and the United States, profound differences stirred. The patriots included both those who reluctantly supported their governments and sought ways to mitigate the ravages and brutality of war as well as those who were intensely nationalistic and militaristic. A different kind of division, scarcely studied, characterized the antiwar feminists: between the majority who clung to their prewar views on the proclivity of women for peace and those few who could no longer posit this. I will sketch out the major lines of their thought.

One of the most exasperating features of the wartime divisions among feminists is that they do not lend themselves to easy analysis. Political consciousness and political behavior usually correlate with certain social variables such as class, race, gender, age, religion, marital status, and (in more recent research) sexual preference. But these variables do little to enlighten us on why certain feminists supported World War I and others did not.

Divisions occurred not just across class but within families. The British Pankhursts—all feminists of one sort or another—divided sharply over the war. Sylvia and Adela Pankhurst adopted a passionate pro-peace position, while Christabel and the mother of all three, Emmeline, were no less ardently pro-war. To be sure, Adela and Sylvia were socialist feminists, but this is not sufficient to explain their antiwar stance: Many socialist feminists were prowar. Nor does the radicalism of Christabel and Emmeline Pankhurst account entirely for *their* pro-war position, since many of their radical feminist sisters in the WSPU quit the party in disgust over the war fervor within.[20]

Many antiwar feminists tended to be politically left, but many on the left (both male and female) became prowar. Clearly, there is no easy equivalence between socialism and pacifism in the early stages of World War I. In France, few socialist women opposed the war. In Germany, Clara Zetkin (and later Rosa Luxembourg) in her war opposition stood only with a tiny socialist minority. If neither class, nor family, nor nationality, nor left-leaning explains feminists' varying attitudes toward World War I, the crucial factors evidently lie elsewhere.

Pro-war Feminists

At least one strand of pro-war feminists argued their case within the tradition of pro-feminist theory. Few feminists, as we have noted, had been pure pacifists opposed to all wars. Most had sought only "justice" in domestic and foreign affairs. Thus, their reading of the "justness" of their nation's military action would pretty much shape the position they would take on the war. In other words, their pro- or antiwar stance would turn on which side, in their view, was the aggressor.

Not surprisingly, most German feminist-pacifists blamed the Allies. Gertrude Baumer, President of the Federation of Germany Women's Associations, said the war was "thrust" upon the Germans and that national unity was "crucial" for survival. Most French and British thought the Germans and Austrians were at fault. Germany was portrayed as the "big bully" and as the rapist of Belgium (something the Germans actually wished the Allies to believe as a way of frightening civilian populations into capitulation). Christabel Pankhurst described what Germany did to Belgium as "hacking" and worried that Greece and England would be next. Not all radical feminists shared these views, for, as we have remarked, many left the WSPU over Christabel and Emmeline's war fervor.

In milder tones, Millicent Fawcett, leader of the NUWSS, called upon women to demonstrate their right to citizenship. "Let us show ourselves worthy of citizenship," she wrote, "whether our claim is recognized or not."[21] Since Fawcett believed the Allied cause to be just, citizenship meant loyal support of the British government in its "mortal" struggle to preserve English liberties. On pragmatic grounds, wartime would turn out to be—for both the British and American feminists—a good time to

150

deal. Ironically, on this issue, Fawcett and two of the Pankhursts, Christabel and Emmeline, once pre-war arch opponents, were in total accord.

Fawcett, Rachel Strachey, and others saw a pro-war stance as helping overthrow the rigidities of role stereotyping: men as protectors, women as protected. As mere protected beings, women were (and would remain in the eyes of society) passive, inferior, "irrelevant creatures to be fought *for*, whose only personal function [in war] was to sit home and weep."[22] It was on that premise that women had suffered second-class citizenship. If women now shared the tasks and risks of wartime, they might demonstrate their courage, loyalty, and moral conviction to be as vigorous as that of men. And then . . . of course the vote. One of the claims made for suffrage before the war was that there was a "depth of female bravery" and "moral stamina" to be added to the nation, once women were able to vote. Wartime was the time to make this claim come real.[23]

Now the very logic that had fed pacifist thinking before the war was refashioned to arouse patriotism. Women's protective responsibilities, it was argued by prowar feminists, could only be met if the *nation* was protected. Mothering required not simply mother-care but guarantees that the state be safe for children, and *strong*.[24] That meant sons must be good soldiers (nothing new here), but also that mothers must be prowar.[25] A key refrain within this argument was "service." Women must serve the community beyond the family—protect the nation from its enemies.

Curiously, this very metaphor of the family as expanded to the globe had framed women's peace politics before the war. Now, extended only to the nation, it was used to confine women's loyalties to their particular states. By 1916, the notion of a "global family," which had seemed close at hand to the women who said earlier that the world was their *patrie*, would have struck most nationalists as naive. Still, there were internationalists among the patriots. Some pro-war feminists actually entered relief work and nursing in order to mitigate the violence and to contribute in some way toward the cessation of hostilities.

Pro-peace Feminists

Shortly after Christabel and Emmeline Pankhurst were criss-crossing America, appealing to feminists to endorse the war, no less passionate advocates of peace from Europe were engaged in opposing that mission.

151

On October 30, 1914, well before America entered the war and only five days after the Pankhursts had addressed an audience in Carnegie Hall, Emmeline Pethick-Lawrence spoke on the same platform, urging women to "overstep the miserable bounds of nationality and race" and to campaign for peace.[26] Rosika Schwimmer, Pethick-Lawrence's sometime traveling companion and an acclaimed feminist leader in her own right (from Hungary), exhorted audiences similarly throughout the midwest.[27] Together they called upon American feminists to stop at nothing less than the formation of a Peace Party. Local women's peace committees did form and before long, assisted by Jane Addams, a Women's Peace Party in America was formally in place (1915).

Until 1917, when America entered the war, peace activism enjoyed some popular support among males and females. Once America joined the Allies, however, that support crumbled and, crumbling, sundered the American women's movement just as the issue had divided British and European feminists three years before. The dilemmas were not merely theoretical. Once America was engaged in warfare, feminists and other peace politicians could be prosecuted, certainly harassed. It was far easier for the feminist to row *with* the patriotic tide than to set her oars against it.

In France the hounding of feminist peace advocates was particularly fierce. The nation's very survival was tangibly at stake. Numbers of women were jailed for peace agitation. Notable among these were Louise Saumoneau, who was jailed on October 2, 1915, for distributing antiwar literature; Hélène Brion, who was suspended from her teaching post in November 1917 and later arrested, charged with inciting soldiers to desert the army. With few exceptions, socialist comrades and friends abandoned the women.[28] The police monitored the nonsocialist liberal feminist peace activists so closely that they, too, had to abandon peace campaigning and restrict their efforts to suffrage advocacy.[29] In Germany, Rosa Luxemburg was imprisoned for antiwar agitation, and Clara Zetkin was ostracized by her own party.[30] As for the more "tolerant" United States, Emma Goldman was jailed for twenty-one months and then deported to the Soviet Union for her efforts to form the No Conscription League, while Kate Richards O'Hare was imprisoned for her inflammatory peace addresses under the Espionage Act.[31] Although Jane Addams was not indicted, she was attacked by many of her friends and coworkers.[32]

Only in England were major feminist peace advocates not jailed, though like Addams, they suffered harassment and isolation. Olive

Schreiner, aging and seriously ill, could not find accommodations because of her German surname and her defense of conscientious objectors.[33] The very much admired labor champion and feminist Selena Cooper found that even in the town of Nelson, where long traditions of dissent flourished, she was scorned by neighbors, friends, and kin.[34] It is remarkable that in the face of so much persecution from former female comrades these women continued to believe in female solidarity.

The Hague Conference

The city of Den Haag (The Hague) in the Netherlands was a symbol of internationalism even during World War I. First selected by Czar Nicholas II in 1899 for a major international meeting of heads of state to find means of averting war (and resulting in the formation at The Hague of the World Court), The Hague became the site of additional meetings dealing with issues of *jus in bello* (what sorts of arms would be allowed in war) and a third world conference on peace that had been scheduled there for 1915. Tragically, by 1915 Europe was at war and that Hague conference never met. An International Conference on Women met instead in 1915. (The Netherlands remained neutral territory in the midst of Europe's expanding warfare.) Tellingly, the warring governments very much opposed the conference, and it was in the face of extraordinary governmental resistance that 1,400 delegates attended the first session and 2,400 attended the last session of that meeting.[35]

Among its accomplishments, the Conference set up the International Committee of Women for Permanent Peace, which spawned national branches and undertook a variety of peace missions during and after the war.

The call to the Hague conference, penned by Aletta Jacobs, herself a Netherlander, carried forward pre-war female internationalism. Pitting female "transnational sanity" against "lethal nationalism," the text read: "We feel strongly that at a time when there is so much hatred among nations, we women must show that we can retain our solidarity and . . . mutual friendship."[36] The Call to the Conference and the Conference's final statement of resolutions reflected both theory and practicality. First, there was the restatement of the traditional "distinctive peace interests" of women; then the "urgency" of female enfranchisement. Principles Six, Seven, and Ten of the Resolutions read, respectively: "War, the ultimate 'ratio' of the statesmanship of men, we women declare to be a madness, possible only to a people intoxicated with a false idea. . . . War is brought about not by peoples of the world who do not desire it, but by groups of individuals representing particular interests."

To be rejected as well was the view that war protects women. Wartime propaganda had made much of soldiers "rescuing" women and children. The authors of the Resolutions insisted that warfare did quite the reverse: "The moral and physical suffering of many women are beyond description. . . . Women raise their voices in commiseration with those women wounded in their deepest sense of womanhood [a reference to rape] and powerless to defend themselves." There are *no* benefits of war as far as women are concerned, according to the final document; only suffering, from sexual violation to widowhood and accompanying poverty, mourning the deaths of sons, and caring for the survivors wounded in body and soul.

Among the most arresting new images the writers invoked, so widespread that in time it grew banal, was that of mothers breeding "cannon fodder." This image had already been adumbrated in the preamble to the founding document of the Women's Peace Party in the United States that stated: "Women are charged with creating each [new] generation; war crushes their dreams. And then women are told to bear more sons to be slaughtered." Vida Goldstein used the "cannon fodder" image to oppose compulsory conscription in Australia.[37] Kate Richards O'Hare in an article entitled "Breed, Mother, Breed," used an even more ugly image depicting women as "brood sows raising sons for the Army to convert into fertilizer."[38] But Crystal Eastman, urging the Women's Peace Party to tap maternal feelings in a series of mothers' mass meetings against conscription, talked about women's "greater regard for life, both intellectually and emotionally."[39] Pro-war feminists were arguing that maternal responsibilities extended beyond the protection of one's immediate family to that of one's nation. Hence their support for the war. Antiwar feminists countered that "genuine protection" of the nation was in conflict with wholesale butchery of that nation's young.[40] The sides were drawn over what was to be the "proper" interpretation of the mother's role. The feminists did not clearly differentiate biological and cultural factors. Most assumed both were involved, as when Vera Brittain declared that social structures "reinforce" men's aggressive and domineering impulses, just as they reinforce women's nurturing ones.[41]

From these observations many, but not all, feminists concluded that peace politics required exclusively female organizations. The question of separatism was raised thus during World War I and haunts women in peace politics still today. Separatism was particularly appealing to American women. There was a greater imbalance of men and women in the American peace movement than elsewhere. In England and France, women held prominent positions in mixed gender groups, but rarely in pre-war America. Moreover, American pacifists tended to be more conservative politically, favoring international cooperation and arbitration. Their war analysis repeatedly stopped short of a fundamental challenge to social structures. With the onset of World War I, male peace activists defected from their cause more quickly than did women, leaving women more visibly in charge of the American peace movement. Even then, women still experienced neglect and marginalization in their mixed gender groups. Male peace activists, in the words of Carrie Chapman Catt, then President of the National American Women's Suffrage Association, "over-masculinized" the peace movement, thus spurring go-it-alone women's peace efforts.[42]

There was yet another argument for separatism. Crystal Eastman defended an all-female peace party on the grounds of the "unique history" of women's peace interests in the United States, women's natural international bonds, and the coincidence of the birth of peace and suffrage politics in the West. Eastman hoped the WPP could canalize this new female political energy for the cause of peace.[43] Only by means of an all-female organization, she thought, could peace women assure their maternal/feminist rationale a place in the discourse.

After The Hague Conference

Socialist women also had an international meeting in 1915 at Berne, Switzerland, a meeting initiated by Germany's Clara Zetkin who argued in her call that since women had no political rights, they bore no responsibility for the war. "If men kill, women must fight for peace."[44] The socialist women departed from their sisters in The Hague by creating a mixed-gender peace initiative. Meanwhile, at a follow-up conference of Hague women held in Zurich, an all-female Women's International League for Peace and Freedom (still in existence) was born.

The war was then over and an armistice had been signed. Accordingly, the immediate impetus for the founding of the WILPF was the eagerness of women to resume ties of friendship and support and to find a way to heal the wounds of war.[45] In contrast to that impulse, in their view, the statesmen meeting at Versailles to forge a final peace draft were thinking only in terms of payment and revenge. WILPF demanded an immediate end to the blockade of Germany and relief for Germany's victims. They assailed the peace accord, pointing out that it would cause economic disaster (for the Germans), exacerbate national hatred, and (with prescience) probably cause another war.[46] Ethel Snowden put it well: "I want neither a German peace, nor a French peace, nor an English peace. I want a people's peace."[47]

It is tempting to seek in feminist internationalism some confirmation for more recent theories about female personality. Surely there is evidence that women favored human integration, "wholeness," relations of attachment and empathy, and set themselves apart from male preferences for dualities, separation, and abstracted human relations. For the women meeting at The Hague, in Berne and in Zurich, these "truths" seemed self-evident. But how do we account for other women who did not wish to attack male propensity for war or to associate maleness with war at all? The masses of women, some feminists explained, were heartsore over the war and unwilling to dishonor male kin who had died. Generous as it was, this interpretation overlooked the martial enthusiasm many women had shown during the war and the harassment and criticism peace women had suffered at their hands.

Conclusion

The failure of most wartime feminist peace advocates to wrestle with the reality of female militarism, and their inordinate faith in enfranchised women's peace commitment, reflect a sentimentality about womanhood that was shared by most men and women. The idea of women as peacemakers continued to be the dominant cultural assumption in the interwar years. Pragmatically, it worked to inspire most women peace campaigners. Women's peace marches and associations continued to proclaim, "It is women's work to be the keepers of the young life in this country," and banners read, "Mothers of England, shall Youth be Slaughtered?"[48]

Influenced by prominent female peace leaders, male politicians presumed a considerable gender gap on issues of war. When, for example in America, President Roosevelt in 1935 hesitated to support neutrality legislation, Representative Fred Sisson of New York told the White House that "thousands and thousands of women's votes have been lost by this stalling."[49]

In retrospect, the power of the peacemaker image to enhance women's self-esteem and peace activism has, if anything, been strengthened by the twentieth-century women's movement, despite the critique by many second wave feminists of the equation of female and maternality. The women's movement's attack on male violence—sexual abuse, rape, wife battering, general criminal assault—is at the marrow of feminist and wider female self-differentiation from men and male institutions. And, yet, short of countenancing a global war, most European and American women, with countless feminists among them, support a strong national military establishment (which women are entering in unprecedented numbers). They applaud their nation's military undertakings (e.g., widespread support for Prime Minister Thatcher's war in the Falklands and for Prime Minister Mitterand's approval of bases for American Cruise and Pershing missiles and for President Reagan's invasion of Granada) and are heartened and enlivened by fighting women in liberation struggles, which they can approve. It is fairly easy to be a nuclear pacifist, but a broader antiwar position involves complex ethical distinctions and choices with which feminist theory has yet sufficiently to grapple.

Notes

1. Francesca Sautman, "Woman as Birth- and Death-Giver in Folk Tradition: A Cross Cultural Perspective," in *Women's Studies* 12 (1986), pp. 213–39.

2. Maxine Molyneux, "Mobilization without Emancipation? Women's Interests, the State, and Revolution in Nicaragua," in *Feminist Studies* 11, 2 (Summer 1985), pp. 226–54. See also Cynthia Enloe, *Does Khaki Become You?* (Boston: South End Press, 1983), chap. 6.

3. Sautman, p. 219. See also Sigmund Freud, "Medusa's Head," *Posthumous Writings* 18 (1955), pp. 273–74; Peggy Reeves Sanday, *Female Power and Male Dominance* (Cambridge: Cambridge University Press, 1981), chap. 5; Mary Douglas, *Purity and Danger* (London: Routledge & Kegan Paul, 1966).

4. Enloe, pp. 118–20; see also Marina Warner's discussion of Athena in *Monuments and Maidens: The Allegory of the Female Form* (New York: Athenaeum, 1985).

5. Natalie Zemon Davis, "Men, Women and Violence, the Rally Day Address," in *Smith Alumnae Quarterly* LXVII, 3 (April 1977), pp. 12–16, esp. p. 14.

6. The fate of the biblical Judith is exemplary. According to Marina Warner, *Monuments and Maidens* (pp. 160–72), in medieval Europe the biblical Judith who saved the Israelites by cunningly arousing the lust of the Assyrian General Holofernes so that she might slay him with his own scimitar, was depicted as a

precursor of Mary, as in the fourteenth-century work, *Speculum Humane Salva-tionist*, where Judith's sexy wiles appear secondary to her virtuous intent. Tellingly, in the sixteenth and seventeenth centuries, Judith's image becomes more enigmatic; her similarities with Salome begin to replace her kinship with Mary. By the nineteenth century, her virtue further recedes, climaxing in Gustav Klimt's 1901 painting of her. Judith and Salome are now totally conflated; Judith gazes at us in the guise of a bejewelled harlot of turn-of-the-century Vienna.

7. Patrick Geddes and J. Arthur Thomson, *The Evolution of Sex* (New York: Scribner, 1890), pp. 44–45, 115–17, 248–49.

8. Mlles. Amelie Gayraud, *Les Jeunes Filles d'Aujourdushi* (Paris: G. Oudin, 1914), p. 205.

9. Elizabeth Cady Stanton, *The Original Feminist Attack on the Bible (The Woman's Bible)* (New York: Arno Press, 1974), p. 22.

10. Sandi Cooper, "The Work of Women in Nineteenth-Century Continental European Peace Movements," in *Peace and Change* 9, 4 (Winter 1984), pp. 19–20.

11. Harold Josephson, ed., *Biographical Dictionary of Modern Peace Leaders* (Westport, Conn.: Greenwood Press, 1985). Numerous names of feminist pacifists could be cited among others: Lisa Gustava Heymann (Germany), Anita Augspurg and Rosa Obermayer Mayreder (Austria), Ellen Kay (Sweden), Virginia Griess-Traut, Marie-Anne Hubertine Auclert, Helen Brion, Eugenie Niboyet, Anne-Madeleine Pelletier, and Maria Verone (France), Laura Emma Jamieson and Agnes Macphail (Canada).

12. Patricia Kay Bidelman, *Pariahs Stand Up! The Founding of the Liberal Feminist Movement in France 1858–1889* (West Port, Conn.: Greenwood Press, 1985).

13. Albert S. Hill, "Severine," in Josephson, ed., p. 874; Olive Schreiner to Louie Ellis, April 19, 1887 in S. C. Cronwright-Schreiner, ed., *The Letters of Olive Schreiner* (London: T. Fisher Unwin Ltd., 1924), pp. 114–15; Cooper, p. 20.

14. Mary Wollstonecraft, *A Vindication of the Rights of Woman* (New York: W. W. Norton, 1967), p. 17. See also the discussion in Jean Bethke Elshtain's, *Meditations on Modern Political Thought* (New York: Praeger, 1986).

15. Barbara Steinson, *American Women's Activism in World War One* (New York: Garland, 1982), pp. 22–23.

16. Linda Schott, "The Woman's Peace Party and the Moral Basis for Women's Pacifism," in *Frontiers* 8, 2 (1985), pp. 18–24.

17. Mari Jo Buhle, *Women and American Socialism, 1870–1920* (Urbana: University of Illinois Press, 1981), pp. 311–13.

18. Occasionally, individual liberal feminists maintained their pacifist position, e.g., Celine Renooz, who published *La Paix Glorieuse*, a brilliant radical feminist critique of militarism and war, in 1917.

19. This complex organizational history can be traced in Charles Sowerwine's

study, *Sisters or Citizens? Women and Socialism in France since 1876*. Unfortunately, Sowerwine's discussion is weak on the intellectual content of these groups and their female leaders.

20. Midge Mackenzie, *Shoulder to Shoulder, a Documentary* (New York: Knopf, 1975), pp. 288. Christabel and Emmeline Pankhurst's radicalism is of a curious kind since conservative and authoritarian elements interlace it.

21. Rachel Strachey, *The Cause: A Short History of the Women's Movements in Great Britain* (London: G. Bell, 1928; London: Virago, 1978), p. 338.

22. Strachey, pp. 340–43.

23. Conwright-Schreiner, ed., *Letters*, p. 327. Olive Schreiner to Emily Hobhouse, June 4, 1913; letter from Emmeline Pankhurst to Eleanor Garrison, June 18, 1914, in Garrison Collection, Sophia Smith Collection, Folder 1684, Box 57.

24. Robert Graves, *Good-bye to All That* (England: Harmondsworth, Penguin Books, 1970), pp. 188–91, quoting "A Mother's Answer to 'A Common Soldier,' " appearing in *The Morning Post*. See Jean Bethke Elshtain, *Women and War* (New York: Basic Books, 1987) for a discussion of the literature of male disillusionment with war.

25. Steinson, p. 179. Malcolm Saunders and Ralph Summy, "One Hundred Years of an Australian Peace Movement, 1885–1984," Part I, *Peace and Change* 10, 3/4 (Fall/Winter 1984), pp. 39–56, esp. pp. 46–47.

26. MacKenzie, p. 290.

27. Steinson, pp. 16–17.

28. Sowerwine, pp. 144–46, 150–51.

29. Bell and Offen, eds., p. 264.

30. Sowerwine, p. 147.

31. Philip S. Foner and Sally M. Miller, eds., *Kate Richards O'Hare: Selected Writings and Speeches* (Baton Rouge and London: Louisiana State University Press, 1982), pp. 16–17.

32. Allen F. Davis, *American Heroine: The Life and Legend of Jane Addams* (Oxford: Oxford University Press, 1973), see chap. 13, "From Saint to Villain." For continued harassment of feminist peace advocates in the 1920s, see Joan M. Jensen, "All Pink Sisters: The War Department and the Feminist Movement in the 1920s," in Scharf and Jensen, eds., *Decades of Our Discontent*.

33. Schreiner, *Letters*, Olive Schreiner to Emily Hobhouse, October 1914 (Westport, Conn.: Greenwood Press, Inc.), p. 341.

34. Jill Liddington, *The Life and Times of a Respectable Rebel: Selina Cooper 1864–1946* (London: Virago Press, 1984), p. 254.

35. Jo Vellacott, "Anti-War Suffragists," *History*, vol. 62 (October 1977), pp. 411–25.

36. Eleanor S. Riemer and John C. Fout, eds., *European Women: A Documentary History* (New York: Schocken, 1980), p. 83.

37. Saunders and Summy, pp. 46–47.

38. Foner and Miller, pp. 11, 16–17.

39. Steinson, p. 263.

40. Schott, p. 20.

41. Vera Brittain, *Lady Unto Woman* (New York: MacMillan, 1953), p. 2.

42. Schott, p. 18. See also Anne Garlin Spencer, Lucia Ames Mead, and Jane Addams's similar views.

43. Cook, pp. 266–68. New York City WPP pamphlet, March 1918.

44. Sowerwine, p. 145.

45. Vellacott, p. 417.

46. Schott, p. 22, cites "Address of the French Women to the German Women," *Four Lights*, June 12, 1919. WPP Papers reel 12.19.

47. Liddington, p. 280. In the same tradition is Virginia Woolf's statement. "My country is the whole world" in *Three Guineas* (New York: Harcourt, Brace and World, 1938) and more recently the title of Barbara Deming's book, *We Are All Part of One Another* (Philadelphia: New Society Publications, 1984).

48. Liddington, p. 409.

49. Lawrence S. Wittner, *Rebels Against War: The American Peace Movement, 1933–1983* (Philadelphia: Temple University Press, 1984), p. 4.

Comments

Sheila Tobias's paper is an act of scholarly excavation. She shows what can be discovered if one possesses an interpretive framework that enables the researcher to notice what might otherwise go unremarked. By bringing the saga of soldiering and citizenship to the present, Tobias shows how military service has functioned as a kind of entitlement for a role in civic life. What is fascinating is the extent to which we still rely on the soldier-citizen connection, and how strongly candidates for public office feel the need to describe themselves in this way.

The reader might take note that the historical constructions Tobias unearths have not yet been raised to the level of explicit political debate. Yet, the issues she addresses are as old as the idea of citizenship in the West. Her essay is a flag of warning, urging us to be alert and aware of the frequency with which war rhetoric is brought into campaigns and shapes our notions of qualification for office.

The essay is also a chapter on the origins of the feminine mystique. Betty Friedan refers generally to the impact of World War II on women. But Tobias shows that the loss of female leadership at the national level occurred just when females were going to need it most, just when they were being swamped by the returning G.I.s. But women who lost their war-jobs were not entitled to retraining or any kind of comparable compensation. That issue never came up because, compared to combat, service in war factories was ancillary.

By 1950, the G.I. bill had transformed higher education by enabling

161

veteran males of all classes to enter universities and enjoy broader educational and career opportunities.

What about the concept of participation in the "searing events" of our time? The feminist movement flourished in the 1960s and 1970s during the protests against an unpopular war. Women were participants with men in the war *against* the war. Their lives were wracked by the same momentous activities. During the Vietnam War, much of the "action" was, in fact, at home. Today, middle-class women of that generation can look into the eyes of the males their age and assume that there is nothing they did or saw politically that the former did not. Those shared experiences serve the cause of women's equality, at least for members of this generation.

Some readers might be discouraged by this essay because the patterns Tobias uncovers between politics and war seem so deeply entrenched. If what Tobias says is true, until there is a change in values that disentitles the warrior—something hard to imagine and perhaps not totally desirable—what is to be the compensatory opportunity for women? Must women capitulate by enlisting in the military? Is there any other form of civic activity that confers as much prestige and status as military service? If so, why has it not emerged with clarity, and within the scope of these essays, what changes are required in our thinking to make legitimate alternate routes to full citizenship?

8

Shifting Heroisms: The Uses of Military Service in Politics

Sheila Tobias

Soon after being nominated Republican candidate for vice president in the summer of 1988, J. Danforth Quayle appeared to be disqualified in the minds of many for not having "served his country" in Vietnam. The issue was clouded by innuendo: that favoritism and family connections had eased Quayle's way into the National Guard during the height of the Vietnam War; and by the contrast between Quayle's draft avoidance and presidential candidate George Bush's frequent references to his own World War II combat record.

In Quayle's 1980 Senate campaign, he listed himself ambiguously as a "Vietnam-era veteran," a phrase (later rescinded) that implied an active duty assignment. But the issue of Quayle's maturity, patriotism, and leadership, in 1988 hinged, at least for the first few weeks of the campaign, on his combat avoidance of nearly twenty years before. Thus, the issue of politics and war service, as well as the contrast between service in Vietnam and service in World War II—the twin subjects of this essay—were raised anew in the campaign of 1988. Grave political consequences still exist for those who choose not to serve in combat and for women who may not serve.

To be sure, women have made great strides in politics, but they remain handicapped because men have one insurmountable advantage—experience in war—that matters a great deal in American politics. Despite the American tradition emphasizing civil control of the military, men with military experience have played a more prominent role in our politics than in other democratic countries. As Samuel Huntington points out, ten of our thirty-three presidents (as of 1957) had been generals, and military exploits have helped others into office (e.g., Teddy Roosevelt and John F. Kennedy).[1] By contrast, England since 1789 has had only one prime minister, the Duke of Wellington, who was a successful military leader. The thesis presented here is that during periods when heroism in warfare and leadership in politics are strongly linked, women will experience real obstacles to their political ambitions. To explore this hypothesis two periods will be compared: the period immediately after World War II when returning G.I.s made claim to leadership in Congressional elections; and the 1986 elections when Vietnam veterans were asserting their claims. The essay ends with a consideration of Geraldine Ferraro's 1984 vice-presidential candidacy, which may have foundered on the issue of women's inexperience in war; for in the minds of the voters, she would have been, as vice president, a heartbeat away not only from the presidency, but also from becoming commander-in-chief of the armed forces.

Early in the 1986 election season, "Duke" Tully, the legendary publisher and king-maker in the state of Arizona, had to resign his several offices and disappear from the political scene when it was revealed that for nearly thirty years he had lied about his military service in the U.S. Air Force and about the decorations he proudly wore from his tours of duty in Korea and Vietnam.[2] Later that year, Royall Switzer, Republican candidate for governor of Massachusetts, gave up *his* candidacy when it was disclosed that he had "embellished" his military service. Switzer claimed to have been a Vietnam combat veteran, a captain in the Special Forces, a Green Beret. In truth, he had only served in the peacetime army with the rank of sergeant and merely visited Vietnam once in 1962.[3]

In 1986, eight Vietnam veterans were holding or running for major public office. Unlike Tully and Switzer, their resumés were legitimate, but the fact of their candidacies, a bare eleven years after America's most unpopular war had been brought to a much-delayed and brutal close, raises questions about the degree to which participation in war continues—even into the nuclear age—to be a test of political leadership, a test that women are virtually certain to fail.

The importance of this connection emerges in a comparison of the electoral campaigns of World War II with those of the 1970s and 1980s. The two American wars were very different—World War II being broadly supported, the Vietnam War was mired in controversy. In the case of the post-World War II campaigns, not surprisingly, references were commonly made to war-related exploits and "duty" willingly performed. In the post-Vietnam War elections, the claim to leadership appears to reside not so much in the war's clarity of purpose and its resounding success (as with World War II), but in its ambiguities. Still, war service is presented to the voter as an appropriate apprenticeship for leadership, the ultimate school for those aspiring to public office.

In 1946, the political claims of women *as a class* were not yet articulated. In the 1980s, however, the fact that women's role extends beyond the family is widely recognized. Still, in both periods, women candidates for public office have not served in war. Hence their claim to leadership, quite as much as their right to "citizenship," must be posited elsewhere.[4] While individual women, such as Indira Gandhi, Margaret Thatcher, and Golda Meir, have demonstrated their ability, and perhaps more importantly, their willingness, even eagerness, to lead their nations in war, they all have achieved political power by other than military prowess. In this country, to the extent that Vietnam or any American war is seen to be a legitimate, even an appropriate apprenticeship for politics, lack of military experience could reduce the political currency of women candidates. Whether it does or does not bears directly and even urgently on feminist theory and politics.[5]

The analysis begins in irony. According to conventional wisdom, modern war was liberating for women. And indeed, as many scholars have documented, World War II did free American women from certain role restrictions and social clichés in mobilizing them for war work at home and some limited military and nursing service abroad.[6] But there was also tremendous resistance to change in gender ideologies and women's status, especially in the military. So, from a political perspective, just as women were being "liberated," they were also being deprived of the most searing experience of their generation: military service, especially front-line combat abroad. Their absence from war may well have caused the resurgence of gender stratification at the end of the 1940s, called by Betty Friedan, the "feminine mystique."

It would be an enormous exaggeration to suggest that in the political

165

rhetoric of the 1946 campaigns there were "feminist" or even "anti-feminist" themes. But there was a war-related intergenerational struggle that would affect women's political fortunes both in the short and in the longer run. Younger men, trying to wrest seats from older incumbents, used their war experience to compensate for their youth and political immaturity. It is easy to show that the political fortunes of certain men, notably Dwight Eisenhower and John Kennedy, were helped enormously by the war. Whether younger women would have benefited too had they fought in World War II, is a speculation that goes beyond the scope of this essay. The experience of women during colonial struggles in Cuba, Algeria, and China suggests the contrary: that after a period of thankfulness to all who cooperated in overthrowing the foreign power, the revolutionary government returns to a policy of female exclusion. In Europe, where an entire generation of men was lost in the two world wars, women's political participation first rises and then falls as the demographics change and the next generation moves in. And in Israel, where women serve in the military (though not in combat), they remain greatly underrepresented in political leadership.

The hypothesis presented here is not that women must (or ought to) go to war to win their place in the political process; rather, it is that popular wars are bad for women's political claims and that even unpopular wars may disserve them.

How, then, are we to account for intermittent periods of women's political success? From the point of view of this analysis, one could reason that if no subsequent war were to be as popular as World War II, women would not be inhibited in reaching for political power. This would explain why a Second Wave of Feminism appeared in the 1960s and 1970s when America's war in Korea was not much celebrated and the war in Vietnam was deeply divisive. If a war lacks consensual support in a particular historical period, warriors will not be much admired. Thus the conventional wisdom: no heroes, no heroism. The reverse may also be true: no heroism, no heroes. Women, running for political office during such a time will, then, not be particularly disadvantaged by their absence from war. On the contrary, one could argue (as I did during this period), that middle-class activist women of the 1960s and 1970s *did* share in the searing events of their time (which were, incidentally, very war-like) in their struggle against the war in Vietnam and for civil rights.

Toward the end of the 1970s and the beginning of the 1980s, however, a number of Vietnam veterans began to emerge in politics. While these candidates range in political coloration from unreconstructed supporters of that war (Jeremiah Denton, R-Ala.) to antiwar activists (John Kerry, D-Mass.), their campaign rhetoric represents but a variant on a much older theme. It was not duty or physical heroism alone that was demonstrated on the battle field, but a moral ripening caused by the ambiguity of Vietnam, the troubling experience there, and the advantage of that perspective and its discipline in qualifying them for public office. Two Vietnam veterans, Denton and Senator John McCain (R-Ariz.), first became known when they were prisoners of war, hardly "successful" as warriors in the narrowest sense of that term, yet "heroes" nonetheless. One, John Kerry, made his name opposing the war. There are no comparable cases after World War II in which ex-POWs or war-protesters could have capitalized on these particular "war experiences" when running for office. While the parameters of heroism may change, the basic phenomenology appears to remain the same: war is the vital playing field, the grooming ground, for politics.

The Elections of 1946

The year 1946 witnessed the first postwar national election. One-third of the Senate was at stake as well as the entire House of Representatives, and many governorships, state legislatures, and other local offices as well. The Democratic party had enjoyed nearly fourteen years of popular New Dealism, and a bipartisan wartime collaboration that deferred interparty dissension. But the honeymoon with the Republicans and with a depression-wracked citizenry was over. In 1946, the Democratic party finally experienced defeat. But it was not the only political sector to lose. The newspapers did not notice, but a feminist historian must: of the eleven women who had served in the House during (and before) the war, only five were returned. Two more women, first elected that year, would join them in the 80th Congress. The turning point for women in American politics was 1946, an event that would not be repeated until well into the 1970s.[7]

Only in one or two instances did World War II veterans defeat these women directly. But even where the contest was not one-on-one, seasoned women lost and young men won. The year 1946 was a good year for returning veterans like John F. Kennedy, Richard M. Nixon, and Gerald R. Ford (first elected in 1948 but part of this World War II veteran "class" of politicians). For these men, the way to the White House was paved first by war and then by their early post-war elections to Congress.[8]

Congressmen Go to War

Not all the veterans who ran for office in 1946 were in fact young. Jacob Javits, Republican from New York, won his first Congressional race in the 21st district in 1946. He had served with the Chemical Warfare Division in both the European and Pacific theaters and had won the Legion of Merit and the Army Commendation ribbons. He had entered the Army in 1942, at forty-two years of age as a major, and was discharged with the rank of lieutenant colonel three years later.

Joseph McCarthy achieved intense notoriety and power a decade after the war by investigating "un-American activities" while a member of the Senate's permanent investigations sub-committee. But in 1946, he was just a returning G.I. ("Tailgunner Joe" as he liked to call himself), looking to restart his political career. He had been elected Wisconsin circuit judge in 1939 from which post, although protected from the draft, he had resigned in 1942 to join the Marines. Biographer Jack Anderson believes he was trying to compete with a Milwaukee mayor, his chief competitor as a rising young Republican, who resigned to join the Navy. Whatever his motives, McCarthy's semifictionalized version of his war service begins with his recruitment. He claimed to have enlisted as a "buck private" but actually had a commission. Although he claimed to have been wounded, and for that wound requested and received, in 1952, a Purple Heart, he actually broke his leg by accident. Although he claimed to have been a pilot, he was only a passenger on combat aircraft, occupying an empty tailgunner's seat. Although he claimed to have done a lot of shooting at the enemy, others say he generally unloaded his tailgun at the end of a run on coconuts.[9]

Sometimes there were "14 dive-bombing missions;" sometimes "17 official missions in the South Pacific;" sometimes even thirty. The point is (and was then) that McCarthy recognized the value of war service for his political career. While still in the service, he ran for Senate in 1944 and lost; he tried again—all the while building up his service record—and ran successfully in 1946.

It is interesting to examine the dossiers of the half dozen men who entered the military from elected seats in Congress.

The United States Constitution unambiguously requires an elected representative to resign from office upon entering (or reentering) the military, and prohibits a career military officer (unless and until he retires) from running for public office at all. But it was not at all clear at the beginning of World War II that this Constitutional requirement would

168

be enforced by the president. The war was so popular that there was a rash of enlistments on the part of Congressmen and Senators when war was declared, and it was not until mid-1942, when Franklin Roosevelt actually invoked the Constitutional requirement, that his legislators found themselves having to choose between Washington and the front. After June 1942, certain Congressmen and Senators resigned their military commissions to resume their seats and to run for reelection. Certain others resigned their Congressional seats instead.[10] Among those who resigned from Congress were James Edward Van Zandt (R-Pa.), Albert Baumhart (R-Ohio), Robert Secrest (D-Ohio), Will Rogers, Jr. (D-Calif.), and Henry Cabot Lodge (R-Mass.). All were returned to Congress in due course.[11]

The case of Lyndon Baines Johnson captures the politics of war-time service. During Johnson's campaign for an unexpired Senate term in 1940, he promised his would-be constituents that "If the day ever comes when my vote must be cast to send your boy to the trenches [a reference to the fighting environment of World War I], that day Lyndon Johnson will leave his Senate seat and go with him."[12] This promise was repeated in every major speech Johnson made that year in what biographer Robert Caro calls, even then, "hawkish Texas." Johnson was already a House member in 1940 when he ran (unsuccessfully) for that Senate seat. Texas did not require an incumbent to resign if he ran for another office, so when the "day came" on December 7, 1941, Johnson had no choice. He had already joined the Navy and had himself commissioned Lieutenant Commander in the Naval Reserve sometime during the summer of 1941. On December 11, 1941, he was placed on active duty, at the age of 33. Rising in the House on that day he said, "Mr. Speaker: I ask unanimous consent for an indefinite leave of absence," and got it.[12]

Johnson may have been trying to have his political cake and eat it, too. In May 1942, he put his name on the ballot for reelection to the House. On June 26, Roosevelt issued the directive mentioned before, giving Congressmen on active duty the choice either to resign from the service or from Congress. While Van Zandt, Baumhart, Secrest, and later Lodge would choose fighting for their country over legislating for the duration of the war, on July 17, three weeks after the President's directive, Lyndon Johnson resigned from the military and came back home.

It would be wrong to infer from these comings and goings that the public was of one mind in terms of its delegates' obligations. Indeed, there was so much criticism of Lodge for being both Senator and soldier during 1942 and 1943, that the Senator felt he had to resign from

Congress if he was to be able to run again after the war. Later, he would say of his decision, "I was only doing my duty, like millions of others."[14]

Also indicative of the spirit of the period are two other quotations preserved for history by Lodge's biographer and published in 1947. When Lodge went back to war for the second time in 1944, he wanted a guarantee, before formally resigning from the Senate, that he would have a combat position and not be assigned some "chairborne role," as he put it. "Cabot," FDR is alleged to have said upon saying good-by to the Senator, "That's splendid. I wish I were going with you."[15] Later Senator Vandenberg was to write of Lodge's departure:[16]

> In all my twenty years in the Senate, no single episode ever thrilled me so deeply as the quiet drama which saw young Lodge in his usual Senate seat on a late afternoon in February and the next morning heard his resignation read at the desk after his overnight departure to the fighting front. It was typical of him. He made no valedictory speech to his colleagues and there was no band to escort him to the station. He just quit the Senate and went to war.

Nixon vs. Voorhis

The wartime service of Richard Nixon, like Nixon's entire career, is mired in the manipulation of public perception. Brought up by a Quaker mother in a Quaker town and educated at Whittier, a Quaker college, Nixon's departure for armed service during World War II represented a break from what must have been a strong family resistance to war. After the war, in his first race for Congress in 1946, Nixon's opponent was Jerry Voorhis, a Democrat who had been first elected in 1936 and had served in Congress throughout the war. Taking advantage of his war service, Nixon circulated flyers during the campaign depicting Voorhis as one who "stayed safely behind the front in Washington" while Nixon was the "clean, forthright American who fought in defense of his country in the stinking mud and jungles of the Solomons."[17]

As Garry Wills, one of Nixon's several biographers, wrote in 1969 long before Watergate permanently fixed history's perception of the man, Nixon's group was "not exactly a combat unit."[18]

> It is true that Bougainville [where Nixon was stationed] was bombed while he was there, but his assignment was to move from island to island *behind*

the line of advance, part of the lengthening umbilical cord of supply. He got to know his fellows, not in foxholes (as he would later claim), but across the table during endless war-time poker games. Later, much later, Nixon modified his own claims. Speaking to a reporter on NBC on September 23, 1952, Nixon said more modestly: "My service record was not a particularly unusual one. I went to the South Pacific. I guess I'm entitled to a couple of battle stars. I got a couple of letters of commendation, but I was just there when the bombs were falling, and then I returned."[19]

Winners and Losers: Women Running for Congress in 1946

The 79th Congress ended in 1946, thirty years after Jeanette Rankin broke the all-male barrier by becoming the first female member of the House of Representatives. At that time, eleven women were members of the House, three of them had been selected to fill the unexpired terms of their husbands who had died in office; there were no women in the Senate.

The total number of women appointed or elected to both houses of Congress between 1916 and 1946 was only forty-one.[20] But fifteen women felt strong enough to run for election or re-election in 1946. Of the eleven women incumbents going into the race, however, only five would be re-elected: three chose not to run; one was defeated in the primary process; two were defeated in the election. Two women who were not incumbents in the 79th Congress won new seats in the 80th. While not a rout, the results signified a downturn for women in Congress.

In an election post-mortem, Malvina Lindsay, writing in the *Washington Post* on November 8, 1946, attributed the women's loss neither to prejudice nor to a voter preference for returning servicemen. Rather, she wrote of the "conservative political and social trend now sweeping the nation."[21] Comparing the poor showing of women in the American Congress (seven) to that of the French Assembly (thirty) and the Japanese Diet (thirty-eight), Lindsay attributed their success in Europe and Japan to the success of liberalism there. She wrote:

> The great majority of [U.S.] women candidates, both in the primaries and in the general election, were political liberals. So far, women in this country and in Europe have shown most political activity in liberal groups. In Europe they have reaped the political advantage of the general leftist trend.

In the U.S. they went down with the liberals, she concludes. But not all women running for Congress were liberals, or even Democrats. Who

171

were these women? What brought them to defeat? Can we find any pattern in what happened to them in 1946?

Tables I and II tell the story of the winners and losers in 1946.

Taft Douglas vs. Stratton

In one race, the woman candidate believed it necessary to identify herself with a returning soldier—her husband—even though she could not claim to have fought in the war herself. The actress, Emily Taft Douglas of Illinois, and her husband, Paul Douglas, had an unusual marriage. Both had political ambitions, and together they had a kind of ten-year plan to run alternately for Congress from their home state. Initially, it was Paul Douglas who was to stand first as the at-large candidate from Illinois. But war came, and he enlisted as a private in the Marines. He spent several years overseas in Asia and in June 1945 was discharged with the rank of Lt. Colonel wearing a Bronze Star. While he was away, Emily Taft Douglas ran successfully for Congress in 1944. Thus, when the election of 1946 rolled around, she was the incumbent, and her husband was an important supporting member of her reelection team.

Emily Taft Douglas had her work cut out for her during the 1946 election. Her opponent, William Grant Stratton, later governor of Illinois, was not an incumbent, but he had been in Congress, in the very seat Mrs. Douglas now held, prior to World War II. He had also held the office of State Treasurer from 1943 to 1944, and then gave up this office to enlist in the Navy in 1945. The delay in his service may have been the result of his personal politics. Prior to the outbreak of hostilities, Stratton had been an isolationist. Only after four years of war did he decide to enlist. Thus, returning after but one year of service, Stratton was a veteran without combat experience. His opponent's husband was, however, a decorated Marine—a fact that the Douglases tried to exploit to their advantage.

Mrs. Douglas focused her campaign on the needs of peace. She worried openly about the "bomb" and talked at length of the hazards of a boom-and-bust economy.[22] Gender loyalty could not be taken for granted in 1946. Several women's groups came out against her candidacy, some largely Republican in membership, and a group calling itself "Housewives against Scarcity" supported Douglas's opponent, Stratton.[23] Meanwhile, to counter Stratton's appeal to veterans, Mrs. Douglas unabashedly associated herself with her husband's war experience. He usually ap-

172

Table I   Women Incumbents in the 79th Congress

Name	D/R	State	Win/Lose	Remarks
Luce	R	Conn.	No run	Personal reasons alleged.
Sumner	R	Ill.	No run	
Norton	D	N.J.	Wins	Pro-labor in working-class district. Easy win.
Rogers	R	Mass.	Wins	Strong Republican district.
Bolton	R	Ohio	Wins	Strong Republican district.
Smith	R	Me.	Wins	Strong Republican district.
H. Douglas	D	Calif.	Wins	Loses to Nixon in 1950.
Mankin	D	Ga.	Loses	Lost primary; also a write-in. Finally lost to a veteran of WW I.
E. Douglas	D	Ill.	Loses	Lost to WW II veteran.
Woodhouse	D	Conn.	Loses	Entire Connecticut delegation loses.
McMillan	R	Ill.	Wins	Ran vs. Goldman. Only 1946 race between two women.
Pratt	D	N.C.	No run	Appointed to office only six months before.

Table II   Women Newcomers in the 1946 Elections

Lusk	D	N.M.	Wins	No incumbent.
St. George	R	N.Y.	Wins	Strong Republican district.
Goldman	D	Ill.	Loses	To incumbent.
Falvey	D	Mass.	Loses	J. F. Kennedy, WW II veteran, won.
Murray	R	Va.	Loses	To incumbent.
Sharp	D	Mass.	Loses	To incumbent.
Hughes	D	Tx.	Loses	To military academy graduate.
Afflis	D	Ind.	Loses	To incumbent.
Laisli	R	N.Y.	Loses	To incumbent.
Watson	R	Okla.	Loses	Carl Albert, WW II veteran.
Barry	D	N.Y.	Loses	WW II Navy veteran.

Note: The three women incumbents who ran and lost, lost to veterans. Of the nine women newcomers who ran and lost, all lost either to an incumbent or to a veteran, except for Sarah Hughes. The fact that Edith Rogers, who won reelection, had a long history of working for veterans' benefits is also telling. Rogers had been the "President's Representative in Charge of Assistance to Disabled Veterans" under Presidents Harding, Coolidge, and Hoover. While in Congress, she had co-sponsored the creation of the Women's Army Auxiliary Corps (WAC) in 1940. Hence her identification with the military was secure.

peared with her in full uniform, and in her newspaper advertisements, she ran a picture of herself, her husband, and their thirteen-year-old daughter over the caption: "Congressman-at-Large Emily Taft Douglas (left) shown with her husband, Major Paul Douglas, who has just returned after four years of Marine Corps service, and their 13-year-old daughter, Judy."[24]

Late in the campaign, Paul Douglas began to wear civilian clothes.[25] But the identification of the Douglases, one with another, and both with the recently concluded war in the Pacific, was meant to be a key factor in their campaign strategy. Still, Mrs. Douglas lost to Stratton on November 5th.

Kennedy vs. Falvey

John Fitzgerald Kennedy was twenty-nine years old in 1946 and had never held a civilian job when he decided to become one of ten candidates for the open Democratic seat in the 11th District. Catherine Falvey was another aspirant for that seat—not his most formidable opponent, but the race is of interest because Falvey was a woman lawyer, a former state representative, and a WAC major still in active service. Wearing her dress whites while campaigning, Falvey referred to Kennedy as the "poor little rich kid," but she and eight others did not properly estimate what power, wealth, and charisma could do.

"I realize," Kennedy said in a post-election interview, "that people voted for me because of the things I *might* do rather than for anything I have done. Getting the veteran a job and a place to live is something the voters probably thought I might help on. Perhaps if elected, I can do something about it. [For this reason] the veterans and their mothers, most of them without experience in politics, were, I believe, the backbone of my campaign."[26] Later in the interview, there was a reference to the death of Kennedy's brother Joe in World War II and the political mantle falling to the younger brother.

Kennedy ran unabashedly on his war record. According to the private polls funded by his father, this is what people were interested in. At one point during the campaign, Kennedy headquarters mailed to every registered Democratic voter in the 11th District a copy of the condensed *Readers' Digest* version of John Hersey's *New Yorker* article about Kennedy's heroism. Much local newspaper space was devoted to his war record, and in nearly every public address, Kennedy told the PT-109 story over again, always in the third person, as if it were happening to someone else. "The commanding officer of the PT-109, believing it to be a Japanese destroyer, turned the bow of his PT to meet a torpedo attack."[27]

Ambassador Kennedy, John F.'s father, according to the Lasky biography, believed that the election of 1946 would be determined by the men and women "who'd experienced the war as a jumping-off point in their lives."[28] Perhaps he was right. In a district in which there were thirty-seven different ethnic nationalities, "veteran's status" was a common denominator. In the end, Kennedy outpolled all his opponents, winning 42 percent of the vote. Catherine Falvey came in fifth.

Dave Powers, campaign director for JFK's 1946 race, recently acknowledged that the decision to emphasize the war record was based on a more sophisticated analysis and strategy than simply offering the voters an opportunity to vote for the soldier who made it home. In an interview broadcast on Boston's WBZ "Evening Magazine" in the spring of 1986, Powers said that at the time their biggest fear was that Kennedy's wealthy Harvard background would be a serious liability in a largely working-class district. To guard against this, they developed a particular strategy in regard to the war record. The plan was to emphasize not just the heroism but the *ordinariness* of Kennedy's war experience, to depict Kennedy as a man who had fought side by side with working-class boys. The campaign staff would regularly march the candidate with veterans in parades and have him speak to veterans' groups, not only as their candidate but as one of their mates. John Kerry (one of the Vietnam veterans in office in 1986), also from a privileged background, is said to have used a similar strategy with similar effect.

Vietnam

For a long time after the War in Vietnam was over, few expected that many national political leaders would emerge out of that war, both because of its unpopularity and because of the massive middle-class evasion of service in that conflict. For the most part, as far as the Americans were concerned, the war was fought by career officers and largely ethnic, Southern Appalachian, and minority enlisted men.[29] Still, by the 1980s, a number of Vietnam veterans began to run successfully for political office.

175

It is difficult to date with any precision when attitudes toward Vietnam veterans began to change for the better. The "Vietnam Veterans Against the War" was the first organization to surface during the 1960s, and John Kerry, now the junior Senator from Massachusetts, came out early with a collection of photographs and personal statements by soldiers in Vietnam published as *The New Soldier*.[30]

Soon, organizations of Vietnam veterans were being coordinated nationally. Later, public sentiment flowed their way when the tragic effects of Agent Orange, among other toxic substances used in the war, began to be assessed. By 1982 when the Vietnam War Memorial was dedicated in Washington, D.C., Americans would feel just as much reverence and sympathy for the Vietnam War's dead as for those of World Wars I and II. *Newsweek* called 1982 a "good year for Vietnam Vets."[31] Still, there was little electoral activity among Vietnam veterans until 1980. John Kerry is the exception. Kerry was on the "right side" of the protest, and his activism gave him the name recognition and respect that translates, certainly in Massachusetts where he ran first for the House and in 1984 for the Senate, into political power.

By 1986, however, a number of Vietnam veterans had surfaced in national politics (including one, the former governor of the state of Nebraska, who ran in 1988 for the Senate). What is interesting about these men is that they share neither party affiliation nor significantly similar political points of view. They are not even in agreement on the Vietnam War. Some, like John Kerry, took early and forceful stands against that war. Others, most notably Jeremiah Denton (R-Ala.) and John McCain (R-Ariz.), do not regret either their military service or the conduct of the war itself. While the military service of the cohort varies from career-long to two-year stints, what unites them is the shared theme of their official biographies: how military service, whatever the ultimate political meaning they take from that experience, provides background and political legitimacy—the best way to spend at least some part of their youth.[32]

The political biographies of those eight Vietnam veterans in politics set the stage for the most explicit rendering of the issue of women, war, and American politics in recent times: the 1984 strategic Ferraro-Bush debate in which a woman's competence in military, strategic, and international affairs was publicly challenged not only because she was a woman, but because she had never participated in war.

176

Vietnam Veterans in Politics

In 1986, Jeremiah Denton failed reelection to the Senate. One of the Republican Senators elected in the sweep of 1980 who President Reagan hoped would be returned, Denton's performance had not much to do with his prisoner-of-war status in Vietnam. Nonetheless his campaign relied heavily on that prior history. Over his signature in a widely-circulated fund-raising letter, distributed nationally early in 1986, appeared the following description of the election campaign he saw ahead:

> Although I endured seven and one-half years of captivity as a POW in North Vietnam, my upcoming reelection campaign presents me with the toughest challenge of my life. Back then, as every day dawned, I was forced to summon the strength and spirit to save my life—to make it one more day. But the issues confronting us today involve not only my life but the lives of my family, your family, and those of men and women across our great nation . . . courage, compassion, moral values, fiscal sanity and a strong national defense.[33]

In 1986, Denton was not a young man. A graduate of the Naval Academy, he had been a career naval officer since the 1940s, entering active duty just after the end of World War II. After he retired from the Navy in 1977, he became executive assistant to the president of a college, his first civilian job. In 1978, he ran successfully for the House from Alabama, a position from which he ran for Senate in 1980, becoming the first Alabama Republican to win state-wide office. He received nationwide attention during a 1965 press interview arranged by the North Vietnamese. During the interview he blinked out in Morse code the word "torture," giving the American government its first indication that American prisoners were being tortured. Later he said he was tortured both before and after that interview.

John McCain, another POW, was first elected to the House of Representatives from Arizona in 1982, one year after he moved to the state only, his detractors say, in order to run for public office. Like Denton, he was discharged from the Navy, having endured POW confinement in North Vietnam for seven and one-half years. In 1985, when Barry Goldwater, long-time Republican Senator from Arizona, announced his retirement, Congressman McCain was unopposed for his party's nomination for that seat. Unlike Denton, McCain won his Senate race in 1986.

177

But like Denton, he frequently refers to his wartime experiences as bomber pilot and POW as having "matured" him.

McCain's is an interesting case because he might have had a considerable Navy career had not the North Vietnamese shot him down. Both his father and grandfather were admirals, and he might have achieved that same rank himself had he not been captured. Later, working as a Naval liaison in the office of Senator John Tower (R-Tex.), McCain was urged to find himself a state in which to run for office himself. He first tried Florida, and when he could not find a district there in which to run, he moved to Arizona.

McCain's opponent in the 1986 Arizona Senate race had never served in the military. While McCain did not exploit that difference, his television commercials displayed him limping off the plane that had brought him back from Vietnam. Talking to voters, he said: "I wasn't drafted. I wanted to serve." And, as for his bad luck in being shot down, he played it "cool": "As they say in Vegas, you play your cards, you take your chances."[34]

Senator Larry Pressler (R-S.Dak.) served neither as a professional soldier nor draftee in Vietnam. The son of a South Dakota farm family, Pressler was on a Rhodes scholarship in England in 1966, when he volunteered for two years of Vietnam war duty. Whether he was motivated by a sense of obligation since his age-mates were fighting and dying on his behalf, or whether he felt that voluntary service in Vietnam would support a future political career, Pressler returned from Vietnam to complete the prepolitical academic program that would all but guarantee him a successful entry into politics: an M.A. from the John F. Kennedy School of Government at Harvard, and a J.D. from the Harvard Law School in 1971.

One is tempted to describe Denny Smith (R-Oreg.) as "to the manor" born. An officer in the U.S. Air Force for ten years, where he flew 180 combat missions in a single year, he was decorated with the Air Medal with six oak leaf clusters before resigning from the Air Force to become chief executive officer of his family's newspaper corporation. He ran successfully for Congress in 1980 and was reelected in 1982, 1984, and 1986. The son of a former Governor of Oregon and a family that publishes a number of local newspapers in the state, he could easily have used the family business to help launch his political career. But instead of going into the newspaper business, Smith became a military and, later, a civilian pilot. It is not clear whether the newspaper career would have brought him to national office sooner than his years in the military. But

178

it is clear that his years in the military did not hurt, and his military service made it possible for him to be critical of defense spending. In Congress he is known as a "cheap hawk."

A somewhat similar role is played in the politics by Vietnam veteran Bob Kerrey (not to be confused with Senator John Kerry of Massachusetts), Governor of Nebraska from 1982 to 1986, and a candidate for Senate in 1988. But unlike Smith, Kerrey is not simply critical of defense spending but of the entire Selective Service System and even of the Veterans of Foreign Wars (VFW). During his 1982 election campaign, Kerrey was criticized for his efforts to organize a Vietnam veterans group independent of the local Nebraska VFW and for his notion of a required "universal service," not necessarily military in function.[35]

Partly because of the confusion of his name with antiwar activist John Kerry of Massachusetts, Bob Kerrey's campaign for governor was haunted by allegations that he had once thrown his Vietnam war medals into a coffin during an anti-draft rally. However, Kerrey was virtually attack-proof on these issues. Wounded in Vietnam during a Navy commando raid in 1969, he spent eight months with other wounded men in veterans' hospitals. He talks about these experiences not without bitterness: "I never dreamed explosive charges could do such damage to flesh and leave the body to survive," he said more than once during his 1982 campaign. "The ward was full of the refuse of that war. We were its end product."[36]

Still, during the 1982 campaign, his opponent, Governor Thone of Nebraska, predicted that Kerrey's campaign "would founder when people found out he dropped medals into a coffin at the rally."[37] But Thone was wrong. While Kerrey's response tends to be low-key when his position on military issues is challenged, the fact that he won a Medal of Honor in Vietnam gives him, it seems, license to take unpopular military stands. Kerrey himself does not talk much about his Medal of Honor, but it is mentioned in all his campaign literature, and his physical disability from the loss of the lower part of one leg in battle, is a visual reminder of his war service.

Even before Dan Quayle's putative draft avoidance surfaced during the 1988 Presidential campaign, the public knew quite well which of the primary candidates had fought for his country, and where. Democrats Bruce Babbitt and Jesse Jackson and Republican Jack Kemp had been neither inductees nor volunteers. All other candidates served their country either in World War II (Haig, Dole, Bush, and Simon), Korea (Robertson), or Vietnam (Gephardt and Gore). To counter the "wimp factor" in his public image, Bush relied on his dramatic bail-out from a B-

29 that, at the age of nineteen, he was piloting in the Pacific Theatre; Haig relied on his "leadership" as a career officer during three of America's wars; Dole relied on his paralyzed left arm, a grim reminder of years in hospitals and the loss of his first love, athletics. Of the Vietnam veterans, Albert Gore, Jr., as it became known during his campaign, was initially opposed to America's role in that war but finally joined up for a two-year rotation in order to appease his father's political advisers who feared that his nonparticipation would hurt his father's reelection campaign in 1970. Gore joined, served in Vietnam, and his father lost anyway.

Gore is one of a category of Vietnam veterans that includes Senator Tom Harkin (D-Iowa) for whom Vietnam war service occurred briefly and represented neither a career (as in the cases of Denton, McCain, and Smith) nor major milestone (as in the cases of Pressler, Kerry, and Kerrey). Gore enlisted and served for two years. Harkin went to college on an ROTC scholarship and spent five years in the Navy as part of his contract. For two of those years, he ferried disabled jet aircraft out of Vietnam. In his 1984 Senatorial campaign, Harkin was opposed by another Vietnam combat veteran who disparaged Harkin's war record on the grounds that, while Harkin's mission had been dangerous, he had not technically been in combat, i.e., under enemy fire.

These varied biographies make very clear that service in war gives veterans a stock of political capital that they can use at will. Whether as career military, enlisted men, or draftees, they can claim familiarity with the military in addition to personal sacrifice and patriotism. The voters will accept a retired professional soldier as an appropriate political representative. There appears to be little negative fallout from military service, even service in an unpopular war. Rather, there is a halo effect and an assumption of leadership quality. As retiring Senator Barry Goldwater said in his 1986 endorsement of Evan Mecham, then candidate for Governor of Arizona and a former Air Force officer like himself, "You know a man when you know him in the air," meaning at the controls of a military plane.[38]

But how do you know a woman? And how can she demonstrate her experience, her patriotism, and most important, her competence in matters of foreign and military policy, when service in the armed forces is not part of her background? Geraldine Ferraro, Democratic candidate for vice-president in 1984, found out how difficult this is.

Ferraro vs. Bush

It was the second of the much-touted presidential debates of the 1984 election. This time, the vice-presidential candidates were in the spotlight.

Ferraro was trying to maintain the slight debating advantage Walter Mondale had won for the team during his first encounter, one week before, with President Reagan. First came George Bush's patronizing treatment of "Mrs. Ferraro". In a discussion of the terrorist attack on American marines in Lebanon, Ferraro had asked: "Are we going to take proper precautions before we put Americans in situations where they are in danger?" to which Bush had rejoined, "Let me help you with the difference, Mrs. Ferraro, between Iran and Lebanon."

Then came the final, and what Ferraro, reflecting on the debate two years later in her official autobiography, called "the inevitable question" from a reporter at the debate:[39]

> Congresswoman Ferraro, you have had little or no experience in military matters and yet you might find yourself someday Commander-in-Chief of the armed forces. How can you convince the American people and the potential enemy that you would know what to do to protect the nation's security, and do you think in any way that the Soviets might be tempted to try to take advantage of you simply because you are a woman?

Ferraro didn't hesitate as she recalls: "Are you saying that I would have to have fought in a war in order to love peace?" She went on:[40]

> Equating military experience with the ability to defend our country is about as valid as saying you have to be black in order to despise racism, that you'd have to be female in order to be offended by sexism. . . . If I were in a position of leadership when the Soviet Union were to challenge our country militarily, the Russians would be assured that they would be met with swift, concise, and certain retaliation.

The last sentence was clearly planned to eliminate any notion that the lady was a wimp.

In his closing statement that evening, Bush returned to the theme. He stressed his experiences in World War II as a qualification (Ferraro's later interpretation) for keeping the peace.[41]

> Yes, I did serve in combat. I was shot down when I was a young kid, scared to death. And all that day I saw friends die, but that heightened my convictions about peace.

Note that Bush did not depict himself as "cool" or even as heroic. The important point he made and wanted the viewers thoroughly to appreciate, was that he was *there*.

181

Ferraro's conclusion, two years later:[42]

What a pointless resumé for leadership, excluding half the population. If you hadn't fought at the Halls of Montezuma, ran the argument, you couldn't understand the need for peace on the shores of Tripoli.

The issue, as Ferraro recalls, did not stop with the debate. Three days later Marvin Kalb on "Meet the Press" asked candidate Ferraro if she thought she was "strong enough" to push the button. If her candidacy as a woman were being judged the same as a man's, she asked in turn, would she still have to answer questions like that? The question of "button pushing," Ferraro argued, was such a simplistic one. The discussion was never about[43]

whether force should be used only when every other avenue is exhausted or whether or not I had the knowledge and the intelligence and the fortitude to move towards arms control negotiations so that pushing the nuclear button never would become a necessity. No, my "strength" in ordering the destruction of the world dominated the controversy.

It is interesting that Ferraro presents a far more "feminine" position on war/peace issues in this post-hoc reconstruction of her thinking, than she did during the campaign when confronted with challenges to her capacity to lead the nation in war. When she was a live candidate, she selected, rather, the tough-lady approach. But with hindsight, it appears to have been the absence of *experience* in war rather than any lack of toughness that took the greater toll on the Ferraro candidacy. We can only speculate how she would have been perceived by the voting public and the press and how she would have handled George Bush had she served in Vietnam, or had she been a downed pilot, or a wounded combat veteran returning from that war.

Conclusion

American women were also present during the war in Vietnam; 10,000 of them served their country in that war, 7,000 as nursing staff. But, while more and more women are volunteering for the military, particularly as previously restricted classifications are being opened to them, it remains most unlikely that any significant number of American women will seek military service in the coming decades the way some men do, as a convenient stepping stone for politics. Therefore, it will be necessary for feminists and others who support women in politics to think through positions on defense, defense economics, and strategic issues that will render American women candidates more credible in their competition for national office.

So long as women cannot display either medals of honor or missing limbs as signs of service to their country, the issue of war and politics for women will remain on the cutting edge of feminist theory and a constraint on the future of feminism itself.

Notes

1. Samuel P. Huntington, *The Soldier and the State* (Cambridge, Mass.: Harvard University Press, 1957), p. 157. I am grateful to Sanford Lakoff of University of California at San Diego for pointing out the Huntington finding and for suggesting some of the formulation for this introductory paragraph.

2. Andrew Radolf, M. L. Stein, and John Consoli, "Confession in Phoenix," *Editor & Publisher* (January 4, 1986), pp. 14, 52, 62.

3. Mike Barnicle, "Farewell to the Captain," *Boston Globe* (June 6, 1986), p. 21.

4. Linda Kerber, "May All Our Citizens Be Soldiers and All Our Soldiers Citizens" (this volume).

5. In her Introduction to *Woman, Culture and Society*, Michelle Rosaldo comments on women's general exclusion from legitimated authority. She suggests that it is not simply that women's exclusion from the military disadvantages them in politics, but that their exclusions from both may derive from the same source(s).

6. Karen Anderson, *Wartime Women* (Connecticut: Greenwood Press, 1980). Sheila Tobias and Lisa Anderson, "What Really Happened to Rosie the Riveter?" in Linda K. Kerber and Jane De Hart Mathews, eds., *Women's America: Refocusing Our Past* (New York: Oxford University Press, 1982), pp. 354–73.

7. Betty Friedan dates the origins of the feminine mystique in a later period. I believe the losses suffered by women in the elections of 1946, 1948, and 1950 presaged that development and, as importantly, left non-traditional women with fewer role models and significantly diminished access to national power.

8. To appreciate the significance of eleven women in Congress going into the elections of 1946, note that in the 1980s there were only eighteen women in the House and two in the Senate, after nearly fifteen years of feminist activism.

9. Jack Anderson and Ronald W. May, *McCarthy: The Man, the Senator, the Ism* (Boston: The Beacon Press, 1952), pp. 54–71 passim; also Richard M. Rovere, *Senator Joe McCarthy* (New York: Harcourt, Brace and Co., 1959), pp. 93–105 passim.

10. The full text of the directive is as follows: "All members of the House and Senate now serving in an active status will be placed on inactive duty July 1, 1942, or immediately on returning to the United States, or remain on active duty for the duration of the war."

11. Secrest lost the 1946 election, but was reelected in 1948. Baumhart did not run again until 1954, but then was continually reelected until 1961; Lodge's case is a little more complex. He went to war from the Senate in December 1941; became inactive in 1942 to run for reelection in 1942; resigned again in 1944; in 1946 he won a surprise upset against a seventy-three-year-old incumbent for Senate.

12. Robert A. Caro, *The Years of Lyndon Johnson: The Path to Power* (New York: Knopf, 1982), p. 752.

13. Caro believes that Pearl Harbor derailed LBJ's career because he was planning to run in the primary in the summer of 1942 for the full six-year Senate term he had missed in 1940. The war made the 1942 race impossible for him, so he had to wait six more years to run for the Senate (successfully) in 1948 (Caro, p. 764).

14. William J. Miller, *Henry Cabot Lodge* (New York: Heinemann, 1967), pp. 2–3. Lodge was the first Senator since the Civil War to resign to serve on active duty. The Civil War combatant was Senator Baker of Oregon, who was killed at Ball's Bluff, Virginia. Baker is honored with a statue in the "great space" under the Capitol dome in Washington, the only non-president to be there.

15. *Ibid.*, p. 188.

16. *Ibid., pp. 2–3.*

17. *Gary Wills, Nixon Agonistes* (Boston: Houghton Mifflin, 1969), p. 82.

18. *Ibid.*, p. 72.

19. Quoted in Schnapper, M. B., ed., *Quotations from the Would-Be Chairman Richard Milhous Nixon* (Washington, D.C.: Public Affairs Press, 1968), p. 34.

20. Derived from Martin Gruberg, *Women in American Politics* (Oshkosh, Wisc.: Academe Press, 1968).

21. Malvina Lindsay, "In Politics Too, Women Will Have the Last Word," *Washington Post*, Nov. 8, 1946, p. 3.

22. *The Chicago Tribune*, October 20, 1946.

23. *The Chicago Tribune*, October 25, 1946, p. 12. See also *The Chicago Tribune*, October 30, p. 8, and November 3, 1946.

24. *The Chicago Tribune*, Monday, Nov. 4, 1946, p. 20.

25. *The Chicago Tribune*, Nov. 2, 1946, p. 2.

26. *The Boston Daily Globe*, Wednesday, June 18, 1946, p. 2.

27. Victor Lasky, *JFK: The Man and the Myth* (New York: Macmillan Co., 1963), chap. 5. For more details about John F. Kennedy's primary campaign, see also Leo Damore, *The Cape Cod Years of John Fitzgerald Kennedy* (Englewood Cliffs, N.J.: Prentice Hall, 1967), chap. 5; John H. Davis, *The Kennedys: Dynasty*

and Disaster, 1848–1983 (New York: McGraw Hill, 1984), chap. 19; Herbert S. Parmet, *Jack: The Struggles of John F. Kennedy* (New York: Dial Press, 1980); J. and C. Blair, *The Search for JFK* (New York: Putnam, 1976), chap. 18; and Peter Collier and David Horowitz, *The Kennedys: An American Drama* (New York: Summit Books, 1984), chap. 1.

28. Peter Collier and David Horowitz, *The Kennedys: An American Dream* (New York: Summit Books, 1984), p. 151.

29. "Of the 26 million draft-age men from 1964 to 1973, 16 million never served, and most took positive steps to avoid service. During the Vietnam era, the law encouraged legal draft evasion, and society, especially for the privileged classes, condoned it. . . . By 1971, the Selective Service System was processing more applications for conscientious objection a month—12,000 to 14,000—than were being inducted into the armed services." James Reston, Jr., *Sherman's March and Vietnam* (New York: Macmillan, 1984), pp. 215, 219.

30. John Kerry, *The New Soldier* (New York: Macmillan Co., 1971).

31. *Newsweek Magazine*, May 17, 1982, p. 16.

32. Even peace candidate George McGovern, who ran in 1972, made frequent reference to his service as bomber pilot during World War II—references meant to legitimize his anti-Vietnam War stand in his bid for the presidency.

33. Letter from Jeremiah Denton, November 1985.

34. *Arizona Daily Star*, April 25, 1986.

35. C. David Kotok, "Leaders of Both Parties: Kerrey on 'Defense,' " Omaha (Nebr.) *World-Herald*, June 25, 1982; see also *World-Herald*, June 16, 1982, p. 10.

36. *Ibid.*

37. *Ibid.*

38. As reported in *The Arizona Republic*, Oct. 9, 1986, p. B-6.

39. Geraldine A. Ferraro, *Ferraro: My Story* (New York: Bantam, 1985), p. 261.

40. *Ibid.*, pp. 261–62.

41. *Ibid.*

42. *Ibid.*

43. *Ibid.*, p. 273.

Comments

For most Americans, the possibility of nuclear war is a preeminent concern. We contend less with the question, or problem, of militarism. By this we mean the regimentation of society on a model of military discipline, the militarization of civilian society, the policing of that society, and the bankrupting of societies through military escapades and excesses. Women in Latin America have confronted this problem more directly. Historically, their lives have been profoundly molded and controlled by military juntas and dictatorships.

Cynthia Enloe, a political scientist and feminist scholar, draws a connection between the politics of "capitalist imperialism" and the denigration of women in Third World countries. She insists that the machismo within Central America, in particular, is intensified by U.S. militarization of that region. Drawing upon Marxist theory, Enloe puts gender politics into the picture as a central consideration. She points out that many leading male theorists and critics of imperialism have omitted any discussion of women's lives. Enloe's thesis is shared by other feminist scholars. In her book, *Male Dominance, Female Power*, Peggy Reeves Sanday, a cultural anthropologist, demonstrates the ways in which male dominance evolves as resources diminish and group survival depends increasingly on aggressive acts of males.[1] Sanday takes note of the fact that in some precolonial African societies there was rough sexual equality, and that an imbalance in favor of male dominance was generated with the coming of Western colonial force.

Enloe deploys the category "militarism" to cover a range of phenomena

187

that involve not just actual war-fighting, but also a cluster of forms of domination that preparation for war and war by other means trails in its wake. What she omits from her analysis, given its focus, is this question: what kind of military *should* prevail in a democratic society? In other words, if we defeat militarism as she understands it, would we still have a *military?* Can we envisage an acceptable form of defense and what part would women play in it? Because Enloe is not a pacifist, she accepts the fact that collective violence at times may be necessary. Can she, or we, envisage any violence on the part of American men and women that would be acceptable as we enter the last decades of the twentieth century?

Note

1. Peggy Reeves Sanday, *Male Dominance, Female Power* (Cambridge: Cambridge University Press, 1981).

9

Bananas, Bases, and Patriarchy

Cynthia Enloe

I first began thinking about the piece that eventually became "Bananas, Bases, and Patriarchy" during an afternoon spent at a "Remember Vietnam" symposium. As one male speaker after another told of his experiences during the late 1960s and early 1970s, I realized that women's experiences were being completely left out. It was as if Vietnamese, American, and Cambodian women's lives and thoughts added nothing to our understanding of the causes and consequences of that destructive and controversial war. That afternoon, both the history of the war and the "lessons" we're still trying to extract from it were being masculinized. In the 1980s, two of the regions of the world being most rapidly militarized are the Caribbean and Central America. What will we lose—in our capacity to understand and to act—if we leave women out of our analyses of that militarizing process?

The well-known commentators who occupy the stage of almost any critical discussion of imperialism or interventionism apparently believe that there is almost nothing to be gained by looking at women's lives.

An earlier version of this essay appeared in *Radical America*, vol. 19, no. 4, 1985, pp. 7–23.

Emmanuel Wallerstein, Walter Rodney, Samir Amin, Perry Anderson, Noam Chomsky—some of these men are from the "First World," others from the Third. Together, they have helped fashion the intellectual tools many of us use to explain how EXXON, NATO, the IMF (International Monetary Fund), and Hollywood have come to distort relations between the world's rich and poor. But they have developed this critical world view without much consciousness about gender. They almost never ask whether it matters that the Third-World's investment-attracting "cheap labor" is *made* cheap by being feminized. They scarcely ever wonder whether the IMF's standard package of austerity measures imposed on Third-World governments changes the relations between women and men in those countries. They also seem to believe that the expansion of Third-World militaries due to foreign arms sales and the influx of military aid does not depend at all on changing notions of what constitutes "masculine" behavior in those countries or in the donor country. When reading these commentators, we are almost never prompted to try to figure out what the connections might be between international debt, foreign investment, and militarism on the one hand, and violence against women, and domestic work, on the other. The message one comes away with is that the former are inherently "serious" and "political," whereas the latter are "trivial" and "private."[1] Surely everything we have revealed in the last twenty years of the women's movement suggests that we should be very wary of any theory that presumes the economic and emotional relations between women and men to be outside the pale of serious politics. What would be helpful in moving beyond those unexamined presumptions about the peripheral role of gender, at least in the anti-intervention movement, is posing some questions about women's lives. Perhaps by asking where women are and what they are doing, we can start to imagine what a distinctly feminist analysis of international politics would look like.

Where Are the Women?

It seems like such a simple question, why is it so rarely asked? What, in fact, would we see if we looked at women's lives in Central America and the Caribbean, for example? One possibility is that we would understand how the policies of the American government and its local allies intensify the hardships of women's lives. If we take women's lives seriously, we cannot assume that local or international politics affect

190

women and men in identical ways. For example, some of the issues named and contested by feminism become visible as integral parts of U.S. intervention policy. The denigration of women intensifies with the U.S. militarization of Central America. There is a higher incidence of rape and battering during war time. The male role as protector and sexual exploiter is affirmed and extended; prostitution is a mainstay of preserving military organization. More difficult, but equally important, we need to understand the full costs of Nicaraguan militarization to the future of the revolution. While U.S. policy has forced such a mobilization, the way in which the Nicaraguan government views its defense and appeals to its people to join the effort may deepen the power of men over women, as well as endangering democratic goals.

There is a second possibility. If we keep asking, "Where are the women?" we may find that we will have to modify our understanding of the requirements for U.S. politics to succeed in the Third World. In other words, it might be that women's lives are worth considering not only for the sake of detailing the *impact* of militarism and imperialism, but also for the sake of clarifying their basic underpinnings—how U.S. power locks into existing power relations within the countries it seeks to control. At this stage we don't have a fully articulated feminist theory to explain how imperialism and militarism have structured our relations with Central America and the Caribbean. But we do have the makings of such a theory. We do know enough about how power operates *inside* societies to urge that men-as-men and women-as-women be made visible in any investigation of how power operates *between* societies.

Colonialism and the Reproduction of Gender

Sugar. Coffee. Cotton. Limes. Cocoa. Bauxite. Rice. Bananas. These are the raw products for which the countries of Central America and the Caribbean are famous. Each has its own peculiar politics. Each has its own history. These products have been nurtured not just by the region's warm climate and rich soil, but by foreign capital and hierarchies of class and skin color. When militaries have been sent into these countries, it has usually been to protect those hierarchies and the rewards they have garnered from their control of sugar, coffee, bananas, and other products for export.

In the last decades, other, less traditional industries have been added:

tourism, cattle, garment-making, electronics assembly, oil refining and, most recently, office work.

Both the more traditional and the recently introduced products have been enmeshed in global power struggles from the outset. The colonizing governments (Spain, Britain, the Netherlands, the United States, France) and the internationally competitive companies (Gulf and Western, Tate and Lysle, Bookers, United Fruit, Alcan, Kaiser, Del Monte, and Dole) have waxed and waned in their fortunes, have bargained and fought each other, and have withdrawn from some places in order to intervene in others. The remaining constant has been the extreme vulnerability of the local peoples to decisions made outside their own societies.

Most historical accounts we have of these decisions and how Caribbean and Central American people have tried to cope with, or at times resist, these decisions are written as though no one ever had considered gender. But is this true? For instance, did British and Spanish colonizers never consider whether female Africans made less valuable slave laborers than male Africans? New work being done by black women historians suggests that it is misleading to imagine that sexist assumptions didn't shape the ways in which racism was developed to rationalize and organize slave labor. They suggest that these early uses of sexist strategies have had lasting effects, helping to sustain patriarchal notions within the black communities, notions that present obstacles to effective political action even a century or more after slavery's abolition. What then of the present-day politics of Jamaica, Trinidad, Dominica, Guyana? It seems unwise to theorize about post-slavery "plantation societies" of the Caribbean as if women and men experienced slavery in identical ways, or as if the politics of post-slavery communities were free of the legacies of the colonists' patriarchal strategizing.

Essentially we would be asking how divisions of labor have been constructed, divisions that have made the cultivation of sugar and bananas, for instance, profitable enough that they reaped profits for the overseas companies and their local allies. Furthermore, questions about how racist bases of such profitable divisions are dependent on sexism aren't relevant solely to those countries in the region with histories of slavery. In Central American societies, where colonists' use of African slaves was less prevalent, racism nonetheless was wielded in order to create domestic stratifications of color that served to coopt the Hispanicized and exploit the Indian. Were the formulation and, even more interesting for us today, the persistence of these divisions of Central American labor accomplished without any dependence on sexism?

We have heard a lot about the potency of *machismo* ideology, about how women in the insurgent movements of El Salvador, Guatemala, and Nicaragua have had to struggle against the presumption of male privilege inside their own organizations, but we rarely ask how *machismo* has supported the racist stratifications on which most of the coffee, sugar, and banana companies depend for their own operations. We often proceed as if ideologies of male dominance have their place in Central American history, ideologies of Indian inferiority in turn have their place, and never the twain shall meet. Moreover, in most of our political organizing it is the latter that gets treated with more seriousness as if Hispanicization and its complementary exploitation of Indians is what "really" explains how profits are squeezed out of sugar cane, banana trees, or coffee beans. *Machismo*'s role in the process is hardly considered, or, if it is, it is not discussed in ways that could tell us how sexual divisions of labor have been used to support racial and class divisions of labor.

Take the banana. The banana's history is embedded in the history of European colonial expansion and, later, North American neocolonial control. It is also integrally tied to the ways that women's relations to men have been shaped by local governments and foreign companies, bolstered from time to time by U.S. military intervention. So the banana, perhaps, is a good place to start in our fashioning of a feminist analysis of American militarization of the region.

The banana is not native to Central America. Its original home was Southeast Asia. By the 1400s, the banana had spread westward to become a basic food on the Guinean coast of Africa. When Spanish slavers began raiding the coast and shipping captured Africans to the West Indies and South America, they shipped bananas as well. The banana, then, entered this hemisphere as the slavers' choice of a cheap and popular African staple to feed enslaved women and men.

The yellow bananas familiar to North American consumers were not developed as a distinct variety until the nineteenth century. They were first served at the homes of wealthy Bostonians in 1875. United Fruit's corporate empire, which over the next century came to behave like a surrogate state in much of Central America, grew out of the American popularization of this humble globe-trotting fruit. That market success wove an invisible but crucial political link of interdependence between the women of North America and the women of Central America.

In the 1950s, United Fruit took the lead in launching a brand name for its own bananas—"Chiquita." Standard Fruit, its chief competitor, followed quickly on its heels with its own brand name—"Cabana." Thus began a marketing war to win the allegiance of American and European housewives and their local grocers. Today, the goal remains to persuade predominantly female consumers that bananas from one company are of higher quality and possess longer shelf life and greater overall reliability than those from another company.

The conventional way of thinking about how and why it's "banana republics" that American officials want to preserve—by force, if necessary—in Central America is one that focuses on class alliances made by United Fruit and Del Monte executives with local political and economic elites on the one hand, and with Washington policy-makers on the other. They all have a common stake in keeping banana workers' wages low and their political consciousness undeveloped. But who are these workers? Pictures that I have seen of Honduran banana-worker union members always appear full of men. Do only men work on the major banana plantations, or is it only the male workers who are employed in the banana industry in ways that allow for unionization? Where are the women? One reality—that women do work—makes bananas profitable for this triple alliance of elites, but the work they do (weeding) is so marginalized that they develop a different sort of political consciousness and are excluded from the unions by their fathers and brothers who imagine their conflicts with management more "political," more "serious." Another reality is that women do not do any wage-paying work on the plantations of United Fruit or Del Monte: they are at home doing unpaid subsistence farming, child care, and cooking. Feminists in scores of industrialized and Third-World countries have revealed how even mining and agricultural operations that recruit only male workers still depend on women's work. For without women doing the hard but unpaid work of subsistence farming and household maintenance, the companies would not be able to pay their male workers such low wages. The unpaid work that women do allows for the survival and reproduction of those paid workers.

Given these realities, the "banana republics" that U.S. militarization is intended to sustain are patriarchal in at least two ways. First, the colonially-seeded culture of *machismo* serves to legitimize local class and racial stratifications in ways that make the subjugation of all women perpetuate low wages and attenuate union organizing. If we thought these propositions were worth investigating, we would also find how they operate *together* so as to sustain the kind of internationally dependent, militarized society we have come to call a "banana republic."

The economies of Central America and the Caribbean have been undergoing important changes during the 1970s and 1980s. Most of those changes have been initiated by foreign corporations and government in order to resecure their hold on the region. In part because of the growing militarization and its resultant social unrest and in part out of their own inhouse global strategies, some of the largest banana companies are threatening to cut back their Central American operations. Both Honduras and Nicaragua have been told that countries such as Ecuador and the Philippines now look more promising for banana operations. The corporate decisions have been reported in terms of their effects on unemployment in already fragile Central American economies. Scarcely anything has been said about what it has meant for relations between women and men.

If we knew that women and men in Nicaragua and Honduras had identical roles in the international banana industry, then it would be superfluous to ask those questions. But we know this is not the case. Women and men have been affected by these recent corporate decisions in different ways. For instance, it is reported that Honduran peasant women are trying to develop cash-generating projects such as the making of straw hats and the processing of cashew nuts. This is a political development, a step women are taking to reduce their earlier dependence on exploitative middlemen *(coyotes)*, and to gain some social autonomy as women. But the pressure to start these new cooperative projects is also coming from the ripple effects on men compared to women of the banana companies' cutbacks. For the unemployed banana workers are overwhelmingly the men in these women's families. Women as mothers and wives are joining women's straw hat and cashew nut cooperatives at least in part to offset the decline in household income. But what are the long-range implications of male banana workers' unemployment and women's cash-producing projects? Will the political prominence of the Honduran women demand a larger say in leftist political organizations? It is not unreasonable to predict that whatever change or resistance to change does occur will be played out not in the plaza but in thousands of peasant homes.

Women in the region have been making their own critiques to address the presumptions of gender's political irrelevance or women's uninvolvement. For instance, the Jamaican populist women's theater collective, *Sistren*, has created a play about women sugar workers. They are reminding Jamaican poor women (and us, as well) that though Jamaican postindependence politics has been dominated by men in part because it was men who led and filled the ranks of the preindependence militant sugar workers unions, the sugar industry was not an all-male affair. Women too worked to make profits for the giant British company. Yet they and their labor have been made politically invisible in ways that continue to obstruct Jamaican women's entry into the nation's political life.

Similarly, before the U.S. military invasion, Grenadian women were organizing to make their work in the cocoa industry (a principal export sector) more visible. Grenadian women in the revolutionary movement began to insist that the men take their work seriously. Beyond that, they began developing government policies that would dismantle the sexual divisions of labor on which the island's cocoa business has relied. These important sexual politics were cut short by the landing of the U.S. Marines. It is likely that the postinvasion Grenadian society is being "developed" on a rigid sexual division of labor by the expansion of the tourist industry and by the (not terribly successful) attempts by Washington officials to "secure" Grenada by inviting American light industries to establish cost-cutting assembly-line production.

A Nation of Chambermaids

As landlessness increases in Central America, women and men may be making quite different choices about how to survive. There is no reason to believe a priori that landlessness is any less gendered than plantation labor. One indication that this is happening is the increase in numbers of women migrating from the countryside to the towns to seek jobs as low paid seamstresses and, if they are less lucky, domestic workers. According to one estimate, 64 percent of all women working for wages in Guatemala City today are employed as domestic workers. Many of these women are Indian women working for Latino families. Many of these women are the sole caretakers of children.

The fact that more Latin American women work in domestic servant jobs than in any other type of wage-paying employment is an important clue to what kind of class transformations are occurring in the 1980s as a consequence of changes in the international economy. Having household servants is one of the most visible signs of middle-class status. The push of more and more peasant women out of the countryside, where they no longer can support themselves and their children, and into the towns, where they must accept low-paying jobs with minimal workers' rights, allows more and more Central Americans with relatively secure incomes to imagine that they have arrived in the middle or even upper-middle class. For many a man of this class, it is an arrival that is accompanied by peculiarly masculine privileges, such as sexual access to a young rural woman under his own roof who has only minimal resources with which to resist his demands. For the woman of this growing middle class the role of employer—of another woman—may serve to reconfirm her sense of upward mobility and blunt her sense of shared destiny with other, poorer women in her own country.

Simultaneously, prostitution is being integrated into this gendered and globalized political economy. A woman working as a domestic servant may be fired by her employers if she becomes pregnant—by the man of the house who wants to cover up his own actions, or by the woman of the house who prefers to deal with her husband's "indiscretions" by turning her anger on the victim. Those women, as well as women from the countryside who never were lucky enough to find jobs (or who found jobs in a factory assembling bras or transistor radios only to be laid off soon afterwards), still have children or parents to support. Thus they often turn to the last resort, prostitution.

Our understanding of what changes are occurring in Central America needs to go beyond mere talk of "landless peasants" or "peasant mobilization." What kind of politics does a woman learn from being the sole caretaker of someone else's child? What are the understandings gained from being the sole parent of one's own child as well as surrogate mother to someone else's child? What are the understandings about power that come from working as an Indian maid in a Latino home? At what point does sexual harassment by the father or son of that household begin to inspire resistance—resistance supported by whom?[2]

In the Caribbean as well, the resort to domestic work has been a growing trend among poor women. Some of those women have sought domestic servant jobs in their own countries. Thousands of women have migrated to Canada, the United States, and Europe in search of income with which to support themselves and their children. Some of them have started to overcome the isolating effects of such work to speak out and to organize. In the United States, one such organization includes both Caribbean and Central American women as well as U.S.-born Latina and black women.[3]

Even more striking and noticeable than the increase of domestic work has been the emergence of the tourist industry. Tourism seems to be the Caribbean replacement for the world's declining sugar demand. Sometimes the shift happens very explicitly, such as in the Dominican Republic

197

in 1984 when Gulf and Western sold off more than 200,000 acres of sugar cane fields to American entrepreneurs who plan to turn the land into tourist havens. By 1984, tourism had already leaped ahead of sugar as the Dominican Republic's top foreign exchange earner.

Typically, this rapid rise of foreign-capitalized tourism is condemned by critics because it is turning the countries of the Caribbean into "nations of busboys." That is, it is in the very character of these sprawling Holiday Inn chains to de-skill their workers, institutionalize racism, and keep crucial decision-making prerogatives in the overseas headquarters. Furthermore, the lengths to which Holiday Inn, Club Med, and others will go to make their American, Canadian, French, and British patrons comfortable with familiar foods and decor ends up siphoning off whatever foreign exchange the friendly regimes may hope to keep for themselves.

But is it a "nation of busboys" that is replacing the region's plantation society? Is this the most accurate way for us to make sense of the kind of transformation that is taking place in Grenada, Jamaica, Barbados, the Dominican Republic, and other countries? Fear of becoming a "nation of busboys" may raise insecurities around manhood to seriousness within nationalist political mobilizations, but it may not reflect the real gender dynamics of tourism.

Observers who bother to put on their gender-glasses note that tourism is a blatantly feminized industry in its lowest ranks. Approximately 75 percent of all the 250,000 Caribbean tourism workers are women.[4] Many of these women are seeking hotel jobs in the wake of jobs lost in agriculture. Many women are also in desperate search for income because it has been women who, even more than men, have had to find daily ways of coping with their government's decisions to give in to International Monetary Fund pressure to cut public services and raise food prices.[5] In other words, one way we might understand how the Reagan administration is transforming American influence in the Caribbean is to trace the lines between the decline in foreign-funded agribusiness, the growth of tourism, imposition of the IMF austerity programs, and the spread of U.S. control. It appears that each of these trends, as well as their underlying connections, is illuminated by taking the experiences of Caribbean women—as workers, as copers, and as challengers—seriously.

Women and "Light Industry"

Light industry is the newest economic sector to be opened up in the Caribbean and Central America. Much of this development is based on

198

the lessons derived from Puerto Rico's earlier "Operation Bootstrap," a thoroughly feminized formula that depended on forced sterilization and lowering of women's wages. "Light industry" usually encompasses labor-intensive forms of manufacture used in garment and toy manufacture, food processing, and electronics assembly. Taking a page out of the textile industry's history book, light industry's executives have defined their operations' assembly jobs as "unskilled," i.e., they require a high toler-ance for repetition without loss of precision and pay poorly, and thus, are ideal for women.

President Reagan's advisers urged friendly regimes of the "Caribbean Basin" (which includes Central America and Colombia) to accept more light industry foreign investment. The aim was not so much the promo-tion of Caribbean economic development or even American profits. Rather, the aim was to cement a security alliance between those weaker regimes and the United States with the glue of economic dependency. But such security schemes can't work unless the local regimes and American investors can attract women workers. This, in turn, will depend on their success in sustaining those myths of masculinity, femininity, motherhood, skill, and family that together make and keep women's labor cheap. Women who write plays about wife battering, women who risk overseas migration, women who unionize, women who demand more training, these and others will not be the sorts of women that will guarantee the success of the Caribbean Basin Initiative and the security objectives it is designed to serve.

Along with older light industries, corporate newcomers are taking up Washington's invitation, however. Office work is becoming globalized. American Airlines has been in the forefront, shifting its reservations operations to Barbados. Thanks to the wonders—and cost-effectiveness—of satellite communications, companies in the insurance, banking, credit, and reservations business have begun to look outside the United States for office workers. International lending agencies like the World Bank and the IMF have been enthusiastic. A Washington-based organization called the "Free Zone Authority" is currently urging Jamaica's Seaga regime to open up a "teleport." It has the added attraction of being only a stone's throw from Jamaica's tourist mecca, Montego Bay.

It is clear that the feminization of cheap labor, plus the legacy of the English language in postcolonial countries, is making this new stage in the global reach feasible. As one of the off-shore office work boosters told a journalist, "These workers are really good. . . . Typing skills are impressive, and accuracy is about 99 percent."[6] They also can be hired at wage rates far below those paid their American counterparts.

Diana Roos, researcher for the national office of "9 to 5," says that American executives are still weighing alternatives. They are busy comparing the costs, productivity, and controllability of three groups of women office workers: American women employed at the companies' own offices; American women contracted to do office work as home work in the suburbs (without the costs of overhead and in a setting that is harder to unionize); finally Caribbean and Asian (especially Indian) women working in their own countries.

For American feminists this corporate strategizing presents at least two interlocking challenges. First, politically active office workers and their supporters must find ways to understand these global maneuvers and to insure that they don't play into the hands of "divide and rule" union busters. Second, office workers and their supporters here and in countries like Barbados, the Bahamas, and Jamaica will have to try to get the attention of women and men active in the anti-intervention movement. In the future, anti-intervention campaigns will have to be shaped out of an awareness of how women in the United States and other countries of the region are being linked to one another in ways that could serve to smooth the way for Caribbean militarization or, alternatively, *could* permit them to subvert Washington's grand security scheme.

Bases and Patriarchy

Feminists in the Philippines, South Korea, and Thailand have described in alarming detail just how U.S. military bases have distorted the sexual politics of the countries. A military base isn't simply an installation for servicing bombers, fighters, and aircraft carriers, or a launch-pad for aggressive forays into surrounding territories. A military base is also a package of presumptions about the male soldier's sexual needs, the local society's sexual needs, and about the local society's resources for satisfying those needs. Massage parlors are as integral to Subic Bay, the mammoth U.S. naval base in the Philippines, as its dry docks.[7]

Lucy Komisar, a freelance reporter, has written an account of how sexual politics in Honduras are being fashioned to meet the alleged needs of the American military there.[8] Komisar went to visit the shanty town of brothels that has grown up near the Palmerole military base, one of the bases used by the U.S. military in its series of "Big Pine" joint maneuvers.

200

She found Honduran women serving as prostitutes to both Honduran and American soldiers. Her report revealed in microcosm what Honduran public health officials have noted more generally: that there has been a notable rise in the number of cases of venereal disease in Honduras in the three years since the start of the U.S. military build-up. Hondurans refer to the particularly virulent strain of V.D. as "Vietnam Rose." While the nickname wrongly blames the victim, it suggests that Hondurans see the Vietnamization of their country in terms of sexuality as well as money and hardware.

Lucy Komisar lets us hear from some of the people behind the statistics. First there are the young Honduran women, some as young as sixteen years, who have been virtually kidnapped and brought to the brothels as captives. One woman who tried to escape was caught and returned by Honduran policemen. There are other women who, on the surface, seem to have come to the brothels "freely," driven by the need for money. They split their fees with the owners of the shabby cantinas where they conduct their business. But many of the women living on the fringes of the base fall somewhere in between. They have been drawn so deeply into debt to the men who supply their food and minimal housing that they never seem able to pay off their debts and gain their freedom.

The men involved are both American and Honduran. Komisar found that local policemen acted as the enforcers of the prostitution system. They, in turn, are controlled by Honduran army officers, a reflection of the growing capacity of the military to intimidate other Honduran institutions. American men involved are from both the enlisted and officer ranks. It may be the construction of militarized masculinity that is most responsible for American enlisted men's belief that one of the prerogatives due an American male G.I. overseas is the sexual services of local women. It is not yet clear how this presumption is being affected by the fact that, unlike Vietnam where most American military women were nurses, American field units in Honduras include several dozen women soldiers. So far the most common complaint that these women have had is that they have not been issued proper sanitary supplies. But where do American women soldiers go for *their* "R and R" when their male comrades head for the cantinas?

It would be wrong to imagine that this sort of sexual exploitation is sustained solely by Honduran military intimidation and diffuse American patriarchal culture. As is true in other base towns around the world, the system requires explicit American policy-making. Komisar reports, for example, that it is American army doctors from the Palmerole base who routinely conduct medical exams on Honduran women working in the nearby brothels. Their job is to insure that American male soldiers will get access to the sex they want without jeopardizing the army's operational readiness.

The Militarization of Gender

In our attempt to discover just how much militarization is a gendered process, that is, a process that won't "work" unless men will accept certain norms of masculinity and women will abide by certain strictures of femininity, we might consider three other dynamics in addition to military prostitution. The first is *rape*. The second is *military recruitment*. The third is the *ideology of national security*. How far is each of these necessary for the American-sponsored militarization of the Caribbean and Central America in the 1980s? How far is each of these dependent not just on notions of gender but on patriarchal relations?

We can only be suggestive here, but we might at least raise the level of genuine political curiosity. For instance, it seems remarkable that there hasn't been more curiosity, more committed political questioning, about why male soldiers' rapes of civilian women have been so widespread in Central America. Typically, rape is listed among an assortment of repressive acts, as if rape were not qualitatively different both in its motivations and its repercussions. But why, in fact, do male soldiers in Guatemala or Contra soldiers in Nicaragua engage in sexual assault on women so insistently? Is it one more product of masculinity militarized? Is it part of some self-conscious officer-level policy of intimidation? Of whom? Of the women themselves or of their husbands, sons, and fathers whose sense of male honor is tied up in their capacity to protect "their" women? Guatemalan army commanders have been quoted as saying that killing Indian women and children is part of a deliberate strategy of counterinsurgency: the foundation of the Indian guerrillas' organization is seen to be the "family nuclei." Therefore, whole families have to be murdered if the insurgency is to be crushed.[9] But this still doesn't explain the reports of rapes and sexual tortures of women that soldiers engage in before they murder Indian women. Some Latin American feminists now believe that masculinity is being militarized for the sake of a wider militarization of the society.[10] If this is true, then we will have to focus our political energies much more on finding out how U.S. soldiers are trained and what sexual assumptions are woven into the training we provide to soldiers and police of other countries.

We will also have to listen more carefully to women and men in El Salvadoran and Guatemalan insurgent movements. Have the experiences of rape, direct and indirect, had different effects on their political mobilization? It may well be that a woman who herself has suffered rape by a government soldier or who has seen her mother or sister raped will think about power and injustice rather differently than her male comrades who either have not been politicized by rape at all or who have, but assign different meanings to that experience.

Finally, there are the gendered politics of military manpower. When I hear that Barbados is expanding its military manpower, here are some of the things I wonder about. I wonder how it is that Barbadian standards of masculinity can be transformed so that the cricket player can be overtaken by the soldier (or the militarized policeman). Not all societies, and certainly not most of those in the Caribbean and even some in Central America (e.g., Costa Rica), so merge soldiering and manhood that they become almost indistinguishable. Certainly it makes the military recruiter's task easier if to be a soldier proves a man is masculine. But the two are analytically and historically separable. If they weren't, governments would not need to waste their credibility by trying to enforce conscription laws.

So when the Reagan administration set out to urge governments in the Caribbean and Central America to increase their numbers of soldiers, it was asking them to engage in some tricky cultural maneuvers. Unless those regimes can count on young men enlisting simply to escape the despair of unemployment or the threat of repression—and both of these are available to Caribbean and Central American recruiters—they will also have to convince women in their countries that men who join the newly expanding armies are more genuinely "real men" than are men able to get decent civilian jobs. What is happening to Barbadian and Costa Rican women's beliefs about masculinity? Are they changing in ways that will ease Washington's militarizing plans? If women in these countries are resisting such cultural changes, then it is likely that their alienation from their governments, and possibly from the men in their lives as well, is intensifying.

We could perhaps understand militarization better if we looked at how "national security" is defined and how it is gendered. I think it is useful to try to figure out just how much militarization of *any* society requires its citizens to rethink what they need to feel secure. Feminists who have studied European and North American societies in wartime have shown the differences between the beliefs of men and women about what they need to feel safe. They have also revealed how governments intent upon legitimizing their expanded wartime powers have used propaganda emphasizing women's need for protection and men's duty to serve as protectors to win that legitimation.

There's strong reason to believe that some of the same efforts might be needed if Caribbean and Central American regimes are to gain their people's acceptance of the larger manpower quotas, greater security budgets, wider emergency powers, and more foreign bases on their soil that Washington is fostering. Does this mean that the U.S.-fueled militarization of these countries is dependent on an even more entrenched version of *machismo*? This may not be easy as we enter the 1990s. Today, there are more women in these countries raising children on their own, farming on their own, learning how to read and write for themselves, joining crafts cooperatives. These are not the sort of experiences that will encourage women to accept national security doctrines that portray them as the objects of male protection.

The militarism of the United States and other countries needs us all to behave *as women*. Otherwise their militarizing goals won't be achieved. They need some American women to feel protected by a massive arms build-up and by their sons and husbands in uniform. They need wives of soldiers to accept the extra duties of household maintenance when their husbands are on maneuvers in Honduras and El Salvador without worrying too much about the rumors they've heard about the Honduran brothels. They need some—not too many—American women to view the military as the place to prove their equality with men. Still, among American women, the military needs some Latinos, maybe new arrivals from war-torn Central America, to work in Silicon Valley's electronic factories making the latest electronic weaponry, and other Latinos to see their boyfriends answering the army recruiter's call as a step toward Americanization.

In Central America and the Caribbean, militarization seems to require women to work for low wages for foreign companies or to support those companies' low-paid male workers by performing family work that is rewarded with no pay at all. It also requires women to do the stress-inducing juggling of household budgets so that the government can cut their social service budgets in order to live up to agreements with the IMF. If local poor women can't manage this demanding task, or if they refuse to privatize their economic struggles and instead take to the streets, then the U.S.-fostered militarization will be jeopardized by faltering local governments.

What this suggests is that we have just begun to understand how the relations between women and between women and men—in movements, in families, on military bases, on plantations—are the prerequisites for American-promoted military expansion. Even with the fragmentary clues we now have, we should be able to insist that gender in general and patriarchy in particular be made central topics in any movement dedicated to rolling back militarization.

Notes

1. The vol. 19, no. 1 issue of *Radical America* offered a good example of this. Three of the four feature articles made virtually no mention of gender. On the other hand, *RA's* graphics designers obviously did have gender on their minds, for the photos surrounding the texts of these three articles were filled with messages about the interplay of masculinity, feminity, and militarism.

2. For moving descriptions of the daily lives of domestic workers in Lima, Peru. see the new book by Ximena Bunster and Elsa Chaney, *Sellers and Servant* (New York: Praeger, 1985). Other excellent descriptions of working women's lives in Central America are contained in the writings of Laurel H. Bossen, *The Redivision of Labor: Women and Economic Choice in Four Guatemalan Communities* (Albany: SUNY Press, 1984), and Audrey Bronstein, *The Triple Struggle* (Boston: South End Press, 1982). The U.S.A.I.D. Women and Development section has also published a statistical overview of selected Latin American and Caribbean countries, *Women of the World* (Washington, D.C., May 1984).

3. Interviews with West Indian women working as domestic workers in Canada are included in Makeda Silvera, *Silenced* (Toronto: Wallace Williams Publishers, 1984), distributed in the United States by Kitchen Table Women of Color Press in New York. Latina, black, Asian, and white women have organized Household Workers' Rights, 330 Ellis St., Rm. 501, San Francisco, Calif. 94102.

4. This figure comes from one of the few general books critiquing neo-imperialism in the Caribbean to include information on women: Tom Barry, Beth Wood, and Deb Preusch, *The Other Side of Paradise* (New York: Grove Press, 1984).

5. Lynne Bolles, "Kitchens Hit by Priorities: Employed Working Class Jamaican Women Confront the IMF," in June Nash and Maria Patricia Fernandez-Kelly, *Women, Men and the International Division of Labor* (Albany: SUNY Press, 1983). Another excellent discussion of the domestic politics of underdevelopment in the Caribbean and women's responses is *Daughters of the Nightmares: Caribbean Women*, 1984. This useful short booklet and others like it about and

by women from Chile, Peru, Ethiopia, Thailand, and the Philippines can be obtained by writing Georgia Ashworth, Change International Reports on Women, 29 Great James St., London WCIN, England.

6. *Boston Globe*, Sept. 15, 1985.

7. Concern about AIDS does seem to be dampening business somewhat.

8. The full version of Lucy Komisar's article appeared in *Honduras Update*, vol. 3, no. 11, 1985, available from them at *Update*, 1 Summer St., Sommerville, Mass. 02143.

9. Michael McClintock, *The American Connection State Terror and Popular Resistance in Guatemala*, vol. 2 (London: Zed Press, 1985), p. 245.

10. For instance, see Ximena Bunster, "The Torture of Women Political Prisoners," in Kathleen Barry *et al.*, eds., *International Feminism: Networking Against Female Sexual Slavery* (New York: Women's Tribune Center, 1984).

Part IV

Thinking What We Are Doing: Toward a Feminist Theory of War and Peace

Comments

Philosopher Janet Radcliffe Richards raises a number of provocative points, not so much about the *existence* of all-female antiwar protest but about the kinds of *justifications* given for why such efforts must exclude men. Through closely reasoned argumentation, Radcliffe Richards insists that the apparently radical claim that ridding the world of *male* values and creating a new society based on *female* values—belligerence and desire for war being "male" on this construal—is, in fact, profoundly conservative and harkens back to old traditionalist insistencies concerning separate spheres.

Radcliffe Richards builds her case by returning to the attitudes and arguments of opponents of feminism and going on to show how many radical feminists share the assumptions of their ostensible protagonists. If the reader finds her argument persuasive, it follows that, in Radcliffe Richards's words, there may be many "good reasons for keeping an all-female camp at Greenham," but the "idea that peace is a feminist issue is not one of them." Here is a cautionary note, requiring that feminist and peace activists and thinkers take greater care to sort through the implications of their guiding assumptions and justifications.

10

Why the Pursuit of Peace Is No Part of Feminism

Janet Radcliffe Richards

It is an important fact about practical politics that people who are united in their support for some objective may differ considerably in their reasons for that support. Agreement about *what* should be done may rest on serious disagreement about *why*.

For the purposes of any particular campaign it may not matter much whether its supporters differ in their opinions about what its justification is, and it may not matter even if many of them have motives that are too hazy or confused to count as justifications at all. They may still be able to agree about what needs to be done, and cooperate efficiently in trying to bring it about. In the long run, however, underlying disagreements and confusions matter very much. The reasons people have for trying to achieve some political purpose will determine what they support in other contexts, so that people who have different reasons for being allies in one campaign may well find themselves opponents in another, and anyone whose reasons are confused will be unable to form clear and effective sets of political policies at all. It is therefore extremely important that people

211

who have no doubt about which political side they are on should be equally clear about why they are on it.

I say this at the outset to emphasize that although this paper takes the Greenham camp as its starting point, the question to be discussed is not whether it is a good thing that there should be an all-female protest camp outside a missile base. That is something about which I have no doubt, and shall take for granted throughout. My concern is only with the kinds of *justification* that may be given for it, and in particular with one very familiar one: the idea that the camp should be restricted to women to reflect the idea that peace is a *feminist* issue, and that part of the business of feminism is to oppose such typically male assumptions as that the best way to resolve disagreements is to fight about them.

This kind of justification of Greenham is by no means the only one given by its supporters, and often not the only one given by the ones who do give it. However, it does seem to be a very prominent one, and it is particularly important because of the far-reaching consequences ideas of the same kind have for the rest of feminism. Peace is only one issue among many. It is now widely held that one of the main aims of the movement should be to rid the world of *male values* in general, and create a new and better society based on female ones.

The idea behind this relatively new aspect of feminism is not at all difficult to understand in 'a general way. It is essentially that since all social institutions and norms were established during millennia of male supremacy, they must inevitably be permeated by maleness, and that there must in consequence be a limit to the value of what can be achieved by women's seeking only (as Germaine Greer said) "equality of opportunity within the status quo; free admission to the world of the ulcer and the coronary."[1] The old feminism of equal rights, equal opportunities, and equal consideration ("equal rights feminism" for short from now on) is regarded as dealing only with the surface of the problem, and offering women nothing more than the illusion of liberation in a world constructed by men to suit themselves. The new feminism, by contrast, is seen as *radical,* going far beyond equal rights feminism in calling into question all patriarchal values.

Peace as a women's issue can, therefore, stand for this aspect of contemporary feminism as a whole; and the claim I shall defend here is that in spite of the attractiveness and plausibility of the new direction the movement has taken, it is a mistaken one. I shall argue that this new "women's values" kind of feminism is not, as is widely thought, a radical extension of the equal rights sort, espoused by women who want a

212

thoroughgoing solution to the problems of patriarchy rather than cosmetics. Although it looks radical, in demanding more changes than the equal rights feminism, it is really dangerously conservative, actually *opposed* to what most people (and most feminists) normally regard as central concerns of the women's movement, and tending to entrench serious aspects of the traditional subjection of women.

From this it will follow that although there may be excellent reasons for an all-female protest camp at Greenham, the idea that peace is a feminist issue is not one of them.

Since the main claim of this article is that the women's values kind of feminism is actually incompatible with what is here called the equal rights kind, it is important to start with some clarification of the nature of equal rights feminism. There are three main points to be made. The first concerns the distinctness of this kind of issue from questions of social values; the second concerns how much feminist work of this kind remains to be done; the third concerns equal rights feminism as a political movement. The second and third of these claims, at least, are controversial, and all three need far more explanation and defense than they can be given here, but it is important for the argument that they should at least be stated.

The first claim, then, concerns the nature of the equal rights issue, and its distinctness from questions about social values.[2] The original aim of equal rights feminism of course was (and in many parts of the world still is) to remove the vast structure of legal and institutional devices that made women the property of their husbands, kept them out of education and most kinds of occupation, and deprived them of many civil rights and all political power. But these formal restraints were only the most conspicuous manifestations of a much more complex web of social devices and attitudes that pervaded every aspect of life and divided the sexes into their traditional *separate spheres*, to the systematic overall advantage of men. The concern of present-day equal rights feminists is whatever aspects of that total differentiation still remain, to the disadvantage of women, even now its most conspicuous extremes have now disappeared in many parts of the world. However, it is important to be clear about the precise nature of this traditional differentiation, since traditionalists often manage (whether by accident or design) to disguise it, in ways that are directly relevant to the arguments of this paper.

Traditionalists have always defended the separation of the sexes' spheres by means of a very simple claim: that any good principle about how to treat people must specify that different kinds should be treated in different ways, and that since men and women are different it must of course follow that they should be treated differently. Who would argue that the sick should be treated in the same way as the well, or the strong in the same way as the weak? For just the same kind of reason it would be absurd to treat men and women in the same kind of way.

In other words, they argue that the sphere separation follows from general principles about how people of different sorts should be treated, conjoined with particular claims about the differences between men and women. Not surprisingly, therefore, the usual feminist response has been to claim either that tradition is completely wrong about the natures of women and men, or (directly relevant to this discussion) that the social values that determine how different people should be treated are misguided or, of course, both at once.

Now of course there can be no doubt that many traditional beliefs about female nature are scandalously wrong, nor that many traditional social values leave a very great deal to be desired. However, the trouble with raising issues of this sort in the context of the separate spheres controversy is that it lets traditionalists get away with what in one sense is the most fundamental mistake of all. The point is that their argument, as presented here, makes the separate spheres out to be nothing more than a natural consequence of general principles about how people should be treated: principles that happen to have the effect of differentiating men and women just because of natural differences between them, in the way that a general principle about how to treat the strong and the weak would have the effect of differentiating those. But, in fact, the traditional sphere separation was never anything like this. The separation of the sexes never came about through the application of *general* social standards, applying equally to everyone, and which *happened* to have the effect of differentiating women and men: it was brought about by a quite distinct set of *sex-specific rules*, which treated the sexes differently *as such*.

Perhaps the traditionalist thinks this makes no difference to the argument. If, for instance, it is right to have a social rule that the strong should protect the weak, and men are strong and women weak, then surely this justifies a sex-specific social rule that men should protect all women. In fact, however, it does no such thing. If you already have a social rule that the strong should protect the weak, and if it is true that all men are strong and all women weak, then certainly it will follow that all men should protect all women. But that cannot justify the *addition* of a rule, specifically about men and women, to the existing general rule. You cannot justify the existence of a social rule by pointing out that what it is supposed to bring about would happen anyway, without it. The only point of any rule is to bring about what would *not* otherwise happen.

Suppose, on the other hand, you take what is anyway the only faintly plausible interpretation of the claim that men are stronger than women: that men are *on average* stronger than women. Then the sex-based rule certainly has a purpose: it brings about something that the sex-neutral rule does not. But precisely what it brings about is an *overriding* of the sex-neutral rule. What it does is make sure that in some circumstances—where individuals are not typical of their sex, and men are weaker than women—the weak must protect the strong. And whether or not that can be justified, it certainly cannot be justified by appeals to principles about the strong helping the weak, since it actually contradicts them.

In other words, you cannot reach a justification of policies that differentiate men and women simply by appealing to general principles about how people of different types should be treated, *even if* your principles are themselves good, your beliefs about sexual differences are true, and your principles would as a result tend to bring about differential treatment of the sexes. Either the specific sex-based rules are redundant, or they *undermine* the general principles that are supposed to be their justification.

Now this does not in itself prove that no justification for sphere separation can be found: the fact that this most familiar line of traditionalist argument fails does not mean that no other could succeed.[3] However, what it does make clear is that the two issues—the separation of the sexes into their respective spheres and the issue of social values in general—are quite distinct. The general question of what values there ought to be, even if such values would *tend* to result in differential treatment of men and women, is quite separate from the question of whether there ought to be sex-specific rules, which, if they have any effect at all, override those general values.

To put the matter in a helpful if not entirely accurate way: the separate spheres issue can be seen as more or less the familiar issue of *double standards*. A complaint that standards are double is quite distinct from a complaint that any standard is wrong. Any feminist campaign to change social values, therefore, is necessarily different from any campaign to get men and women treated according to the *same* set of values, which is what equal rights feminism is about.

The second claim about equal rights feminism to be made here concerns how much work of this kind there is yet to do. Of course, no feminist needs to be persuaded that there is still a great deal to be done, or that the task is in many ways harder than ever, since so many of the differentiating pressures that remain are invisible to the untutored eye. Still, from the fact that feminists whose main concerns are of this kind are frequently referred to (rather disparagingly) as liberal—as opposed to radical—feminists, it seems that there is considerable room for disagreement about how much change can be justified by considerations of this sort. My own view is that, *properly interpreted*, this so-called liberal feminism[4] covers a very wide range of ground, and is potentially extremely radical.

This is partly because its concerns must obviously go far beyond laws and formal institutions to include all social conventions that differentiate the sexes to the advantage of men, and also the many related ways in which people treat the sexes differently—as research conclusively shows—without the faintest idea that they are doing so. It must also be concerned with the mistaken and deeply entrenched beliefs about women's nature that are in various ways the direct consequences of the sexes' differential treatment, and survive to become the cause of more such treatment.

But in addition to all this, the campaign for equal treatment must also extend to wanting women's *interests* taken into account equally with men's. Since all social institutions were established during millenia of male supremacy, this requirement turns out to entail the rethinking of all social arrangements and policies that may suit the interests of women less than those of men. The differences that stem from the bearing of children alone demand radical reassessment of all our most basic social institutions: marriage (including its existence), the family, arrangements for child care, the whole organization of work and housing, and innumerable others. And that is even before changes needed to cope with any tendencies to difference between men's and women's inclinations and temperaments are taken into account. Equal rights feminism therefore turns out, when properly understood, to be exceedingly radical, even on its own.

The final claim about equal rights feminism concerns its nature as a political movement, and in particular the question of who can be involved in it. It is important that there is relatively little about this kind of feminist campaign—involving as it does the identification and elimination of differentiating treatment that puts women at a disadvantage to men—which is by its nature such that only women can work for it. Recognizing, objecting to, and working against the differential treatment of women and men have nothing to do with knowing what it *feels* like to be a woman: you can be a woman without understanding these things at all, or be a man and understand them very well. Unjustified differential treatment can, in principle, be observed by anyone looking for it, and often demonstrated conclusively by controlled experiments. It can also, in principle, be campaigned against by anyone; and even though many men are doubtless too deeply ingrained in their preconceptions about their role to be of much help, this is equally true (as feminists know all to well) of a great many women. Perhaps there may be some need to keep a special watch on men who get involved in any feminist campaign, since their motives may often be open to suspicion; but there can be no doubt that many men are seriously committed to the cause of feminism, just as many women are not. In other words, the campaign *for* the equal treatment of women need not, as history has shown, be carried out *by* women.

This does not entail the facile conclusion that all separatism amounts to discrimination, and that feminists must never exclude men from anything. A full understanding of the unequal treatment of women can be used to justify a great deal of feminist separatism; not all aspects of the equal rights movement must involve men and women working together. For instance, women must obviously be the ones who decide what kinds of arrangements would suit women. And since the traditional relationship between the sexes means that women are still actively (if subtly) discouraged from acquiring a great many important skills—particularly those needed for leadership—there is probably a good deal to be said for women's taking themselves away from men in many contexts for a time, in order to try to develop these hitherto neglected abilities. These are, of course, familiar ideas; and since they are (when seen in this way) techniques to bring about more equal treatment of the sexes, they are in no way at odds with the ideal of equal treatment. Some separatism may well be useful in the campaign for equal rights.

It is interesting that this is one kind of argument often given in favor of the Greenham separatism, and (I think) one of several *good* ones. Nevertheless, the allowability of many kinds of separatism does not vitiate the point that the struggle *for* the fair treatment of women need not, in most of its aspects, be conducted *by* women.

All feminists, presumably, must agree that one essential aim of the movement must be to eliminate all that still remains of the differentiating

217

norms that have kept women in a position of inferiority to men, and of the prejudices that have resulted from them. The question to consider now is of whether the movement can or should be made more radical by the addition of another project: that of changing the nature of prevailing values, and replacing bad, male ones with enlightened, female ones. Should feminists not only try to make sure (for instance) that *if* men are encouraged to be militaristic and aggressive *then* women should be treated like that too, but also try to bring about a society where this happens to neither sex?

On the face of it, there seems to be no problem at all about aiming for both these things. As has already been said, it seems obviously true that no matter how radical the equal rights kind of feminism may actually be, it must nevertheless be more radical to aim for both kinds of change than only one. It does also seem plausible (and anyway can certainly be accepted for the sake of this argument) that a great many social attitudes, including all those that involve encouraging militarism and violence, are badly in need of change.

However, even though such change may be very desirable, its desirability is not enough to show that its pursuit should be regarded as part of *feminism*, and that is the question at issue now.

It is easy to see in a vague and general way why it seems as though it should be: the idea is that violence and so on are essentially male. However, as the analysis of traditionalist argument has shown, it is dangerous to leave parts of arguments fuzzy. There are different grounds on the basis of which something might be described as male or female, and at least two possibilities need to be distinguished here, since they lead to different accounts of why the elimination of militarism might be considered a feminist project. One is the idea that militarism is male in the sense that men (but not women) *enjoy* war and aggression, so that it is to men's *advantage* that society should be militaristic; the other is that it is male in the sense that men *cause* wars and other kinds of conflict (whereas women, if they had power, would not). Of course militarism might be male in both these ways at once, but there is no reason in principle why the two should go together: it is common for people to value what they cannot bring about, or to dislike what they do bring about. The two possibilities must therefore be considered separately.

First, then, suppose that militarism is male in the sense that men enjoy war and the preparations for it, whereas women do not. In that case, peace may be regarded as a feminist issue simply on the grounds that the present militaristic state of things is one indication among many of the way women's interests have been disregarded under patriarchy, and that a world that was fair to women and took their interests properly into account would give a much higher value to peace.

If such claims about the natures of the sexes are true (which we can accept at least for the sake of argument), then peace is indeed in this sense a feminist issue. However, if this is the justification for a feminist peace movement, and the ground for seeking peace is that women's interests should not be regarded as less important than men's, it means that the pursuit of peace is only one part of the pursuit of equal rights for women. If peace is pursued for this reason, it is pursued (as it were) only incidentally: what is really wanted is *whatever is in women's interests*, and peace is valued only as something that is in women's interests. The feminist peace movement, when understood in this way, is only part of a properly understood equal rights movement. This is another illustration of the fact that equal rights feminism is really much more radical than is generally thought, since it includes any campaign to change social values *for this reason*.

Even if some part of the motivation behind the feminist peace movement is concern for women's legitimate interests, however, it seems most unlikely that many of the women involved in it would regard it as the whole. There can be little doubt that most of them would, once the matter had been presented in this way, claim that militarism and war were straightforwardly *bad*, not just bad for women. And if feminists do want to pursue peace simply because it is better than war, rather than because it is good specifically for women, this certainly makes the feminist peace movement quite distinct from the equal rights movement.

In that case, however, we need another account of why the campaign should be counted as feminist, since it is no longer feminist in the sense of being *for* women; and it is here that the idea seems to be needed that militarism and war are male in the sense that men *cause* them, and perhaps fail to see how bad they are. Men may be the cause of war even though war is really as bad for them, in the long run, as for women. Peace in this case must apparently be seen as a feminist issue in the sense that it is women who can best bring it about.[5]

This distinction between what is done *for* women and what is done *by* them is extremely important; and it is particularly important in the context of this discussion, because it differentiates from a quite different point of view the two strands of recent feminism that are the subject of this essay. The equal rights feminism is feminist because its aim is to achieve something *for* women—something women are morally entitled

219

to—even though (I have argued) the campaign need not be conducted *by* women. Here the situation is just the opposite. If the feminist peace movement is to be understood as having concerns beyond equality of rights—a commitment to peace not just as something women want, but as something desirable in itself—the *justification* for it has nothing to do with women in particular, and it is therefore not feminist in the sense of being *for* women. If peace is a feminist issue at all, therefore, it must be so in virtue of some other characteristic; and the only possible candidate seems to be the idea that peace is something to be brought about *by* women. War and militarism are male in the sense that men were the *producers* of them; women, in contrast, will produce peace.

This must presumably be the kind of idea that leads some supporters of Greenham to claim that the camp should be entirely female because peace is a women's issue.

If this is indeed the idea, as I think it must be, it is clear that we have returned to familiar terrain. The claim that some area of activity is the appropriate preserve of one sex sounds remarkably like the traditionalist claim about separate spheres. That should be quite enough to signal a need to take care here; and in particular to clarify precisely what is being claimed.

The traditionalist argument, it will be remembered, derived part of its plausibility from the conflation of two very different claims: first, that if everyone were treated according to *general* principles specifying how different kinds of people should be treated, women and men would, as a result, happen to be treated differently; and second, that men and women should *as such* be subject to different social norms and institutions. Any feminist idea that peace is the business of women needs clarification of exactly the same kind. Is the claim that peace is a women's issue supposed to mean simply that if you start a movement for peace and open it to all who are good at bringing about peace, it is women rather than men who will (as it happens) qualify as activists? Or is it, on the other hand, supposed to be a women's issue in the sense that only women (and perhaps even all women) *should be* involved?

There may be no clear answer to the question of which any particular feminist really means, since unless the distinction has been noticed and thought about what is actually believed may be some vague combination of the two.[6] However, when supporters of the Greenham camp defend its separatist policy by means of the claim that peace is a women's issue, it is evident that at least some feminists, at least some of the time, must be committed to the second and stronger position. The policy at Greenham is not that the *belligerent* should be excluded from the camp, with the incidental consequence that the camp has turned out to be all female; it is that *men* should be excluded. This is precisely the counterpart of the traditionalist conclusion that men and women should as much be treated differently, and that the separation of spheres should be *imposed*.

It is also certainly true that there are to be found in feminism (not by any means consistently or universally, but unmistakably nevertheless) widespread indications of ideas that precisely mirror ones already familiar from traditionalist arguments about the sexes' proper places. These also support the idea that some feminist ideas about appropriate activities and treatment for men and women have the same general structure as those of the traditionalist.

For instance, the traditionalist argument, as I have argued, depends on claims about the differences between the sexes, and traditionalists as a result are well known for a set of devices to keep suitable beliefs about female nature intact in the face of contrary evidence. They may, for instance, dismiss apparent exceptions to the traditional ideals of womanhood or manhood with claims that these are not *true* women or men, or that they have been *corrupted* by various means (interfering feminists, nagging wives, and the like). In just the same way, it is now quite common for feminists to say similar things of women who fail to act in ways this kind of feminist theory says they should: either their thinking and acting as they do may be explained by patriarchal conditioning, or they are not true women (I have many times heard this said in reply to the accusation that Mrs. Thatcher hardly bears out feminist predictions about what the world will be like when women are in power). Corresponding ideas are also held about men. Men are now to be found who claim with some pride that their feminist friends count them as honorary women; and certainly there are feminists who say of men who show any appearance of virtue that this proves nothing but the depth of their guile, and that experience will always eventually reveal their true blackness of soul. Ideas like these are, of course, not universal in feminism, but they are sufficiently widespread to suggest that a feminist variation on the idea of imposed separate spheres is lurking in the background.

In addition to all this, it seems to me that the very fact of *describing* peace and other such matters as women's issues shows that the division between the sexes is being presupposed. Compare, for instance, describing physics as a boys' subject, or mining as a man's job. Far more is implied by such utterances than a simple prediction that most people good at physics and mining will happen to be male.

Many feminists, in other words, seem to want differential treatment of men and women *as such,* just as their traditionalist opponents do. But since that is so, and the women's values kind of feminism presupposes what are, in effect, imposed separate spheres, it must be incompatible with any movement to eliminate those spheres.

I said at the outset that I wanted to show that the women's values kind of feminism was incompatible with other aims that seemed essential to any form of feminism, and I have so far argued that it is incompatible with any attempt to eradicate the sexes' imposed separate spheres.

The fact that these two conflict, however, is not enough to prove that it is the women's values part of feminism that must be dropped; perhaps it is the equal rights part that should go. Any feminist must oppose the traditional form of differential treatment of the sexes, but of course the traditional norms that differentiated the sexes actually kept women in a position of inferiority to men. Perhaps all feminists need to do is oppose differential treatment of *that* form, rather than differential treatment as such.

This is certainly a possible line of defense. If it is attempted, however, there still remains the problem of justifying whatever kind of differential treatment is proposed in place of the traditional one; and the problem feminists face here is just the same as the corresponding one of traditionalists. A concern for *peace* cannot, at least without considerably more argument, justify a policy that specifies *sex.*

This would technically be the case, as argued earlier, even if the divide between the militaristic and the peace-loving coincided exactly with the divide between women and men. It is, however, obvious to anyone who considers the matter with anything approaching impartiality that there are masses of peace-loving men and not a few militaristic women, so the effect of having a policy based on sex must apparently *undermine* the expressed purpose of the policy. It will leave out of the movement all the men who could, in principle, further its aims, while allowing into it some female snakes in the grass who might sabotage it. This, obviously, cannot be justified, at least without considerably more argument, in terms of a desire to produce peace. Certainly (given the premise about the general nature of the sexes) *if* one sex or the other were on its own to take on the task of bringing about peace, it should be women; but no justification has yet been given for making the divide in the first place, and that is precisely what is needed.

This does not show that there could not be such a justification, but it is not at all easy to see what it might be. The kind of argument I have already mentioned for limited separatism supports nothing as large-scale as this. However, it is not necessary to argue that a reason cannot be found; it is necessary only to say that *until* one is given, we have no reason at all to accept the idea that policies to bring about peace or any other desirable end should take the separation of the sexes as a starting point. At the very least, it seems arbitrary and pointless.

In fact, however, the situation seems even worse than that. Unless an adequate justification can be given, it must be assumed that feminist ideas of this kind depend on nothing better than the separate spheres of patriarchal tradition, which have been the main tool of women's oppression. The women's values kind of feminism seems to rest on the unsupported assumptions and deeply flawed arguments of feminism's opponents, and to accept the very divide men originally instituted for their own benefit.

This is why it seems to me that opposition to the differential treatment of the sexes *as such*, and not simply differential treatment that specifically harms women, must still remain part of feminism. Even if the perniciousness of the separate spheres would be considerably lessened by their being made more equal, that would not eliminate their potential for harm: they would still limit the options for individuals who were unsuited to the specified sexual mold, and damage such enterprises as the pursuit of peace by keeping out people who might be able to advance them. If the imposed differentiation of the sexes does any such harm at all, and if there is no better basis for it than the habits of mind induced by patriarchy, it surely *must* be an essential part of feminism to remove it. And since the women's values kind of feminism is at odds with this, it seems reasonable to claim that it is *that* kind of feminism, rather than so-called liberal feminism, that should be regarded as dangerously conservative, making alterations on the surface while leaving the roots of the trouble untouched.

At least until better arguments appear, it seems to me that we must take a properly understood equal rights campaign to constitute the essence of feminism; and that being so, we cannot have the women's values part.

These arguments may seem to lead to a paradox. It was accepted earlier that it must be more radical to get rid of differential treatment of the sexes *and* change values than to do only one of those things. It was also accepted that values did need to be changed. But now it has been concluded that if feminism also wants to change social values, it undermines the attempt to abolish differential treatment, and is to that extent conservative. It therefore *cannot* be radical in both ways at once.

However, it is probably obvious how this difficulty can be resolved. The conclusion to be drawn is not that women must after all resign themselves to nothing more than seeking equality within the present scheme of things. Once again, it is important to distinguish between the question of *whether* something should be done and *why* it should be done. Nothing has been said here against the need to change social values and to reorganize society; all that has been argued is that, except to the extent that they are part of the equal rights question, these matters are not *feminist* issues, or *women's* issues. It is only if they are seen as feminist issues that they undermine the basic feminist case.

Of course, if feminists are right about the natures of men and women, there will certainly be a connection between feminism and the pursuit of peace and other such desirable things. Anyone who wants peace will be well advised to work for feminism as a means to peace, as well as (or instead of) as an end in itself: if women are good at bringing about peace, giving women their fair share of power and influence will certainly advance the cause of peace. That, however, does not mean that peace is a feminist issue, or that it should be regarded as in some way the special property of women.

According to these arguments there is every reason for feminists to pursue peace, and other changes in social values, just as they now say they should. The only difference is that they should see themselves as pursuing these things not *as* feminists, or *as* women, but simply as people concerned with peace, and willing whenever possible to join forces with anyone else who shares those concerns. Or at least, to do so within the constraints of the limited kind of separatism which, as mentioned earlier, may be justified by the equal rights kind of feminism.

Nothing, therefore, seems to be lost by this view of things except the unsupported assumption that if any cause is worthwhile it must in some way be part of feminism. There is, on the other hand, a great deal to be gained in the possibility of a properly radical attack on the differential treatment of women and men, and in the benefits to society in general of the full emancipation of women.

This is why, although there may be many good reasons for keeping an all-female camp at Greenham, the idea that peace is a feminist issue is not one of them.

Notes

1. Germaine Greer, *The Female Eunuch* (Paladin, Frogmore, 1971), p. 296.

2. For a fuller discussion of some of these matters see Janet Radcliffe Richards, "Separate Spheres" in Singer, ed., *Applied Ethics* (Oxford: Oxford University Press, 1986) and also "Discrimination," *Proceedings of the Aristotelian Society*, supp. vol. LIX, 1985.

3. Traditionalists try various other lines of defense when this familiar one is shown to fail, but they all run into difficulty. There is good reason to think that no adequate justification could possibly be found for separate spheres of anything like the traditional form. See Richards, "Separate Spheres" and "Discrimination."

4. This term is highly misleading, anyway, when applied to the kinds of concern described here, since a campaign for equal treatment could take place against the background of any kind of political theory—conservative or communist just as much as traditionally liberal. The kind of freedom demanded by traditional liberalism has nothing to do with the equal treatment of the sexes as described here.

5. A slight variant is the idea that militarism is bad *according to female values* but not according to male values. This is a more complex matter, but the line of argument presented in this paper still applies.

6. This point applies equally to the earlier distinction between campaigns *for* and *by* women. If the distinction has not been noticed, it is no good asking what is actually said by feminists on the subject; all that is possible is to look at what the implications are generally taken to be.

Comments

Why does it seem to be true that women, especially mothers and a maternal perspective, have historically played such an important role in peace movements and peace thinking? So much so that when a great male pacifist leader like Gandhi wants to think of an alternative to the world he opposes, he evokes maternal imagery. What kind of tradition is this? How has it been grounded in ways that locate women in certain roles? Can we rethink this issue in a manner that empowers women and is efficacious for peace politics?

One of the constructions one has to defeat in order to make possible this latter alternative is the notion that there is an opposition between rational men as against emotional women. Sara Ruddick, a feminist philosopher, begins by unpacking a narrow view of rationality. She does this by tying rationality to the activity of care. Her argument is not anti-reason. Rather, she evokes a particular understanding of reason. And with this new understanding, Ruddick calls for a shift in our appreciation of motivations for war and for peace.

Ruddick works over a set of concerns she has previously tagged "maternal thinking." She takes seriously the complexity of the mother's mind and the subtleties of her ways of thinking, elaborating, and expanding the notion of care beyond that of mothering children to include many forms of care. She points out that women are disproportionately involved in all societal modes of care.

What kind of politics do these recognitions invite? What kinds of interventions in the social and political world? What sorts of peace people are women supposed to become, once they acknowledge the rationality of care embedded in peace activities?

11

The Rationality of Care

Sara Ruddick

To speak with my voice: the ultimate. I didn't want anything more, anything different. If need be, I could prove that, but to whom?—Christa Wolf, *Cassandra*

We'll persuade nurses and mothers to tell the approved tales to their children and to shape their souls with tales more than their bodies with hands.—Plato, *Republic*

And looking into the face of . . . one dead man we see two dead, the man and the life of the woman who gave him birth; the life she wrought into his life! And looking into his dead face someone asks a woman, what does a woman know about war? What, what, friends in the face of a crime like that, what does man know about war?—Anna Shaw, speech to women's peace party, 1915

The dragging of Hector around Patroclus' tomb, the slaughter in the fire of the men captured alive: we'll deny that all this is truly told.—Plato, *Republic*

No woman who is a woman says of a human body, "it is nothing."—Olive Schreiner, *Woman and Labor*

When we went inside we found Socrates just released from his chains, and Xantippe—you know her!—sitting by him with the little boy on her knees. As soon as Xantippe saw us she broke out into the sort of remark you would expect from a woman: "Oh, Socrates, this is the last time you and your friends will be able to talk together!" Socrates looked at Crito. "Crito," he said, "someone had better take her home."—Plato, *Phaedo*

I heard her voice, calling "Mother, Mother." I went towards the sound. She was completely burned. The skin had come off her head altogether, leaving a knot of twisted hair at the top. My daughter said, "Mother, you're late, please take me back quickly." She said it was hurting a lot. But there were no doctors. There was nothing I could do. So I covered up her naked body and held her in my arms for nine hours. At about eleven o'clock that night she cried out again, "Mother," and put her hand around my neck. It was already ice-cold. I said, "Please say Mother again." But that was the last time.—Hiroshima survivor

We surely say that a decent man will believe that . . . being dead is not a terrible thing . . . There is no further need of wailing and lamentations . . . They're useless to women who are to be decent, let alone for men.—Plato, *Republic*

Most women and men support organized violence, at least in "emergencies." Certainly, women have not absented themselves from war. Wherever battles are fought and justified, whether in the vilest or noblest of causes, women on both sides of the battle lines support the military engagements of their sons, lovers, friends, and mates. Increasingly, women are proud to fight alongside their brothers, and as fiercely, in whatever battles their state, cadre, or cause enlists them.

Nonetheless, throughout history there have been women who insist that, as women, they have distinct reasons for rejecting men's wars. This does not mean that women are innately or inevitably peaceful. As Jane Addams put it:

The belief that a woman is against war simply and only because she is a woman and not a man, does not, of course, hold. In every country there are many, many women who believe that War is inevitable and righteous, and that the highest possible service is being performed by their sons who go into the Army.

Nor are women afraid to fight, unable to fight, or morally superior to fighters. In the words of Olive Schreiner:

230

It is not because of woman's cowardice, incapacity, nor, above all, because of her general superior virtue that she will end war when her voice is finally and fully heard.

Rather, to quote Addams again:

The women do have a sort of pang about it. . . . That curious revolt comes out again and again, even in the women who are most patriotic. . . . Even those women, when they are taken off their guard, give a certain protest, a certain plaint against the whole situation which very few men I think are able to formulate.

Both Addams and Schreiner traced women's "curious revolt" against war to their experience as mothers. Addams compared a mother to "an artist who is in the artillery corps, let us say, and is commanded to fire upon a wonderful thing, say St. Mark's at Venice, or the Duomo at Florence, or any other great architectural and beautiful thing. I am sure that she would have just a little more compunction than the man who had never given himself to creating beauty and did not know the cost of it." Schreiner spoke of "so many months of weariness and pain while bones and muscles were shaped within; so many hours of anguish and struggle that breath might be; so many baby mouths drawing life at woman's breasts; all this that men might lie with glassed eyeballs, and swollen bodies, and fixed, blue unclosed mouths, and great limbs tossed." Neither Addams nor Schreiner believed that women became generally wise from being mothers. Schreiner did however attribute to women a quite specific knowledge:

No woman who is a woman says of a human body, "it is nothing". . . . On this one point, and on this point almost alone, the knowledge of woman, simply as woman, is superior to that of man; she knows the history of human flesh; she knows its cost; he does not.

In this paper, I take Addams's and Schreiner's claim seriously.[1] From the work they have done, women have derived a distinctive kind of knowledge that might be put to antimilitarist use. More particularly, women would tell a "history of human flesh" quite differently from a military history. I put to one side the passions and fears that make many women—like many men—militaristic. My concern is only with those women who protest wars and preparation for wars. I also limit myself to one of many bases for protest, namely the caring labor that women have undertaken. Although caring women are expected to be antimilitaristic, their "curious revolt" is not included when reasonable people reflect upon wars and preparations for wars. To "formulate" a reason in women's "plaint" contributes to many complementary efforts to articulate a rationality of care that could strengthen antimilitarist politics.

A preliminary note about terminology: By the "whole situation," which is the object of protest, I mean organized, deliberate, "legitimate" violence, not random assaults and individual aggression or defenses against them but the social violence of which good people approve. Nor will I be concerned with the absolute renunciation of violence, a preoccupation which divides anti-militarists. My concern is with a collective decision to invest funds and energies in armies and weapons, then to rely upon the threat or use of military violence to protect the collective and enforce its will. In order to develop a theory and practice of nonviolent action, people must become suspicious of the rhetoric and reason of deliberate collective violence. It is to this sturdy suspicion of organized violence in the best of causes that protest in the name of care can make a contribution. On the other hand, the sturdiest distrust in violence does not enable a community to get what it needs or to protect those it cares for. Antimilitarist arguments remain unpersuasive in the absence of alternative nonviolent means of collective resistance to violence. Elsewhere, I have discussed the distinctive contribution that a feminist account of caring labor, and of mothering in particular, could make to the theory and practice of nonviolent action.[2] My arguments here are only preparatory to the larger task of imagining a world where nonviolent struggle replaces collective, deliberate violence.

The Rationality of Care

In the past several years, feminist philosophers have developed a critique of "Reason" as it has been defined in Western philosophy.[3] Engaged in a "hermeneutics of suspicion," they have reread the texts of the Great Thinkers with a subversive eye. They have taken with some seriousness the misogynist remarks that pervade philosophical texts. But the issue is more profound than the sexism of great writers. It is not possible to apply impartially to women the ideals of reason that Great Thinkers have formulated. The ideals themselves have been genderized. Standards of rationality are shaped and, from a human perspective, distorted by masculine affective, sexual, and social histories. Although any summary misrepresents the variety and subtlety of critique, let me briefly suggest the argument.

"Reason" is conceptualized as an attainment achieved through a discipline, method, or struggle that creates a rational self. The virtue of "Reason" is defined by a series of dichotomies; reason is achieved when the first of the member of the pair controls or contains the second. As Reason governs passion, so the mind is opposed to and rules over the body; so too the theoretical, universal, abstract, and symbolic are opposed to, govern, and explain the practical, particular, concrete, and material. The rational self is able to persevere in its own being, controlling forces external to reason, whether they originate from others or from internal passion. Reasonable selves are also in agreement with each other. The reality known by reason is one; an abstract order underlying the manifold varieties of speech, nature, and history. Hence, reasonable minds are indistinguishable in their true judgments. Disagreement does not mark difference but a failure of at least one party to see clearly.

Bodily sensations, particular affections, and passionate desires are of course human. Yet, repeatedly, throughout the history of Western philosophy, the dichotomies that define reason also define and reinforce a dichotomy between male and female. Within certain canonical texts, reason is explicitly defined as *not* female. Conversely, the "female" is defined as the antagonist of reason, as what is particular, passionate, changeable, bodily, and sensuous. What is reasonable—abstract, impersonal, passionless—discourse is accordingly associated with what is "male." The rational self controls not only bodily sensation, particular attachment, and passionate desires but also those people associated with the bodily, particular, and passionate. Hence, "reason" grants the right to speak in public and to rule at home.

> [G]ood order would have been wanting in the human family if some were not governed by others wiser than themselves. So by such a kind of subjection is woman naturally subject to man, because in man discretion of reason predominates.[4]

To say that reason is "male" is not to say that actual men are reasonable. Ideals of reason describe an attainment that excludes most people. The point is that to attain rationality requires, for men or women, a separation from and control of sensuous, particular, passionate, concrete attachments, and styles of cognition that mark the "female." "Female" persons are harbingers of disagreement and are therefore of an unruly division that threatens the rational self and rational argument.[5]

Military thinking, the plans and justifications for war, express in exaggerated form those characteristics that render reason "male." Virtually no one denies that military thinking is imbued with masculine values. No more than a man is born reasonable is a boy born a soldier. Becoming a soldier means learning to control fears and domestic longings, which are explicitly labelled "womanly." This much has long been familiar. What is increasingly clear is that becoming a militarist means acquiring a distinctive way of thinking. Feminist critics have underlined the ways in which philosophers honor, even as they construct, conceptual connections between reason, war, and masculinity. The struggle to become reasonable "mustn't be useless to warlike men"; on the contrary, philosophers see to it that those men and (sometimes) women who are called "reasonable" have "proved best [both] in philosophy and with respect to war."[6] Even as the tendency to define reason in opposition to the feminine takes different historical and philosophical forms, even more, the requirements of military thinking vary radically, depending upon political, economic, and technological contexts of war. In our nuclear age, there is a "language of warriors," a "technico-strategic rationality,"[7] which is shared by armers and disarmers, chiefs of staff, and chief negotiators. This rationality exhibits in near caricature the kinds of dichotomization and abstraction that, in other contexts, have been characterized as male. Military theorists

> portray themselves as clear-sighted, unsentimental analysts describing the world as it is . . . a world of self-confirming theorems invites fantasies of control over events that we do not have. . . . Through abstracted models and logic, hyperrationalism reduces states and their relations to games which can be simulated. . . . One of the legacies of war is a "habit of simple distinction, simplification, and opposition." . . . One basic task of a state at war is to portray the enemy in terms as absolute and abstract as possible in order to distinguish as sharply as possible the act of killing from the act of murder. . . . It is always *"the enemy,"* a "pseudo-concrete universal."[8]

Men and women often assume that the abstract, impersonal character of military thinking will alienate women. In a similar way, some assume that when women appreciate the masculine bias of ideals of reason, they will formulate alternative ideals appropriate to their lives. Actually, however, women respond variously to masculinist ideals of reason. In practice, and contrary to myth, these ideals suit many women's intellectual life as well as men's, just as soldiery also suits the temperament and skills of many women. Even women who are alienated by practices of reasoning governed by masculinist ideals want to be included among the people of reason who can speak and be heard in public. These women learn the language of warriors, even as they have learned the language of philosophers, some because they love it and speak it well, others because they want to show they can speak and be heard where it counts. Many such women walk "a path bounded on one side by inauthenticity and the other by subversion." To be "reasonable," when reason is described as not female and rationality is said to depend upon overcoming "female" attachments and obligations, requires of a woman "a radical disidentification from self."[9] On the other hand, if a woman who has learned to be reasonable tries to reason in a different voice she may find she cannot be heard as reasonable. Indeed deconstruction of the ideals of reason is more apt to explain than to overcome women's apparent silence as reasoners.

Nonetheless, many feminist thinkers, emboldened by the deconstruction of masculinist ideals, are determined to "make female speech prevail, to penetrate male discourse, to make the ear of man listen," "to name the nameless so that it can be thought."[10] Despite a variety of theoretical orientations, there are common themes in the articulation of alternative ideals. Ideally, reason is "connected" to the passions that motivate it, and to the people, histories, and symbols it comprehends. Ideally, the reasonable person is cognitively able to see particulars in their complexity, to attend with nonintrusive love to what is real, to speak truly, and to conceive of a truth that is caring. The reasonable person does not fight change but welcomes it, developing concepts that enable her as a knower to change with the changes she experiences. The autonomy for which she strives serves to promote a "differentiation [that] is not distinctness and separateness, but a particular way of being connected to others."[11] She refuses to renounce, though she fears losing, what has been called her "subjective" voice. At the same time, she rejects the label of "subjectivity," striving instead for an objectivity that "aims at a form of knowledge that grants to the world around us its independent integrity, but does so in a way that remains cognizant of, indeed relies on, our connectivity with that world."[12] Although, like the Man of Reason, she often fears people who reason differently, ideally she is conscious of the social construction of many reasons, including her own, and thus makes intellectual humility and nonviolence a consequence of reason.[13]

Although these ideals were identified by feminists who explored women's experience, they are not intrinsically associated with gender. Indeed, feminists who formulate them underline the fact that they are evident in the thinking of many men, including philosophers and scientists. In honoring certain kinds of reasoning, masculinist ideals distort the actual varieties of thinking. Freed from distorted selection, reasoning that has been subordinated in the name of "femininity" will be seen as human. Some feminists are leery of attempting to describe suppressed, distinctive voices as women's voices. They fear perpetuating divisions of gender, including the divisions of reason that describe any womanly thinking as irrational, intuitive, subjective, i.e., not thinking at all. They argue that since reason ideally transcends gender, there is no need to look for distinct and suppressed voices that are, in fact, associated with women.

However, reasoners cannot, at will, transcend the world in which they reason. In a gendered world, thinking is structured by divisions in our lives. Mostly male humans have created not only the practices of science, law, war, philosophy, psychology, and poetry but also our thinking about these practices. At the same time, certain distinctive kinds of work have been undertaken primarily by women. It is likely that out of women's work, just as out of men's, distinctive kinds of thinking would arise. Moreover, unless we learn to look at women's ways of knowing in their specificity, I fear we will drift into the very sentimental dichotomies some feminists fear. We will, for example, consider peace as a womanly, sweetly empty counterpart to men's wars rather than as the myriad kinds of nonviolent actions it must become.

In attempting to articulate ideals of reason, which are in some sense feminine but which ultimately could transcend gender, I have found it useful to draw upon a "practicalist" conception of reason that, though central to current philosophical discussion, differs from the dominant masculinist ideal.[14] According to practicalists, reason arises from and is tested against "practice." Practices are collective human activities distinguished by the aims that identify them and by the consequent demands made upon practitioners committed to those aims. The constitutive aims of a practice determine what counts as reasonable within it, even as a "reasonable" articulation of aims and strategies render the practice coherent and communicable. Not any stretch of discourse counts as reasonable. To be "reasonable," a kind of thinking must make coherent and communicable sense of the activities of practitioners. Yet there is no primary reason, no standard of coherence and communicability that transcends practice. Practices in some ways surprisingly alike, in others strikingly contrastive, give rise to reasons that can be compared and contrasted. Scientific reasoning is distinct from, though in many elements similar to, religious, historical, mathematical, psychoanalytic, or hermeneutic reasoning.

In practicalist terminology, the mothering of children can be understood to be a practice from which a distinctive kind of thinking arises.[15] Maternal thinking, like scientific or religious thinking, attempts to make coherent and communicable the practice whose aims it serves. The work of mothering is, symbolically and psychologically, the central instance of what has come to be called "caring labour."[16] "Care" is a general designation covering many practices—nursing, homemaking, and tending the elderly, for example—each of which is caring because it, like mothering, includes among its defining aims insuring the safety and well-being of subjects cared for. Instances of care cannot, however, be simply assimilated. For example, caretaking always involves "teaching" the subjects of care, and teaching itself can be understood as a kind of caring labor. But the teaching of healthy children differs from the instruction of the ill or elderly or the members of a household by a homemaker, while teaching itself is not exhaustively described in the language of care. To confuse the care of healthy children with nursing, tending the elderly, homemaking, or teaching would be bad for child, patient, homemates, older person, student, and the caretaker herself.

Amidst the varieties of caring, there are elements of the work that, though not present in all cases, are sufficiently common and central to be formative of a rationality of care, just as, despite the varieties of science or religion, we still speak of scientific or religious rationality. However, when articulating in detail the rationality of care it is crucial to distinguish between kinds of caring and the overlappingly similar but nonetheless distinctive rationalities to which they give rise.

Demands of care always arise within particular social contexts. All people need to die in some comfort, in some company, with "dignity." For some this means enough food to ward off painful starvation, some kind of shelter in which to lie, a friendly hand. For others a flexible and humane relation to high-tech medicine. Ideally, caretakers respect the well-being of dying subjects. For some, this means waiting upon God's grace and miracles; for others, respecting the cost and "uselessness" of extended pain. To begin at the beginning, although all children require protection, they are variously threatened by chemical poisons, uncontrolled bacteria, uncovered wells, speeding cars, junk food, and famine. Some must be protected from the police, some are protected by them.

237

In sum, there are radical differences among caretakers even with respect to the simplest acts of care—feeding, sheltering, holding, keeping safe. It *may* be that in situations of harsh tyranny or abject poverty, no one can undertake caring labor. I myself, however, am struck by the resilience of care in situations which make caring nearly impossible.

The rationality of care, like the labor from which it arises, is socially variable. We have barely begun to examine the rationality of care in any culture. It may turn out that concepts central in one social context— attentive love, for example—may be subordinate, perhaps even absent, in another. Given the varieties of caring, it is impossible to predict the applicability *or the inapplicability* of concepts across culture. Rather than attempting to assimilate or control for difference, those who reflect upon care need to listen to different voices without assimilating them, to be precise about the particular social origins of their own perspective, and then to develop an account of care that allows caretakers to act politically while preserving differences.

The rationality of care—like scientific or religious rationality—is potentially genderless. Caretaking is a human activity. A small but weighty fraction of specifically maternal work is ineluctably female. Only women can carry and give birth to infants; where babies are nursed, only women can nurse them. But pregnancy, birth, lactation, and the care of tiny, relatively immobile infants make up a very small portion of maternal work. A scrambling, temperamental toddler in reach of poisons under the sink, a school child left out of a birthday party, a college student unable to write her papers—these children are more emblematic of the demands upon a mother than the smiling infant so briefly quiet on her lap. Of the many kinds of caring labor that are not evidently maternal, most can be done by men and women. Similarly, many women refuse caring work either because it neither interests nor suits them or because of exploitative and confining work conditions. A woman is no more "naturally" a caretaker, no more obligated to caring labor, than a man is "naturally" a scientist or obligated to become one. Both kinds of work should be open to capable and interested women and men.

Although the work of care could transcend gender, care has been profoundly womanly. This is not, in the first instance, because many women are caretakers but, rather, because most caretakers are women. Women have not only borne but have also cared for children. Although the sociological explanations are in dispute, few disagree that in most cultures the work of nursing, caring for the elderly, and even teaching, especially of small children, has been performed by women. Accordingly,

238

to study care would be to study women, even if only a small proportion of women engaged seriously in care. As it is, however, in most cultures throughout the world, many more women than men expect to undertake and identify with caretaking work. Although many women refuse caring labor, women as a group are apparently more likely than men to acquire the abilities of care and to see the world from the vantage it affords. Hence the rationality of care and "women's ways of knowing" are inextricably entangled. When critics, psychologists, artists, and others speak of women's minds, they are speaking also—though of course not only of— the rationality of care. In most cultures now, to articulate a rationality of care is also to ascribe a distinctive intellectual vantage to women.

To speak of women's ways of knowing or of a rationality deriving from work that has, as a matter of history, been women's work is not tantamount to creating a "woman's reason" to rival the "man's." It is a reason that thrives on dichotomy that looks for a female to oppose to the male, a "natural" woman to oppose to man's "culture," a subjective mind to oppose to his objectivity. It is militarists who benefit from the equation of women with irrationality, who call Cassandra mad and defense intellectuals people of reason. The struggle to be "rational"—to see what is real in all its complexity and ambiguity—is a peacemaker's struggle. The task is to reconceive rationalities that will be instruments of nonviolent action, rather than of war.

Because "the feminine" has been defined in part by its exclusion from rationality, and because care is womanly, it becomes a struggle to articulate without sentimentality or abstract simplification a "rationality of care." Women who put pillowcases, toys, and other artifacts of "attachment" against the barbed wire fences of missile bases are prizing the symbols of care from the context where they are expected and harmless. They are "words" of a developing language which is spoken by women in public in order to resist violations of care in care's name.

The rationality of care, as I read it, is consonant with, and indeed often exemplifies, alternative ideals of reason advanced by feminists. At the same time, it contrasts with masculinist and militarist rationalities. For example, since care is constituted by the demand of subjects that they be assisted, the adequacy of distinctions and concepts is tested in terms of responsiveness to need, rather than, for example, by the prediction, control, or destruction they enable. The ability to respond to human needs without undue fantasy or projection requires a nonintrusive attention to specific particulars of persons and of connections and dependencies among them. Such attentive love differs markedly from the intellec-

239

tion of day dreaming, experiment, invention, and strategy, though caretakers may engage in all of these, sometimes in the service of care and certainly in other intellectual pursuits. Since the vulnerable are subject to abuse and neglect, the circumstances of care allow for violence. Caretakers are tempted by sadism, self-indulgent aggression, and self-protective indifference to the real needs of others. They must learn to see and speak truly about these temptations and about the discipline of resisting them. By contrast, increasing vulnerability and aggressing against the vulnerable is an aim of the military. A benign detachment from one's own and others' vulnerability is often an aim of the man of reason.

On the practicalist view of reason, the meaning of "reason," "feeling," and their right relation are given within a practice. Caring work is imbued with disturbingly ambivalent feelings about the subject cared for and the demands of the work. Maternal love, for example, is intermixed with hate, sorrow, and regret; affection for the elderly with impatience and resentment; compassion for the ill with disgust and despair. In a practice governed by the demand to assist and protect, ambivalent and potentially destructive feelings cry out for reflective assessment. Reflective assessment of feeling is, like attentive regard, a defining "rational" activity of caretakers. As attention is itself a kind of love tested in practice, so reflective assessment is itself tested by feelings in the context of the need to assist. Rather than separating reason from feeling and both from action, the practice of care makes reflective, active feeling one of the most difficult attainments of reason. In sum, in the rationality of care, "feelings" are at best complex but sturdy instruments of work quite unlike the simple and separate hates, fears, and loves that motivate military endeavors or are put to one side in many philosophical analyses.

Yet the opposition between the rationalities of militarism and of care, though real, is not simple. I myself have contrasted the "preservative love" of mothering with military destruction. And, indeed, the contrast seems nearly a contradiction. Mothering begins in birth and promises life; military thinking justifies organized, deliberate deaths. A mother preserves the bodies, nurtures the psychic growth, and disciplines the conscience of children she cares for; the military deliberately endangers the same body, mind, and conscience in the name of victory and abstract causes. Mothers protect children who are at risk; the military risks the children mothers protect. Yet I took the term "preservative love" from J. Glenn Gray's account of it in warriors' lives.[17] For Gray, preservative love is poignantly bittersweet in battle where it flourishes because it is threatened everywhere by death. By contrast, the preservative love of care is marked by its unexciting dailiness and a matter-of-fact acceptance of vulnerability and the threat of loss. Preservative love is opposed to military destruction but the opposition is a matter of the weight and context of destruction and love within two systems of thinking.

Ideals of reason are controlling, and, within Western scientific thinking at least, the capacity to control is made a test of reason. Just-war theories control our perceptions of war, turning our attention from bodies and their fate to abstract causes and rules for achieving them. Nuclear thinking gives an illusion of control over events that are profoundly unpredictable. Both the experience of being controlled by alien thought and the value put on control within that thought leads some feminists to reject the idea of control altogether. Indeed, caretakers think about control differently from scientists or generals. When the objects of care are human, they are not objects but subjects. Caretakers are liable to depend upon the dependence of those who depend upon them. They have to learn to relish reciprocity. It is an attainment of reason to perceive those cared for as intentional, self-generating agents, to identify as a caretaker's virtue her respect for the independent, uncontrollable will of the other. If the care is successful, a teacher or mother will protect and enable someone whose will cannot be controlled. Even a nurse or companion to the elderly can protect, as one would a flame in the wind, her subjects' ability to formulate and act on desires of their own. But none of this is tantamount to relinquishing control. Rather, the best control makes room for the limits of control. No one who has cared for a small toddler, supervised a classroom, or helped the learning-disabled in their travels will trust her own or her subjects' spontaneity. Care without control is a horror.

In sum, the opposition between militarism and care is not simple. Central concepts, while including certain commonalities, tend to be differently defined, weighted in ways appropriate to a system of thinking, and put to distinctive uses. I would now like to illustrate this general point by comparing military and caretaking concepts of the body.

The History of Human Flesh

Both militarists and caretakers, unlike philosophers, do their work among bodies. Both are ambivalent about the bodies they work among. Each of them conceives of the body as sexual and sharply gendered. For

241

each, death is a central bodily experience. In sharp contrast to military ideology, maternal thinking weights birth over death, offering a concept of natality as central to the rationality of care. Moreover, despite their shared preoccupation with sexuality and death, the concepts of the body, taken as a whole, differ radically.

One aim of militarist thinking is to develop descriptive and justificatory concepts appropriate to a "history of human flesh" in battle. The central business of war is a trafficking in bodies. Soldiers achieve their aims by threatening to damage bodies or actually doing so—burning, cutting, blasting, pounding, breaking flesh and bones. As Elaine Scarry puts it,

> Injury is the thing every exhausting piece of strategy and every single weapon is designed to bring into being: it is not something inadvertently produced on the way to producing something else but is the relentless object of all military activity.[18]

It sometimes seems that high-tech war is a contest between weapons where damage to bodies is not only described as "collateral" but is also a genuinely lamented secondary effect of the contest.[19] Yet we call these machines "weapons" precisely because with them we can threaten to sicken, mutilate, and burn up human bodies. Soldiers are killed and kill with weapons that are meant to be cruel. "Radiation sickness" and chemical poisons are not merely the "fall out" of "clean" explosions but predictable effects. Napalm purposely includes an ingredient that increases the adhesion of burning petrol to human skin. Explosive (dum dum) bullets, the metal cubes of claymore mines, the fiberglass fragments of cluster bombs are deliberately designed to tear bodies apart not only in pain but precisely in ways that defeat medical skill.[20]

Although some people are military enthusiasts despite—or even because of—war's cruelty, for many others military allegiance depends upon concealing the crude realities of injuring. There is a gap—moral and conceptual—between aims of war and the "glassed eye balls, and swollen bodies, and fixed blue unclosed mouths, and great limbs tossed,"[21] which is war's outcome. Reluctant militarists must keep their eyes fixed on justice despite the absence of moral or political connections between the capacity to out-injure and the cause in which one fights. Whatever the cause, "our boys" must be seen as defenders and victims, not killers. Accordingly, military thinking provides indentifiable techniques of redescription and evasion that focus the mind on strategy rather than on suffering; on sacrifice rather than on killing; and on the cause rather than the bodies torn apart in its name.[22] Primary among these conceptual strategies is the creation of the "just warrior" using interlocking myths of masculinity, sacrifice, and heroic death.

In most armies, in most of history, the just warrior is not only male but manly. Militarists seem nearly obsessed by the division between male and female bodies. Men and women may fight together outside of state power, but once violence is "legitimately" organized, only male bodies are deemed suitable to "carry the battle to the enemy." Military requirements cannot account for such a stringent association of war with masculinity. Many weapons and battle plans do not require the upper body strength that recruiters celebrate and that men, on the average, display. "The male's greater vital capacity, speed, muscle mass, aiming and throwing skills, his greater propensity for aggression and his more rapid rises in adrenalin" may indeed make him on the average "more fitted for physically intense combat."[23] Such specifically masculine strength has little to do with the computer centers, missile silos, bomber cockpits, and armored tanks at the center of modern battle plans. (Women in the Air Force are now members of command teams in missile silos; but they still cannot become bomber pilots.)

Although there is wide agreement that soldiers must be men, there are at least two competing views of manliness. For an enthusiastic militarist, the soldier who is necessarily male, is simultaneously a man who is "naturally" suited to become a soldier. There is little doubt that for many soldiers and strategists, injuring is sexualized and sexually exciting; soldiers themselves often describe their sexuality as compulsive and predatory.[24] Military speech is imbued with masculinist heterosexual metaphors. War is a "pissing contest." "To disarm is to get rid of all your stuff." "Spasm attacks" release "70 to 80 percent of our megatonnage in one orgasmic whump." Military lectures are filled with references to "vertical erectory launchers, thrust-to-weight ratios, soft lay-downs, deep penetration." An invasion of a small island becomes a "pre-dawn vertical insertion"; an outmoded missile is maintained because it's "in the nicest hole."[25] Suspected or captured soldiers, male and female, are tortured in specifically sexual ways. Women, generally, are sexually exploited while "conquered" women are predictably raped. Even children and the elderly are not immune from sexual abuse.

Citing connections between sex, gender, and war, some militarists "explain" the inevitability of battle in terms of men's sexuality. By contrast, those who are only reluctantly militarist, minimize and lament the sexualization of injuring. In order to justify war, they employ a competing, romantic, conception of armed manliness, both hetero- and homosexual. In their planes and ships, as on their battlefields, soldiers participate in a homoerotic romance ("bonding") whose sensual intensity suffuses war memoirs and poetry. The comrade turned heterosexual is no rapist but rather a temporarily celibate though fully sexual partner of the woman and women he excites and defends. As their literature and memories attest, the potentially violent yet vulnerable, dangerous yet restrained protector and warrior is alluring to girl and grandmother, sweetheart and wife.

This restrained sexuality of the just comrade is entwined with ideas of imminent death and sacrifice. The soldier is poignantly and particularly erotic as he becomes one with cause or cadre, relinquishing individual sexual union for the "universal."[26] His romantic death is sacrificial, at best heroic. Yet the ideology of death that serves reluctant militarists sits uneasily with the bodily realities it masks. Ideologically, military dead are warriors although soldiers are at least as able to flee death as the citizens of the villages and cities they bomb and burn. Military deaths are meaningful; the best battlefield death is a courageous, chosen testament to valor. In fact, numerous military deaths are accidental or fratricidal and an individual's death is rarely of even military consequence. A soldier's death is meant to be swift and clean; a sharp sacrifice. In fact, even as death by hemlock is messy and painful in ways philosophical fantasy must obscure, so too dying soldiers, like the assaulted victims who outnumber them, vomit, sob, shit, and scream their life away.

If military thinking must conceive of the body in ways that justify the work of killing and dying, caretakers depend upon a conception that justifies giving birth and sustaining what is born. Like militarists', caretakers' work is done through and with bodies. Mothering begins in some woman's intensely, ineluctably, often shatteringly physical experience. Much caretaking work, including early mothering, is done amidst feces, urine, vomit, milk, and blood. The subjects of care, generally, are physically at risk; their bodies must be tended as they are, not as they romatically might become. Bodies come in various shapes, have distinctive "chemistries," are liable to their own styles of being and acting. In myriad ways, the subjects of care assert themselves: this physical being is here; whoever cares for me, cares for this.

The omnipresence of bodies does not, for the caretaker any more than for the militarist, guarantee respect for the bodily. Caretakers may deny bodily pleasure in favor of suffering, preparing the way for "heroic" birth and the "sacrifice" of children. For these caretakers, pain, danger, and illness—certainly real enough—morbidly overshadow the exhilaration of even painful childbirth, the erotic experiences of nursing and holding, the wonder of children's healthy bodies, and the frequent beauty of even frail or dying bodies. More aggressively, caretakers may conceive of bodily nature as the "enemy" rather than substance of their work. The concept of body-as-enemy arises when caretakers transform the necessary control of their subjects' behavior into dominating rule in the caretakers' interests. Dominating caretakers may be sadistic or self-interested; they may also be fearful or misguided about the meaning of care. Whatever the motives, the "nature" of the subject threatens the caretaker. A mother or teacher sets herself against what she cannot control. Her own bodily and libidinal "weakness," like that of her charges, must be conquered. Wills must be broken, desires ruled. Bodies that are "deformed," greedy, dirty, aggressive, and lustful must be brought to heel. This is the fascist moment of care.

In maternal thinking, the conception of bodily nature as an enemy partly arises from and certainly abets a fearful preoccupation with sexuality. Caretakers, especially mothers, are expected to deny and repress their own passion—especially if it is not legalized, domestic, and heterosexual—and to simplify or deny their children's. Since mothers are blamed and blame themselves for their own "unruly" sexual lives and for unusual sexual proclivities in their children, they are likely to long for bodies that are asexual, sharply gendered, and well behaved.

However, there is latent in the practice of care, an alternative conception of the sexual body. Mothers and teachers of small children witness, to some extent direct, and are frequently the object of infants' and children's erotic desires. Caretakers themselves experience and control erotic responses to their subjects. As participants in and witnesses to infant-child erotic life, caretakers could welcome eros where it begins. This would mean acknowledging surprising desires, both of their own and of the children they tend. It would mean recognizing rather than repressing expansive, complex ways of being masculine and feminine, so evident in children's and adolescents' lives.

A welcoming maternal sexuality would oppose both the predatory license of the "naturally" aggressive male soldier and the romantically mystified allure of the just warrior. Mothers control in themselves and discourage in children the sexualization of injury and destruction. The alluring helplessness of a child who is also stubborn and disobedient can be a powerful stimulus to sadistic excitement both for a mother or teacher or for a larger child. But sadism, however understandable, cannot be visited upon vulnerable subjects. More generally, the most welcoming maternal eroticism cannot justify abusive sexual behavior in the name of natural impulse. Small children, ill or disabled adults, or anxiously sexual adolescents demand restraint. Despite the temptation to abuse or to be passive in the face of abuse, caretakers, ideally, discipline their own desires and resist any predatory sexuality by which their subjects are threatened.

While the marauding male soldier is a fearful apparition, the just defender is a quintessential hero. Mothers will not cease to desire the armed yet vulnerable warrior simply by learning to acknowledge the complexities of their own and their infants' erotic life. The lifting of repressive denial offers more modest hopes. In recognizing the complexity of any desire, mothers could subject military romance to critical reflection. Moreover, if they were allowed and accorded themselves desires of their own, mothers would be less in need of the heightened and distant eroticism the warrior figure provides. By opposing the sharpened division of masculine and feminine, so at odds with the vicissitudes of emerging sexual identities, they would undermine a linch pin of military ideology. Most importantly, enjoying in bodily pleasures, one's own and other's, makes sacrifice and transcendence less necessary or attractive.

Whatever the hopes for maternal eroticism, mothers are now embattled as they insist on the right to name and act on their desires at the same time that they struggle for an understanding of sexuality adequate to the moral complexities of care. While a transformed sexuality might fuel the appreciation of bodies, it is at least as likely that maternal conceptions of the bodily will shape developing conceptions of sexuality. Crucial to maternal thinking as a whole, and to a welcoming of sexuality within it, is our understanding of birth. Men of Reason have written many, many words about the human meaning of death but few about the world seen from the vantage of those who give birth. To be sure, there is a quasi-militarist conception that makes a woman's birthing of a child parallel to the soldier's death, both being sacrifices to the state. This conception, however, concedes maternity to militarism. Medical ethicists struggle to apprehend the meaning of birth in the light of new reproductive technologies. Even as they record "polyglot maternal discourses," they reveal the paucity of philosophic reflection on them.[27] The promises, obligations, and fears of birth are at the heart of maternal practice. To conceptualize natality, with attentiveness to its cultural and technological variety, is an urgent task for maternal thinkers.

246

An exception among philosophers, Hannah Arendt developed a concept of birth as natality that Jean Elshtain has attempted to put to antimilitarist use. Central to natality, as to maternal thinking as a whole, are interwoven notions of beginning, unpredictability, trust, vulnerability, difference, individuality, dependence, and hope. Birth is a beginning whose end and shape can be neither predicted nor controlled. Since the safety of human bodies, mortal and liable to damage, can never be secured, and since humans grow variously, but always in need of help, to give birth is to commit oneself to protecting the unprotectable and nurturing the unpredictable. (A woman giving her child to another to raise acts out that commitment when she transfers the task of protection to others she trusts.) While death might raise a man above mere affections, birth increases affectionate dependencies, first of the newborn on those who care for them, then of the birther on the infant for whom she cares. To actively engage in giving birth is an expression of trust in others and a determination to become trustworthy. It is an expression of hopefulness in oneself and in "nature," one's own and that of the child to whom one has given birth.

> The miracle that saves the world . . . is, in other words, the birth of new human beings and the new beginning, the action they are capable of by being born. Only the full experience of this capacity can bestow upon human affairs faith and hope, those two essential characteristics of human existence . . . that found perhaps their most glorious and most succinct expression in the new words with which the Gospels accounted their "glad tiding": "A Child has been born unto us."
>
> Placed alongside the reality of human beginnings, many accounts of political beginnings construed as actions of male hordes or contractualists seem parodic in part because of the massive denial (of the "female") on which they depend. A "full experience" of the "capacity" rooted in birth helps us to keep before our mind's eye the living reality of singularities, differences, and individualities rather than a human mass as objects of possible control or manipulation.[28]

To weight birth over death is not to deny death's realities. Nor is it simply to accord to vulnerable beginnings and their hopeful protection greater attention than to endings and loss. The weight is not only quantitative but conceptual. Death itself must be seen under the aspect of natality. No more than war deaths are cared-for deaths heroic. Dying bodies stumble, smell, forget, swell, waste away, fester, and shake. But whereas military ideology masks these realities, the practice of care depends upon grasping them accurately. And whereas military strategies grasp the body's vulnerabilities in order to exploit them, caretakers perceive accurately in order to comfort.

The caretaker's regard—a species of attentive love—is a discipline of intellect and action nearly the opposite of the planned cruelty epitomized in the claymore mine or napalm bomb. Any death that results from predictable and avoidable damage to a body—whether from war, poverty, social neglect, or individual abandonment—is a violation of birth's hope. Precisely because of its commitment to beginnings, its basis in trust, the concept of "natality" grasps the betrayal in violent death. By contrast, cared-for death is not intrinsically an assault. To care for dying bodies is to mitigate pain and forestall even the appearance of cruelty. Although caretakers are often unkind, the business of care is kindness.

Dying is an experience quintessentially one's own and unshared. Nonetheless, dying, whether cared-for or military, is also a social experience, incorporating the plans and work of the living. It is the living—those who have cared and those who have killed—who are bequeathed the task of remembering the "history of human flesh." Soldiers, especially victorious ones, may be consoled for the injuries they have suffered and inflicted by reflecting on the necessity and virtue of the Cause. Or they may forget since the "ache of guilt" is frequently the price of memory.[29] Caretakers likewise have witnessed, even though (usually) they do not contribute to the pain of the dying. Even the most "natural" death marks an unnatural end to a human story. Those who minister in kindness must learn to remember in sorrow.

Critic Celeste Schenck has identified an elegaic tradition among women poets that differs from men poets and that seems to me to be opposite. The women poets she writes of reject ceremonies and myths of consolation—even "the dead are bored with the whole thing"—in favor of "more crazy mourning, more howl, more keening," "mourning without end." In the midst of sorrow, they also celebrate continuity rather than separation. Refusing "to render up their dead," they imagine forms of mourning "that arise from a distinctly feminine experience of attachment and loss." Drawing upon Gilligan's work, Schenck ascribes to women a desire for "separation based on attachment and recovery, rather than a severing of ties." Such a resurrection of the dead as a real and benign presence among the living depends upon unsentimental remembering adequate to the ambivalence and complexity of love.[30]

The conceptions of natality and natal death render the caretaker's conception of the body, taken as a whole, antimilitarist. To be sure, caretakers who fear an uncontrolled "nature" and simplify sexuality play into military hands. When wills, bodies, and desires appear uncontrollable, then military discipline can bring them to heel. When sexuality is denied or simplified, the predatory assaultive sexuality of soldiers can be concealed while the allure of the warrior, like the desire of the women who serve him, goes unexamined. Yet there is, in the rationality of care, a sturdy antimilitarist conception of the body. In this conception, the body is not fearful either in its pleasures or in its suffering. Birth is privileged over death, and with that privilege comes a commitment to protect, a respect for ambiguity and ambivalence, a prizing of physical being in its resilience and variety. Bodies are at least as important as the causes that use them. When they are damaged—exploded, burned, poisoned, irradiated, or cut up—no heroic phrases come to the rescue. Although "nature" is, from a caretaker's perspective, "unnaturally" cruel, caretakers assuage rather than abet the cruelty of dying. Caretakers create ways of tending, comforting, and, finally, of surviving and mourning, that allow the living to include the dead among them as the real, complicated creatures they were. Real complicated peoples, caring and cared for, do not make good heroes or good enemies.

A Word about Politics

It is clear that neither the practice nor the perspective of care assures an antimilitarist politics. Caretakers caught up in daily passions and exhausting details easily ignore the political uses made of their work. Ideology reinforces the temptation to abdicate responsibility. Although caretaking is assertive work, and although caretakers frequently must act in anger, caretakers are expected to defer to the opinions of the "reasonable" and powerful on whose support they in fact depend. In so far as they are political, caretakers are meant to serve as an auxiliary to causes and cadres organized by men. Not surprisingly, many relinquish the right, if not the capacity, for angry independent judgments of public good. The political effectiveness of care depends upon a wider feminist and labor politics that emboldens caretakers—especially women—to judge and organize in the name of care on their own and their subjects' behalf.

Even confident caretakers find it difficult to extend care from the intimate to the public. Women are only now learning to conceive of their *own* communities and states under the aspect of protective and nurturant care. It may seem simple to ask of a state or cadre what it needs, what practices will really protect and nourish its citizens. But these questions compete with technological, militarist, and heroic assertions of honor and danger. To care for *alien* states or cadres and the strangers in them is still more difficult, requiring patient identification with different "others" in their particularities. Many women who begin by "rescuing our children" come to see violence when any child hungers.[31] Some are able to see even in "the enemy" real "others" with attachments and obligations like their own. This ability may be increasingly widespread in a world that is endangered, as a whole, by the violence that any leaders plan. Nonetheless, extensive sympathetic identification remains a fragile achievement for those whose lives have been shaped by passionate loyalties to their "own."

Suppose that caretakers acted independently in the name of care. Suppose too that they succeeded in the morally and conceptually difficult task of extending the perspective of care from intimate to public. How does a caretaker's politics connect to other bases of antimilitarism? In particular, what is the relation of the politics of care to feminist peace politics? What are the antimilitarist strategies of care? What hope have we that caretakers could affect the entrenched militarism of most states?

These and other questions require a paper of their own. Let me close on a confident note.

For reasons both deep and banal, it matters what women say and do. Women have serviced and blessed the violent while denying the character of the violence they serve. Because they have played their military parts well, women's mere indifference could now matter. With the tacit collaboration of disaffected women, a smaller group of caretakers can invent a language of outrage and of love. Already, women are creating care's *rational* protest in urban public squares, rural town meetings, churches and synagogues, peace camps, sanctuaries, and around kitchen tables. From the perspective of care, the imposition of suffering by military force is only one, structurally primary and potentially annihilating, instance of the violation of care. To organize in the name of care is to organize against any bigotry, exploitation, and poverty that does violence to the promise of natality.

The rationality of care seems a prime example of what Foucault called a "subjugated knowledge"—"lost in an all-encompassing theoretical framework or erased in a triumphal history of ideas"—"regarded with disdain by intellectuals as being either primitive or woefully incomplete," but liable to become "insurrectionary."[32] People everywhere depend upon the work of care. Yet, politically as well as psychologically, it is dangerous to acknowledge that dependence. The obligations and attachments of care conflict with other public obligations and attachments required for the success of abstract causes. As Hegel put it, "the community only gets an existence through the interference with the happiness of the family. . . . It creates for itself in what it suppresses and what it depends upon an internal enemy—womankind in general."[33] To control women caretakers, contradiction between the work of care and its political abuses is construed as a proper separation of public from private, reason from emotion, male from female, each located within its own sphere. As ideals of reason prove militarist and exclusionary, as women claim speech and battlefields come home, this familiar ideology breaks down, making conceptual and political space for insurrectionary knowledges.

Certainly, a protest in the name of care is only one of many necessary analyses and politics. To make a difference does not require being the only, or even the most important, agent of change. It is sufficient that women caretakers are a potentially subversive element within the militarized societies that depend upon them. Nor do caretakers, themselves changing as they change the world, provide us with "programs" or "ideologies." Caretakers have barely begun to imagine, let alone to achieve, the conditions and disciplines of a caring "peace." What caretakers can announce is that such a peace is the only choice in the face of the nightmare that military protection and honor offers to caring love.

Notes

1. Jane Addams, an account of an interview with foreign ministers, published in *The Survey*, July 1915, printed in *My Country Is the Whole World*, edited by the Cambridge Women's Peace Collective (London: Pandora Press, 1984), pp. 86–87. Olive Schreiner, *Women and Labour* (London: Virgo, 1978, original 1911), pp. 170, 173. Protest in the name of maternal work or caring labor continues today.

2. Maternal practice suggests an ideal of nonviolent action, which imperfectly governs maternal work and organizes its aspirations. This ideal includes a way of conceptualizing and achieving peace that differs from that shared by both arms controllers and just-war theorists. From a perspective that is antimilitarist and feminist, I attempt to identify the limits of maternal nonviolence, then to suggest ways of overcoming them so that maternal nonviolence becomes *one* model of

nonviolent action in the public sphere. See "Preservative Love and Military Destruction," in *Mothering: Essays in Feminist Theory,* edited by J. Trebilcot (Totowa, N.J.: Rowman and Allanheld, 1984), pp. 231–62; "Maternal Thinking and Peace Politics," *Journal of Education,* vol. 167, 1985, Boston University, pp. 97–112; "Remarks on the Sexual Politics of Reason," *Women and Moral Theory,* edited by Eva Feder Kittay and Diana T. Meyers (Totowa, N.J.: Rowman and Allanheld, 1986).

3. There is a vast and growing feminist critique of reason, which I am only summarizing here. Among the many feminist philosophers who have developed a critique of reason, I rely most on Genevieve Lloyd, *The Man of Reason: "Male" and "Female" in Western Philosophy* (Minneapolis: University of Minnesota Press, 1984); Evelyn Fox Keller, *Gender and Science* (New Haven: Yale University Press, 1985); Sandra Harding, *The Science Question in Feminism* (Ithaca: Cornell University Press, 1986); the anthology on gender and reason edited by Sandra Harding and Merrill B. Hintikka, eds., *Discovering Reality* (Dordrecht: Reidel, 1983); Nancy Hartsock, "The Feminist Standpoint," a chapter in *Money, Sex and Power* (New York: Longman, 1983) and also in Harding and Hintikka, *Discovering Reality;* Susan Bordo, "The Cartesian Masculinization of Thought," *Signs* (Spring 1986), pp. 439–56; Elizabeth Spelman, "Woman as Body: Ancient and Contemporary Views," *Feminist Studies* (Spring 1982), pp. 109–32. I take the phrase "hermeneutic of suspicion" from Elizabeth Schussler Fiorenza's four-stage model of feminist critique in *Bread Not Stone* (Boston: Beacon Press, 1986).

4. Aquinas quoted by Lloyd, p. 36.

5. The myth of a male reason is complexly related, psychologically and sociopolitically, to actual women's and men's lives. Although those called "reasonable" have largely been men, many women have shown themselves to be reasonable philosophers, scientists, statesmen, and entrepreneurs in ways indistinguishable from those of men.

6. Plato, *Republic,* 543a, 521d.

7. The phrase, "The language of the warriors" used to include the language of arms controllers, comes from Freeman Dyson, *Weapons and Hope* (New York: Harper & Row, 1984). The concept of technico-strategic reasoning comes from Carol Cohn, "Clean Bombs and Clean Language," this volume, chap. 2. For other feminist critiques, see especially Genevieve Lloyd, "Selfhood, War and Masculinity," in *Feminist Challenges,* edited by E. Gross and C. Pateman; Jean Bethke Elshtain, "Reflections on War and Political Discourse: Realism, Just War, and Feminism in a Nuclear Age," *Political Theory* (February 1985), pp. 39–57; Mary C. Segers, this volume, chap. 3; Nancy Hartsock, "Men, Women, War, and Politics," unpublished manuscript.

8. Elshtain, pp. 49–50.

9. Keller, *Gender and Science,* pp. 174–75.

10. Ostriker, *Stealing the Language* (Boston: Beacon Press, 1986), p. 211. Audre Lorde, *Sister/Outsider* (Trumansburg, N.Y.: Crossing Press, 1984), p. 37.

11. Nancy Chodorow, "Gender Relations and Difference in Psycholoanalytic Perspective," in Eisenstein and Jardine, eds., *The Future of Difference* (Boston: G. K. Hall, 1980), p. 11.

12. Keller, *Gender and Science*, p. 117.

13. In characterizing alternative ideals of rationality, in addition to Ostriker, Lorde, Chodorow, and Keller, I draw especially upon Belenky, Clinchy, Goldberger, and Tarule, *Women's Ways of Knowing* (New York: Basic Books, 1986); Carol Gilligan, *In a Different Voice* (Cambridge: Harvard University Press, 1982); "The Conquistador and the Dark Continent: Notes on the Psychology of Love," *Deadalus*, vol. 113, 1984, pp. 75–95; "Remapping the Moral Domain: New Images of Self in Relationship," in *Reconstructing Individualism*, Heller, Sosna, and Wellbery, eds. (Stanford: Stanford University Press, 1986), pp. 237–52; Hilary Rose, "Head, Brain and Heart," *Signs*, vol. 9 (Spring 1983), and "Women's Work, Women's Knowledge," in J. Mitchell and A. Oakley, eds., *What Is Feminism* (Oxford: Blackwell's, 1986); Hartsock, "The Feminist Standpoint"; Jean Baker Miller, *Toward a New Psychology of Women* (Boston: Beacon Press, 1973); the series of papers issued by Jean Baker Miller and her colleagues from the Stone Center, Wellesley College, Wellesley, Mass. This is only a suggestion of the growing body of literature by women articulating ideals of reason alternative to the dominant ones.

14. Among the practicalists, I include Wittgenstein, Marx, Rorty, Habermas, and Winch.

15. Maternal practice is constituted by the aims of preserving the life of a child, nurturing its growth, and training it in a way acceptable to the social group, of which the mother is a member. To be a mother is to be committed to meeting the demands of preservation, nurturance, and training. I develop these categories more fully in "Maternal Thinking," *Feminist Studies* (1980) and in the papers cited in footnote 2.

16. I take the notion of "caring labour" from Hilary Rose whose thinking on these matters has influenced mine.

17. J. Glenn Gray, *The Warriors* (New York: Harper & Row, 1970).

18. Elaine Scarry, *The Body in Pain* (New York: Oxford University Press, 1985), p. 73.

19. Cohn, this volume, chap. 2.

20. Among the many books on the destructiveness of weapons, I rely especially on Keegan, *The Face of Battle* (New York: Viking, 1976).

21. Schreiner, *Women and Labour*, p. 170.

22. Scarry identifies several separable techniques for omitting or redescribing the injuring of war. See *Body in Pain*, chap. 2; See also Carol Cohn, this volume, chap. 2 on the domestication of destructive weapons.

23. David H. Marlowe, "The Manning of the Force and the Structure of Battle," in *Conscripts and Volunteers*, edited by R. Fullinwider (Totowa, N.J.: Rowman and Allanheld, 1983).

24. Virtually no one contests the fact that, for a significant number of soldiers and military propagandists, injuring is sexualized. See Gray, Marlowe or, for a more recent account, William Broyles, *Brother in Arms* (New York: Knopf, 1986).

25. Carol Cohn, this volume, chap. 2.

26. See Gray, *The Warriors;* Lloyd, "Selfhood, War and Masculinity"; and war memoirs too numerous too mention.

27. For an ingenious elaboration of the heroic concept of birth, see Nancy Huston, "The Matrix of War: Mothers and Heroes," *The Female Body in Western Culture,* edited by Susan Suleiman (Cambridge: Harvard University Press, 1985), pp. 119–38. For especially reflective considerations of polyglot maternal discourses, see Rayna Rapp, "The Power of 'Positive' Diagnosis: Medical and Maternal Discourses on Amniocentesis," in *Childbirth in America,* Karen Michaelson, editor; and Bergin and Garvey, 1988, "Constructing Amniocentesis: Maternal and Medical Discourses," paper for the American Anthropological Association, 1986.

28. First paragraph from Hannah Arendt, *The Human Condition,* quoted in Elshtain, "Reflections on War and Political Discourse," op. cit., p. 52, second from Elshtain's essay, p. 53.

29. See, for example, J. Glenn Gray, *The Warriors,* "The Ache of Guilt," and Karl Jaspers, *The Question of German Guilt* (New York: Dial Press, 1947).

30. Celeste Schenck, "Feminism and Deconstruction: Re-Constructing the Elegy," in Tulsa Studies in Women's Literature, April 1986. She cites "Even the dead are bored with the whole thing" from Anne Sexton; "More crazy mourning, more howl, more keening" from Adrienne Rich; "Mourning without end" from May Straton. These and other specific references are to be found in Schenck's rich and evocative paper.

31. "In the beginning we only wanted to rescue our children. But as time passed we acquired a different comprehension. We understood better what is going on around the world. We know that when babies do not have enough to eat that too is a violation of human rights." Rene Epelbaum, Las Madres de Plaza de Mayo, reported by Jean Elshtain, personal communication.

32. Michael Foucault, *Power/Knowledge* (New York: Pantheon, 1980), "Two Lectures," especially pp. 81–82. The phrase "lost in an all-encompassing knowledge" comes from Sharon Welch, *Communities of Resistance and Solidarity: A Feminist Theology of Liberation* (Maryknoll, N.Y.: Orbis, 1985), p. 19. I am indebted to Welch for providing a different, potentially antimilitarist and feminist way of reading Foucault.

33. Quoted by Lloyd in "Selfhood, War, and Masculinity," p. 72.

12

The Problem with Peace

Jean Bethke Elshtain

The great political philosopher, Hannah Arendt, once remarked that it was far less important (and, one might add, far more arrogant) for the political thinker to tell others "what is to be done" than to help others to "think what we are doing." What Arendt had in mind is something like this: what we do we often do somewhat unthinkingly, repeating inherited patterns, reconstructing familiar identities, re-encoding traditional scripts. Occasionally, rare individuals might break free by disassociating themselves in some radical sense from their own time. But this doesn't happen very often. More frequently, change comes about as the old patterns don't seem to work anymore, leaving individuals discontented, restless, anomic, and alienated.

I have in mind no such notion as "historic turning points" here—those are identified only *post hoc* and usually with the aid of some overarching world view that the editors of this volume explicitly reject. Rather, something subtler yet no less powerful begins to take shape as transformed notions coalesce into genuine alternatives, alternatives made

An earlier version of this essay appeared in the British journal *Millennium* (Winter 1988, Vol. 17, No. 3).

possible by all sorts of other alterations in the way things get done. Arendt enjoins us to *think* that which we, in fact, *do,* to immerse ourselves fully in that present of which we are inescapably a part and to engage ourselves with its constructions. We can never start the world anew but we can think in new ways about the world we did not start. And, although thinking is never a one-way street to clear-cut actions, it is a part of forming intentions that intimate that "things could be different."

The essays in this volume suggest just how difficult it is to take Arendt's injunction to heart. For sometimes when we think we are offering alternatives, what we are doing, instead, is shoring up that which we oppose. Take, for example, our understanding of "peace" itself.

Before "Jerusalem the Golden" of Christian yearnings, the dream of an eternal city of peace and joy and rest where there is neither mourning nor crying nor pain, the ancient Greeks had represented peace, Eirēnē, as a female deity of a decidedly subordinate nature, in contrast to Ares, a male god of great power. Whereas Eirēnē was attendant upon the great gods, Ares dominated, unsurprisingly considering the founding myth that the gods themselves had come to power only after fighting a brutal war against the Titans. For the Greeks, war was a natural state and the basis of society. Manly valor was shown by the spirit with which men pursued honor and fame. The epics of war, of tragedy and triumph, constructed, in and through figurations that have lost none of their power to evoke and provoke, the centrality of war-making with its glories and necessities, and terrible triumphs. Heraclitus deemed war the "father of all things," arguing that it is alone through strife as a natural law of being that anything is brought *into* being. Those dominated by self-interest, those who refuse to fight, became slaves. Not a philosophy for the squeamish. The valiant—they shall prevail.

To be sure, such minor poets (as they have been canonized) as Baccylides and Pindar offer odes that "are eloquent in praise of peace." Baccylides writes of the blessings of peace in terms that evoke images of exuberant celebration: "Mighty Peace brings forth wealth for mortals and the full bloom of honey-tongued song; her gift it is that the fleshy thighs of oxen are burned to the gods in the yellow flame on the carven altars and the youths delight themselves with athletic feats and flutes and revels. Upon the iron-bound handles of the shields the spiders weave their webs and rust destroys the spears and the two-edged swords. No blast of brazen trumpet is heard nor is sleep of gentle spirit which comforteth the heart at dawn stolen from the eyelids. The streets are filled with joyous feasting and songs in praise of youths flame forth."[1]

This Peace of eroticized exuberance and delight in the pleasures of feasting and fabrication is more than an absence of war, though that lack is a necessary precondition for the subsequent efflorescence, the break-out or out-break, of Peace. The Romans represented peace as a rather vague goddess. The *Pax Romana* tapped notions at once legalistic and teleological—agreements or pacts not to fight together with images of *tranquilitas, securitas,* repose. In constructing an altar to *pax,* the Romans feminized the representation as Terra Mater "with fruit in her lap, children on her knees, and sheep and oxen at her feet."[2]

Similarly, in ancient Hebrew thought, peace *(shalom)* is not only the absence of war but also a state of well-being; a combination of material and spiritual conditions frequently following a war; a sphere of security that requires assured dominion in order to come into view, to manifest itself. The point is that all antique peoples shared a dream of a world without war, whether as a permanent or temporary condition, and the picture of such a world drew upon mythologies of a lost golden age of fructifying harmony and full transparency in which none was an enemy to any other, nor, for that matter, even a nuisance. A world without borders, boundaries, strangers, estrangements.

This dream of Elysium was bolstered *and* deconstructed when Christianity burst upon the antique scene. The Christian gospel proclaims peace as the highest good. Peace is a blessing not reducible to the terms of any earthly order (including, or most especially, the *Pax Romana*); nor is peace a sentimental dream of an era of perfect justice on this earth. The image of the warrior and war-god is devalorized. Suffering rather than doing harm is exalted. Peace is both interiorized and externalized, represented as an inner fruition, the peace that passeth understanding, available to all through the redemptive promise of the Christian savior, and as a City of God, an unalienated world without end, amen, but a world not of this earth where the state of peace and freedom is bound to be an imperfect approximation of the ideal in its most grandly teleological realization.

The Christian New Jerusalem was balm for the weary but a vexation for the impatient determined to bring peace to earth, the sooner the better. Sixteenth- and seventeenth-century utopias give vent to the latter urge as social urgency. Not all utopias are, or were, alike, of course, but all are concerned with contrasting the dis-order they find with the perfect order they seek. To tag a text or political program "utopian" is to do more than merely label: it is to invite an immediate evaluation, often as a derogatory epithet in our own time. Contrastingly, political theory as a select canon of texts is distinguished from utopian discourse which has about it the air of something rather fuzzy and flighty. But any sharp distinction between, say, More's *Utopia* and Plato's *Republic* is a false divide. The former was nurtured by the paradisical elements in Judeo-Christian faith; the latter embodies the ancient myth of a beautiful city built by men. The important question is a mimetic one: what has the City of Man to do with the City of God (or the gods or, for that matter, the guardians)?

For utopian discourse traffics in simulacra, in bringing the transcendental down to earth in supreme confidence in human capacities, or at least in some of the capacities of some humans, to enact eschatological feats. And the avowed aim of utopias, whether as literary genre, explicit human aspiration, psychological yearning, and philosophical optimism, is something called "peace." So what, or where, is the problem?

The problem is this: peace is, as I have noted elsewhere, an ontologically suspicious concept.[3] Peace never appears without its violent *doppelgänger*, War, lurking in the shadows. Peace is *inside*, not outside a frame with war—most especially in the most powerful and absolute (utopian, if you will)—expressions of its desirability and realizability. War is threatening disorder; Peace is healing order. War is human bestiality ("male" and "male" alone argue many feminists); Peace is human benevolence ("female" and "female" alone argue many feminists). War is discordance; Peace is harmony. The antinomies may be proliferated almost endlessly with Peace on one side of the ontological ledger.

If the reader is with me thus far, he or she may still be puzzled. Why is the absolutizing of Peace bound to be problematic? Problematic how and for whom and with reference to what? Is it not the case that if one backs down from the grand dream all one is left with is dreary diplomacy, a world of half-measures and desultory trimmings and various pacts with various devils to achieve limited and often inglorious ends? To grapple with these matters I must return, for a moment, to Hellas to consider other features of Greek political life and thought as these revolved around the social practices of settled civic existence, or the rules that pertained *within* the *polis* on the one hand and, on the other, those standard practices that came into play externally, that governed dealings with "foreigners," all who were not members of one's city.

The rules are at once straightforward and complex. Within the *polis*, according to Athenian thinking and it is this thinking that founds several discursive traditions, both "realism" in international relations and political theory more generally, different spheres of rule-governance specified rights and wrongs, the just and the unjust. A sharp internal/external split prevailed. Justice governed relations among citizens within the *polis;* force came into play between Athenians and "others." What would be counted a wrong against a citizen was not so adjudged if it came into play between citizens collectively and some external group. The *locus classicus* of this rule is, of course, the so-called Melian dialogue familiar to all students of politics and history, in which the Athenians proclaim "might" the right that reigns. To be sure, diplomacy and arbitration might mediate relations with external others, but the sharp presumptive divide—them/us; what's wrong in one case may be right in another—holds.

There is a major irritant in this image. Just as occasional arbitration is a limiting case of the general law of external force, relations between citizens and internal others—women and slaves—is a limiting instance of the rule of *polis* justice. For women and slaves cannot partake in the full amplification of goodness and reason that was the common heritage of co-equal participants in the city.[4] The "essential" difference that pertains between greater and lesser persons justifies this relationship by finding a "community of interest" between the naturally ruled and the naturally ruling that is essential to the preservation of each.

Internal relations between the dominant citizen and lesser persons are *not* a perfect mimesis of external relations ruled by force and existing in a kind of ethical twilight zone. Rather, *partial* justice, limits to the application of force, an appropriate ethic for the household as contrasted with the robust equality or justice between citizens, comes into play. The image that lingers then, with its attendant rhetoric and categorizations, is of sharp cleavages between *polis* and others externally, and between citizens and others internally, with shaded areas of overlap where something of the justice of the *polis* is called upon to blunt the sharp edges of the rule of force externally and where something of the goodness and equity that pertains between citizens is called upon to shape domestic governance.

Several beginnings are here signalled: of realist discourse (them/us, citizen/foreigner) and of the discourse of justice, equality, and the bases of internal order central to the tradition of Western political thought more generally. In contrast to realists, "idealists" came to be those who insisted that rules appropriate to internal order could, and should, come into play and eventually triumph in dealings with external others. But this division is too simple by far—too ready to hand to offer us any critical leverage in recasting the problem with peace. For there are realists who elide the distance between internal and external rule, at least before the coming of absolutized civic order (Hobbes comes to mind), just as there are realists whose narrative revolves around a public/private split in which the softer (effeminate) virtues and values are appropriate in one sphere but out of place within and subversive of *realpolitik*. I have in mind Machiavelli who, nevertheless, cannot resist analogizing from private to public in ways subversive of the distinctions he otherwise presumes. His *Prince* valorizes *virtù*, a particular manly virtue, and celebrates collective, armed *esprit*, in contrast to Christian inefficacy in the tough world of men and states. What one does with friends and mates, all other things being equal, would bring ruination in dealings with other *civitati*.

And yet . . . Machiavelli's embodiment of Fortuna as a fickle bitch goddess who must be mastered by the bold prince and bent to his will draws explicitly upon generalized acceptance on the level of folk wisdom of the need to keep wives in place through generous application of the stick. Fortune is "like a woman." Arguing from simile rooted in classical precedent (images of Fortuna draw upon Nemesis), Machiavelli also mines, indeed presumes, the Aristotelianized distinction between form and matter *(forma* and *materia)* in which the male principle gives shape to what would otherwise be a formless mass. The Prince's relationship to his people is akin to that of form to matter as masculinized and feminized representations. There is, then, both a conceptual barrier between private/public in the Machiavellian world that is paradoxically reinforced with free-flow analogizing between private and public imperatives where bringing the feminine "to heel" is concerned. Preventing disorder is the *raison d'être* in each instance.

It is time to weave in the preoccupation with representations of peace with which I began, to show the ways in which the imaginary and the "real," mythology and the so-called "scientific study of politics," power politics and phantasms cohabit. Recall that Eirēnē and Pax were relatively minor goddesses and cults in the overall scheme of Greek and Roman things. The war/father had definite dominion over the peace/mother save in particular moments of harmonious epiphany. A further masculinization of discourse on the level of representations occurs with Machiavelli who thematizes the feminine as a superordinate but undomesticated force.

Fortuna, left to her own devices, embodies the absolutization of disorder and disquietude: she must be mastered by one possessing and possessed by a particular kind of vigor and prowess—the masculinized Prince. The outcome is a draw, most likely, with that Prince who has formed his feminized people—given them shape as an entity of collective *virtù*—perhaps having an edge, for a time, in his never-ending battle with Fortuna. The so-called realist, then, in this classical sense, makes of disorder an absolutized natural given. Anarchy is the defining feature of external relations and, as well, domestic or internal affairs unless or until order is imposed. And that order is inherently unstable, requiring eternal vigilance: *si vis pacem, para bellum*. The irony, or one of many ironic moments in this construction, is the fact that a vast, unruly natural disorder construed as feminized in the sense of fickle, irrational, whimsical, destructive offers up a challenge to the masculinized bringer-of-order whose vision of peace, to the extent he is animated by one, is represented by, and embodied within, other feminized figurations.

Whether as minor deity or *force majeure*, as harmony or as disorder, constructions of "the feminine" in contrast to the "masculine" figure centrally and from the beginning in the genealogy of war/peace discourse. It might seem at first or even second glance that a way out or through the maze I have offered already exists. I refer to what might very loosely be called "the liberal rationalist alternative" or what Michael Howard has traced as "the liberal conscience."[5] This means I am leap-frogging over the strength and complexities of historic just-war discourse in its early Augustinian and later Thomist incarnations with this caveat: the construction of a notion of God's natural law and of an ideal harmonious world from which mankind has taken a rather severe tumble, the insistence that household and city, public and private, do not diverge in kind but are interrelated as parts to whole, sets the horizon for later liberalization of political discourse and philosophy.

Liberal rationalism, whether in its empiricist or deontological forms, is heavily backgrounded (as we are now wont to say) by attempts to tame realism, to offer at least partial alternatives to the discourse of armed civic virtue by putting pressure on masculinized *realpolitik* in and through Christian constructions, themselves a rich admixture of the Hebrew Testament sovereign deity of the law and justice; the New Testament devirilized deity; the valorized Mother as Madonna, fecund and feeling intercessor. It is at once accurate and misleading to signal Immanuel Kant, as I am about to do, as metonym for liberal discourse more generally. The differences between Kant and other liberal modalities are striking and deep.[6] Because, however, Kant represents the liberal rationalist argument at its strongest, its apogee, he is worth unpacking briefly in order to elaborate the problem with peace in its recognizably modernist forms.

Pre-Kant, but assumed and deepened by his discourse, is the thorough-going privatization of the female. Certain sealed social divisions are characteristic of classical bourgeois culture—between home life and public life; peace and war; family and state—what Hegel dubbed the immediacy of desire (feminized) against the self-conscious power of universal ethical life (masculinized). "Women" embodied particular ethical aspirations but were denied a place in the corridors of power. This culturally sanctioned semiotics of womanhood figures both tacitly and explicitly in liberal universal aspirations, including the absolutization of "perpetual peace."[7] Here, then, is why this vision of peace (one many feminist thinkers of the nineteenth and twentieth centuries pay homage to, whether through subversion or inversion) is so problematic.

First, the world of private order, a series of constructions Kant would have us find fully transparent, indeed irresistible, involve layers of mystification and cover-up. Given Kant's transcendental subject, it would appear to make sense that relations of equity pertain across the board. Not so. In Kant's world there are two realms: the noumenal realm of freedom, and the phenomenal sphere of determinism and natural causality. The line of fault, Kant insists, severs a real and noumenal being "in itself" from those phenomenal and determined features of self that inhabit a realm of appearance, the world in which we appear before our fellow men and women. The freely willing self has no phenomenal form.[8]

Kant's account requires that each person insofar as he is a "real, atemporal, noumenal self," free and autonomous by definition, represent himself as a thinking subject in noncorporeal or disembodied terms. The thinking self is not the embodied self but an ageless, sexless, denarrativized abstract entity. Reason "belongs to the inner sense only."[9] It is this interior or noumenal self that is free and equal to others insofar as they, too, are rational agents. Persons *qua* human are endowed by Kant with a moral personality defined as the metaphysical freedom of a rational being who subordinates all concrete aspects and inclinations to the commands of certain maxims. These stipulations, the Kantian categorical imperatives, are cast in universal form and constitute by definition the rational moral order.

Kant presumes a transhistorical moral subject. But are all subjects really in the same epistemological position? Do all human beings as noumenal agents apprehend the prescriptive form of the categorical imperatives? Or is it the case that some are more "noumenal" than others? Remember, this Kantian self is severed from particular situations, is disembodied, disinterested. Kant downgrades human emotions, giving them little moral weight—they lie outside the realm of reason. Women as the preeminent emotional beings, linked in the eighteenth century in a symbolic and mimetic relation to "Nature" (Machiavelli's *forma*), fall under a cloud. Kant similarly downgrades sympathy, compassion and mercy—qualities associated historically with women (for better or for worse, but that isn't the question here)—finding that they don't measure up to his rationalist standards of pure reason.

This, it seems, is terribly abstract, but it figures directly in Kant's account of the "law of domestic society" that provides for the wife's legal possession by her husband. The husband enjoys a property right vis à vis his wife, that is, to her phenomenal being, her "mere" appearance. The runaway can be compelled to return to her husband. This proprietary interest is made secure by contract.[10] Kant is no crude realist, by his own account. He throws no red meat in the direction of the reader. His justification of private dominion is painstakingly sanitized—wholesome tofu salad he would have us believe. Thus, his wife is not his just because "I am at present able to command" her or hold coercive power. No, he possesses her *de jure*. He acquires her not as a thing, because her transcendental noumenal moral personality prevents that by definition.

The husband's proprietary right is fully compatible with the wife's freedom and equality. It is *this* world of *Privatrecht* in which the right of possession is retained but deodorized with coercive dominion vehemently denied and elaborately rationalized away that provides the first tier of Kant's quest for perpetual peace as well as for several layers of cover-up under the transcendental subject banner. Kant's absolutizing of order— here as a rule of private dominion—denies the very *possibility* of moral conflict. Untethered as noumenal agent to particular and diverse ends, objects, aims, and desires, the moral subject obeys imperatives cast as independent of any social order or historic forces. Possession *de jure* exudes a heavenly glow.

Next, Kant's public order. Kant valorizes republican commonwealths. Constitution—Law in its grandest teleological sense—is the true sovereign of the state. Law alone produces a situation in which the rights of individuals are defended and harmony between a Constitution and the Principles of Right pertains. *Whatever* the given Constitution, the citizen must obey; this is an absolute, formal principle. People are enjoined to endure even the most intolerable abuses of authority so long as the lawful constitution is intact. Should a revolution bring a new supreme law into being, so long as it takes the form of universalizable principles, citizens are again enjoined to obey. A world of well-ordered republics is the best and only guarantor of non-coercive domestic peace—domestic not in the private sense but the public, the civic. Obedient but free subjects: that is the story. Yet not even these obedient subjects stand on the same civic footing, for Kant divides citizens into categories of active and passive. "Mere operatives" are ineligible for citizenship as are all women whose disqualification gets termed a "natural one," hence one to which they *cannot by definition* object. And, remember, it in no way cuts into or against their "freedom" as noumenal subjects.

Between this Kantian domestic/public world and his prescription for perpetual peace there is a free-flow. The title of his great essay— "Perpetual Peace"—signifies Kant's metaphysical ambitions.[11] Peace that is not perpetual is a mere truce. A genuine peace must nullify *all* existing causes of war. Peace derives from republican civil constitutions; its origins, like those of bourgeois *Privatrecht*, are pure—the concept of right. A league of purely constituted republics will end war forever. A single rule dominates internal/external relations—in contrast to the world mimed by Thucydides or "realists." Kant's grand design is laced through and through with a grand teleology, willed by Nature, a somewhat capricious "She" who has nevertheless offered up all the necessary preconditions, using even war to gain the absolute of perpetual peace.[12]

For Kant dis/order is a falling away from preternatural wholeness. The peace that follows in his schema is a solipsistic dream that can "exist among like kinds and equals" only, making of the mere existence of "otherness" a flaw in the perfect scheme of things. The cover-up continues for a presumption that otherness is a flaw means, by definition, that it must be eliminated. Kant does so by conceptual fiat. Whatever the differences that exist between Kant and liberal empiricists and utilitarians such as Jeremy Bentham here begin to melt away as each presumes as a precondition for peace cultural and political homogeneity: if this is not now the case it is desirable that it become so, the sooner the better.[13] When difference itself is a blemish, a block to the achievement of one's fondest project, especially one that is teleologically driven, difference must be denied or eliminated. Just as Kant finds a community of interest between the possessed phenomenal wife because she and her husband are both noumenally free, he insists that a world-wide community of interest, of willed right, is both possible and desirable. It is easy enough to point to what gets suppressed—cultural difference, disguised dominion, the list goes on. Finally there won't be anything to fight about because transparency reigns; disorder has been bested. She—Nature— has been mastered, not in a manipulative Machiavellian manner but through the pure conquest of irresistible right.

Women's stake in the problem with peace is great. If peace, as I have argued, requires various ontological endorsements that cover up difference and project a world of ongoing equilibrium, harmony, and perfect order, it would seem to make enormous good sense for women—especially feminists—to eschew its blandishments. For this peace traffics in binary opposites and Manichean constructions that have long relied upon particular constructions of the "feminine," as I have indicated. Such, however, is not the case in any powerful and cogent way. For those feminists who most dominate debates about war and peace are thinkers and ideologists who tacitly or explicitly endorse the ontological ledger I have located and criticized. They simply invert its ranking and evaluations, calling for a free flow from a benevolent, because feminized and transformed, private world to a peaceful, because feminized and transformed, public world.

This feminized version of liberal internationalism finds one spokeswoman proclaiming in the World War I era that women are to be the saviors of humanity, the avatars of pacific Motherhood, the harbingers of the future order.[14] And it finds many spokeswomen now contrasting masculinism, patriarchy, violence, dis-order, with feminism, matriarchy, non-violence, harmonious order.

Feminism, we are told, sees power only in its "healthy form" as a "wholistic understanding" that "leads naturally to the cooperative and nurturing behavior necessary for harmonious existence."[15] The ghost of Kantian categorical imperatives, or perhaps a Kantian angel with wings-a-flutter, sets the horizon of these and similar considerations. Such is the irony of total inversions, which wind up endorsing—indeed requiring—that which they would oppose. Until such absolutist constructions are challenged, not in opposition to but in the name of a critical and ironic feminism, peace will remain a problem.

Notes

1. Cited in Wallace E. Caldwell, *Hellenic Conceptions of Peace* (New York: Columbia University Press, 1919), p. 77. In one of his odes, Pindar praised Peace as the Daughter of Righteousness.
2. Roland H. Bainton, *Christian Attitudes Toward War and Peace: A Historical Survey and Critical Re-evaluation* (New York: Abingdon Press, 1960), p. 18.
3. See my *Women and War* (New York: Basic Books, 1987), pp. 253–55.
4. Here I draw upon my discussion of Aristotle in *Public Man, Private Woman: Women in Social and Political Thought* (Princeton: Princeton University Press, 1981), pp. 41–54.

5. See Michael Howard, *War and the Liberal Conscience* (London: Temple Smith, 1978).

6. See, for example, Michael J. Sandel's *Liberalism and the Limits of Justice* (Cambridge: Cambridge University Press, 1982).

7. See *Women and War* for a critical discussion of liberal internationalism and historic peace campaigns.

8. I draw upon my discussion of Kant in *Meditations on Modern Political Thought* (New York: Praeger, 1987), pp. 21–35.

9. Immanuel Kant, *Critique of Pure Reason*, trans. Norman Kemp Smith (New York: Modern Library, 1958), p. 195.

10. See Immanuel Kant, *The Metaphysical Elements of Justice* (Indianapolis: Bobbs-Merrill, 1965), p. 63.

11. Immanuel Kant, *Perpetual Peace and Other Essays*, trans. Ted Humphrey (Indianapolis: Hackett, 1983).

12. Here, again, a bit of cribbing off *Women and War*, p. 255.

13. Jeremy Bentham outlined his plans for a heavenly earth in *A Plan for a Universal and Perpetual Peace*. See Howard's discussion, *op. cit.*, pp. 32–35.

14. Ellen Key, *War, Peace and the Future* (New York: Garland Publishing, 1972) originally published in the 1920s. Key is one in a plentiful company.

15. Donna Warnock, "Patriarchy is a Killer: What People Concerned About Peace and Justice Should Know," in Pam McAllister, ed., *Reweaving the Web of Life* (Philadelphia: New Society Publishers, 1982), pp. 20–29. The bulk of the essays in this collection share Warnock's presumptions.

Contributors

Jean Bethke Elshtain is Centennial Professor of Political Science at Vanderbilt University. Her previous books include *Public Man, Private Woman: Women in Social and Political Thought,* named by *Choice* as one of the top academic books of 1981–82, and *Women and War,* published by Basic Books in 1987. She is also the author of over one hundred essays in scholarly journals and journals of civic opinion. Professor Elshtain has been a Fellow of the Institute for Advanced Study, Princeton; a scholar in residence at the Bellagio Conference and Study Center, Como, Italy; and a writer in residence at the Macdowell Colony in Peterborough, New Hampshire.

Sheila Tobias is affiliated with three political science departments: the University of Arizona, the University of Southern California where she regularly teaches "The Politics of Peace," and the University of California, San Diego, where she teaches a course entitled "Gender and Politics." She developed one of the first women's studies courses in the country in 1969. Among her writings are: "What Really Happened to Rosie the Riveter?" (1974), *Overcoming Math Anxiety* (1978), *The People's Guide to National Defense* (1982), "Toward a Feminist Analysis of the Defense Budget" (1985), *Succeed with Math* (1987), and "The Case Against Comparable Worth" (1988), *What Makes Science Hard?* (forthcoming), and "Feminism and Antifeminisms: The Schlafly Phenomenon."

Joyce Avrech Berkman is Professor of History at the University of Massachusetts, Amherst. Her teaching and scholarship focus on modern Euro-

267

pean intellectual history and the history of women in America and modern England. In addition to her published articles, she is author of *Olive Schreiner: Feminism on the Frontier* (Montreal, Eden Press, 1979), and a recently completed full-length critical study, *The Healing Imagination of Olive Schreiner: Beyond South African Colonialism* (University of Massachusetts Press, forthcoming). Lecturer, moderator, and commentator at conferences in history and women's studies, Professor Berkman takes particular pride in receiving the University of Massachusetts's Distinguished Teacher Award in 1980.

D'Ann Campbell earned her Ph. D. from the University of North Carolina at Chapel Hill in 1979. She has served as Associate Director of the Family and Community History Center, The Newberry Library, from 1976 to 1979, was Dean for Women's Affairs at Indiana University from 1979 to 1986, and is currently Associate Professor of History at Indiana. She published *Women at War with America: Private Lives in a Patriotic Era* (1984) with Harvard University Press. She has received an NEH research grant to write her forthcoming book on women in the military during World War II.

Carol Cohn is a senior research scholar at the center for Psychological Studies in the Nuclear Age, in Cambridge, Massachusetts, and a research associate in the Department of Psychiatry at the Harvard Medical School. Her article, "Slick'ems, Glick'ems, Christmas Trees, and Cookie Cutters: Nuclear Language and How We Learned to Pat the Bomb," in the June 1987 *Bulletin of the Atomic Scientists*, won the 1987 Olive Branch Award. She is currently writing a book on the language and thinking of nuclear defense intellectuals on a MacArthur Foundation grant.

Cynthia Enloe is Professor and Chair of Government at Clark University, Worcester, Massachusetts. She is also an affiliate of the Women's Studies Program. Her publications include *Does Khaki Become You? The Militarization of Women's Lives*, (1983, 1988); *Of Common Cloth: Women in the Global Textile Industry* (with Wendy Chapkins, 1984); and *Ethnic Soldiers: State Security in Divided Societies* (1980). She is currently working on a book entitled, *Making Feminist Sense of International Politics* (forthcoming, Pandora Press).

Kathleen B. Jones is associate professor of Women's Studies at San Diego State University where she teaches courses in feminist theory, and women and politics. Her articles on feminist theory have appeared in such journals as *Women and Politics, Nomos,* and *Papers in Comparative Studies.* She is coauthor of the *Political Interests of Gender* (forthcoming) and is currently completing a book on political concepts in feminist theory tentatively entitled *Authority, Democracy, and the Citizenship of Women.*

Linda K. Kerber is May Brodbeck Professor of Liberal Arts and Professor of History at the University of Iowa. She is the author of *Federalists in Dissent: Imagery and Ideology in Jeffersonian America* (1970), and *Women of the Republic: Intellect and Ideology in Revolutionary America* (1980, 1986). With Jane De Hart, she is co-editor of *Women's America: Refocusing the Past* (2nd ed., 1987). In 1988–89, she was President of the American Studies Association.

Janet Radcliffe Richards is Lecturer in Philosophy at the Open University, UK, where she specializes in philosophy of science, ethics, and applied philosophy. She is the author of *The Skeptical Feminist: A Philosophical Enquiry* (Routledge, 1980; Penguin Books, 1982) and of various articles on philosophy and feminism.

Sara Ruddick teaches philosophy and feminist theory at the Eugene Lang College of the New School for Social Research. Her book, *From Maternal Thinking to Peace Politics,* will be published by Beacon Press in 1989. She is co-editor of *Working It Out: 23 Women Writers, Artists, Scientists and Scholars Talk About Their Lives and Work* (with Pamela Daniels, Pantheon, 1977), and *Between Women: Biographers, Novelists, Critics, Teachers and Artists Write about Their Work on Women* (with Carol Ascher and Louise De Salvo, Beacon, 1984).

Mary C. Segers is Associate Professor of Political Science at Rutgers University in Newark, New Jersey, where she teaches courses in political philosophy and women's studies. She is also Henry Luce Fellow in Theology at the Harvard Divinity School. She is co-author, with James Foster, of *Elusive Equality: Liberalism, Affirmative Action, and Social Change in America.* Her articles have appeared in *Polity, The Review of Politics, Feminist Politics, Political Theory, The Hastings Center Report,* and other journals. She has also written for *Commonweal, Tikkun,* and *Christianity and Crisis.*

269

Amy Swerdlow is the director of the Graduate Program in Women's History at Sarah Lawrence College. She has been a peace activist for the past twenty-five years, and an historian of the women's peace movement for the past decade. She is the author of a narrative history and critical analysis of the Women's Strike for Peace forthcoming from the University of Chicago Press.

Index